READINGS IN APPLIED TRANSFORMATIONAL GRAMMAR

Mark Lester

University of Hawaii

HOLT, RINEHART AND WINSTON, INC.
New York   Chicago   San Francisco   Atlanta
Dallas   Montreal   Toronto   London   Sydney

PREFACE

The essays in this anthology deal with aspects of transformational grammar. They were written by the leading scholars in the field, and all were intended for a nontechnical audience. The anthology is divided into two parts. The essays in Part I deal with psycholinguistic questions, in particular, how language is acquired. Those in Part II deal with various applications of transformational grammar: literature and stylistic analysis, composition, second language teaching, and reading. Within each area, the essays are arranged roughly in order of increasing difficulty.

With the exception of several essays that contain their own introduction and summary, each essay is preceded by an introduction that attempts to paraphrase the main ideas and arguments of the essay. Many of the essays in Part I are followed by notes explaining technical points. Most of the essays assume some prior knowledge of transformational grammar. If a reader is totally uninitiated into the mysteries of transformational grammar, he would be well advised to begin with Kellogg W. Hunt's article "How Little Sentences Grow into Big Ones" (p. 170), which contains a brief overview of how the syntactic component of a transformational grammar works.

On the whole, the essays in Part I are more technical than those in Part II. However, an understanding of the applications of the grammar depends completely on a clear grasp of its basic psychological tenets. If a reader has little prior acquaintance with traditional psychology, he would find the first few pages of Leon Jakobovits' article "Implications of Recent Psycholinguistic Developments for the Teaching of a Second Language" (p. 253) very helpful.

I would like to give special thanks to my very able colleagues Ruth Crymes and Ted Plaister, without whose libraries this anthology could never have been compiled, and to my good friend Kellogg W. Hunt, whose sage advice has been most helpful.

M. L.

Honolulu, Hawaii
December 1969

CONTENTS

SECOND LANGUAGE TEACHING

READING

PART I

*The Transformational View
of Language Acquisition*

ERIC H. LENNEBERG

The Biological Foundations of Language

INTRODUCTION

This article, a brief summary of some parts of the author's book by the same title, masses the clinical and developmental evidence relevant to questions about the physiological nature of language and the way that language is acquired. The main thesis of the article is that

> all the evidence suggests that the capacities for speech production and related aspects of language acquisition develop according to built-in biological schedules. They appear when the time is ripe and not until then, when a state of what I have called "resonance" exists. The child somehow becomes "excited," in phase with the environment, so that the sounds he hears and has been hearing all along suddenly acquire a peculiar prominence. The change is like the establishment of new sensitivities. He becomes aware in a new way, selecting certain parts of the total auditory input for attention, ignoring others.

Put in different terms, Lenneberg is asserting that there is (1) a normal developmental pattern for language, and (2) this pattern appears to be in

Reprinted by permission of the author from *Hospital Practice*, December 1967, pp. 59–67.

large part independent of the child's environment. In support of the first point, Lenneberg sketches the stages through which normal language development goes.

The evidence that this development is according to a "built-in biological schedule" and is not the result of environment comes from clinical data. For example, children born to congenitally deaf parents learn to speak at a normal rate, moving through all the predicted stages. Even some institutionalized mentally retarded children, who "live under badly overcrowded conditions, and are comparatively seldom spoken to" manage to make "amazing progress." If a 2- to 3-year-old child is stricken with cerebral trauma, he loses all the language he has learned and starts all over again, "in almost every case and often at a faster rate than the first time. He runs through each stage of infant vocalization all over again, from babbling on." In aphasia there are no "reruns." If the patient is between 4 and 10, he simply picks up where he left off. After the age of 18, however, "complete recovery is the exception rather than the rule." Lenneberg concludes that

> language development thus runs a definite course on a definite schedule; a critical period extends from about age 2 to age 12, the beginning and the end of resonance.

Lenneberg then asks the question of "what it means to say that language is a biological phenomenon." One implication of the statement is that the child does not rely on the parent to "teach" him his language. Children "have their own rules, which we do not know and hence could not teach even if we wanted to." A second implication of the statement is that "the course of language development somehow seems to be related to a unique characteristic of the human species." Man is born helpless and remains helpless longer than any other primate. His mental maturational processes continue long after birth, and consequently his brain has a "capacity for change and growth, long after birth. There is reason to believe that one of the primary selective values of prolonged cerebral immaturity may be to make language possible" and also to provide a long period of linguistic and cultural flexibility.

Lenneberg draws a distinction between understanding and speaking, arguing that "understanding may not only come before speaking, but that it is in some way simpler and more basic." He points out that in all the early speech activity of the child, the child is "recognizing patterns and making increasingly refined distinctions."

The greater part of the remainder of the article is devoted to the question of "bringing language to congenitally deaf children." Lenneberg argues that the cognitive ability of deaf children is probably as great as that of hearing children. Furthermore, there is experimental and clinical evidence indicating that loss of one sensory channel "may have relatively minor central effects." Lenneberg points out one area in which the teachers of the deaf misapprehend the nature of language. The use of writing and pictures has been discouraged because these might "interfere with the achievement of vocal skills." Lenneberg returns to his former point and argues that understanding and "knowledge of language precedes speech and may exist without speech."

The coming of language occurs at about the same age in every healthy child throughout the world, strongly supporting the concept that genetically determined processes of maturation, rather than environmental influences, underlie capacity for speech and verbal understanding. Dr. Lenneberg points out the implications of this concept for the therapeutic and educational approach to children with hearing or speech deficits.

An astonishing spurt in the ability to name things occurs at a definite stage in language development. It represents the culmination of a process that unfolds very slowly until the child reaches the age of about 18 months, when he has learned to utter between three and 50 words. Then, suddenly and spontaneously, the process begins to gather momentum. There is a burst of activity at 24 to 30 months, so that by the time the child completes his third year, give or take a few months, he has built up a speaking vocabulary of more than a thousand words and probably understands another 2,000 to 3,000 words that he has not yet learned to use.

This "naming explosion" is only one of the extraordinary activities which mark the coming of language, perhaps the most human and least understood form of our behavior. As far as we know, it occurs at about the same age in every healthy child throughout the world. The specific factors responsible, the underlying cerebral mechanisms, are still unknown and promise to remain unknown for some time to come. But investigators are mounting renewed attacks on the problem. Recent studies have served as ground-clearing operations, helping to eliminate or at least reduce many of the confusions of times past and, even more important, indicating directions for the research of the future.

One noteworthy aspect of these studies is a shift of emphasis from the outer to the inner world, from culture to biology. Less attention is being directed to such environmental factors as imitation and conditioning and the approval of parents and rewards and punishments— and more to elements rooted far more deeply in physiological reactions. The primary focus is on the development of language as a biological phenomenon which, like the development of walking and other pre-dominantly innate varieties of neuromotor coordination, proceeds in response to genetically determined changes taking place in the matur-ing child.

The emergence of this viewpoint illustrates a key fact about re-search: Discovery often depends on the synthesis of established evidence from many sources as well as on the gathering of brand-new evidence. To be sure, new information about the nature of language and language production has been obtained during the past few years. But valuable insights have also come from the bringing together and analysis of information that has been known to neurologists and other specialists for some time—observations and experimental findings con-cerning the behavior of normal children, congenitally deaf children, and patients suffering from various language disorders.

As a result, workers in a number of disciplines are becoming aware of the possibilities of applying current knowledge more widely and of the need for new knowledge. There is no doubt that the language education of deaf children may be improved by instituting programs designed to take fuller advantage of the biological capacities they share with hearing children and with hearing teachers. Further progress depends above all on basic studies of the brain and its development, studies which may be expected to provide the information required for more sophisticated theories about the development and evolution of language.

The theories will have to account for a rather subtle course of events. Indeed, there is no better way of indicating the magnitude of the task ahead than to take a closer look at how normal children acquire lan-guage. In the beginning nothing spectacular seems to be happening. When the infant is not quiet he is crying or fussing. The first change, which as a rule appears by the sixth to eighth week, consists of cooing, initially characterized by the production of sounds resembling vowels and later of sounds resembling consonants (although spectrograms show they differ acoustically and functionally from true speech sounds).

Further changes follow at a relatively gradual pace. For example, syllable-like babbling generally begins to replace cooing during the sixth month, while the first natural-language feature is observed about two months later in the form of intonations such as those heard in questions and exclamations. A still later step involves the appearance of primitive versions of some phonemes, the 40-odd fundamental speech sounds which in various combinations make up words, as the infant gains an increasing measure of control over his vocal apparatus.

By the 12th month or so he is beginning to produce a few sounds acoustically identical to what you might hear in more mature speech.

The most striking changes occur from here on, of course, at least as far as readily observed behavior is concerned. The buildup of a working vocabulary starts during the second year of life, and identifying the infant's first word has probably been an established family tradition ever since there were words to identify. Even before the naming-explosion stage he uses words to serve as the equivalent of one-word sentences ("daddy," for example, meaning "here comes daddy!" or "where is daddy?" depending on the intonation); soon he forms two-word sentences and begins to communicate actively with those around him.

As already indicated, the naming explosion itself is one among a number of major developments that proceed spontaneously and at about the same time. The child is also learning the rules for forming questions, negations, past tenses, plurals, and so on. Indeed his progress is so rapid that investigators have difficulty keeping track of it or isolating any single change for detailed analysis. By the age of four the child has managed to master the essentials of his native tongue, the complexity of his utterances being roughly equivalent to that of colloquial adult speech.

Although language comes so easily and naturally that we take it for granted, what lies behind the process is anything but self-evident. The sheer mechanics of speech production demand a fantastically high order of integration, an entire complex of special physiological adaptations. For example, respiration alters in a manner observed during no other form of activity. We inhale somewhat faster than is the case when we are at rest and not talking, and exhale a great deal more slowly—so that the net effect is a sharp reduction in respiratory rate, from some 18 to as few as four to five breaths per minute.

At the same time, respiration becomes much deeper. With every breath we inhale 1,500 to 2,400 cc of air, or about three to five times the average at-rest volume. These changes are all the more remarkable considering our extreme sensitivity to any change in normal breathing. After all, even a moderate amount of hyperventilation is sufficient to produce light-headedness and dizziness. Yet we are able to tolerate the comparatively drastic respiratory adjustments that take place automatically as we talk.

The extra air is used to do a very specific job. Held in the lungs as in a bagpipe, it must be released at precisely controlled rates and divided into precisely measured packets to produce the unique kind of "music" known as speech. Such behavior is based on the workings of elaborate neuromotor mechanisms, the coordinated activity of more than a hundred muscles in the tongue, lips, larynx, thoracic and abdominal walls, and so on. The production of a single phoneme requires that the brain send an appropriate message to each one of these muscles, specifying its state of relaxation or tension, and we are capable of talking at a rate of some 840 phonemes or 120 words per minute—for hours on end if the occasion arises.

All the evidence suggests that the capacities for speech production and related aspects of language acquisition develop according to built-in biological schedules. They appear when the time is ripe and not until then, when a state of what I have called "resonance" exists. The child somehow becomes "excited," in phase with the environment, so that the sounds he hears and has been hearing all along suddenly acquire a peculiar prominence. The change is like the establishment of new sensitivities. He becomes aware in a new way, selecting certain parts of the total auditory input for attention, ignoring others.

A vivid example of the change is provided by observations of children who suffer a total loss of hearing practically overnight, usually following virulent meningeal infection. If the attack occurs before the end of the second year, before the start of accelerated speech learning, the child is in precisely the same position as the congenitally deaf child. He must undergo precisely the same training and progresses to the same limited extent. On the other hand, children who become deaf after as little as a year of speech experience respond much more favorably to training. Even a brief exposure to oral communication, provided it takes place during the resonant period, seems to bring with it an enduring advantage.

Language not only appears at a fixed time in the individual's life, it appears at its own pace. Although it seems to be highly sensitive to age, to maturational factors, within limits it appears somewhat more resistant to the impact of environmental factors. Children in orphanages live lives that are deficient linguistically as well as in many other respects; not unexpectedly, tests administered to three-year-olds show that they are frequently well below average in speech development. But the language deficit tends to disappear during subsequent growth, and follow-up tests show that most of them have caught up by the time they are six or seven.

Further insights into the development of language behavior in drastically impoverished environments are furnished by several studies that I conducted some years ago at the Children's Hospital Medical

Center in Boston with my associates Irene Nichols, Freda Rebelsky, and Eleanor Rosenberger. In one study we compared the emergence of vocalization during the first three months of life among infants born to normal parents and infants whose parents were both congenitally deaf—and who thus heard far less adult speech and elicited no responses to their own vocalizations. (Deaf mothers cannot easily tell whether or not their infants' facial expressions and gestures are accompanied by sounds.)

There were no significant differences in total amount of vocalization and age of onset. Extensive tape recordings indicate that vowel-like cooing appeared in both groups at about the same time. Moreover, subsequent development continues in normal fashion. We have observed a dozen older children of deaf couples, children who heard only the vocalizations of other adults and their playmates, and in every case they passed without delays through the regular stages from babbling to full command of the language. Incidentally, by their third birthdays or shortly thereafter they were essentially "bilingual," using special sounds and gestures to communicate with their parents, and normal speech for the rest of the world.

The most extreme examples of environmental impoverishment are undoubtedly found among institutionalized mentally retarded children, including microcephalics, patients with phenylketonuria, and so on. In general they live under badly overcrowded conditions, and are comparatively seldom spoken to. Yet considering the circumstances, some children make amazing progress. Although language development is severely limited in the great majority of patients, those who manage to acquire some skill may do surprisingly well. They may not be able to talk, but occasionally they achieve an impressive measure of understanding and show quite clearly that they follow what you say.

Judging by these and other studies language apparently has a kind of self-propelling, driving quality. As a matter of fact it is extremely difficult to suppress its development, even in the most restricted environments encountered. Once the process has been triggered it continues with the pace and rhythm of an organic force until its time is up, until the "switch" that was turned on with the coming of resonance is turned off—at which point there is nothing we can do to extend the period of learning.

Progress in language development usually ceases after the age of 12 or 13, after puberty. One sign of the change may be seen in the learning of a second language. The extent of a foreign accent is directly correlated with the age at which the second language is acquired. At the age of three or four practically every child entering a foreign com-

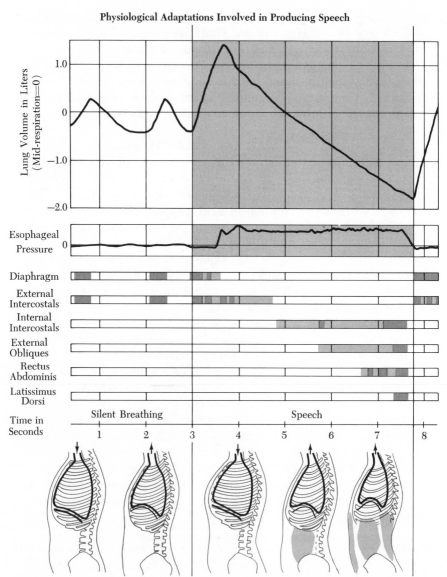

Physiological Adaptations Involved in Producing Speech

Profound alterations in respiration are needed to provide the expired air that drives human speech. In silent breathing, muscular work is largely confined to increasing the volume of the thoracic cage, which produces the negative pressure that causes air to be inhaled. Except in special situations, only the diaphragm and inspiratory muscles are involved. With speech, after a much larger volume of air has been taken into the lungs, the inspiratory, expiratory, and abdominal muscles work in sequence to expel this air gradually and in a controlled manner. In the drawings above, changes in lung volume are shown by the heavy black line superimposed upon the ribs, the sequences of muscular action by the tinted areas. Interval between breaths is increased threefold.

munity learns to speak the new language rapidly and without a trace of an accent. This facility declines with age. The proportion of children who speak the second language with an accent tends to increase, but very slowly, so that by about the age of 12, perhaps 1% or 2% pronounce words differently from native speakers. A dramatic reversal of form occurs during the early teens, however, when practically every child loses the ability to learn a new language without an accent.

A similar cutoff point exists for language development generally, and we can learn something about this development from studies of children suffering from acquired aphasia. As a rule, the earlier the condition occurs, the more complete the recovery. Cerebral trauma occurring during the period from two to three, the period of most rapid acquisition, may in effect erase all the language the patient has learned. As a result he must start from scratch—which is precisely what he proceeds to do, in almost every case and often at a faster rate than the first time. He runs through each stage of infant vocalization all over again, from babbling on.

There are no "reruns" when aphasia strikes between ages four and 10, patients simply picking up where they left off. Recovery may take place over a period of several years, but is complete in most cases. Puberty again marks the cutoff point. Aphasias which appear after puberty or which have not cleared up by this time usually leave traces in the form of peculiar pauses, searching for words, and other symptoms. Among adults, that is, after the age of 18 or so, complete recovery is the exception rather than the rule, and symptoms that have not

Chronological Aspects of Language Growth

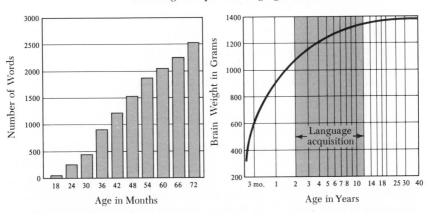

disappeared within five months following the aphasic attack are likely to be permanent.

Language development thus runs a definite course on a definite schedule; a critical period extends from about age two to age 12, the beginning and the end of resonance.

So far we have concentrated chiefly on some of the overt changes under way during this period. The problem of understanding language, however, involves going beneath the descriptive level to a consideration of deeper processes. Above all it involves spelling out in as much detail as possible just what it means to say that language is a biological phenomenon and, more specifically, a phenomenon of developmental biology.

For one thing the statement implies an important but limited role for the environment, particularly for parents. Separate studies of actual speech records, done by Martin Braine of the Walter Reed Army Hospital, Roger Brown of Harvard, and Susan Ervin of the University of California, indicate that contrary to former beliefs children do not learn language by parroting what their parents say. Their utterances are truly creative. Phrases such as "daddy allgone," "more up," "hi, milk," etc., represent the children's original combinations, not something they have heard and are repeating. Furthermore, we are not their teachers. We do not decide to instruct our offspring in grammar and syntax. This is fortunate because they have their own rules, which we do not know and hence could not teach even if we wanted to.

Children will never learn language unless they hear it, and we fulfill our function simply by talking, the more the better. Beyond that and offering moral support there is little for us to do, because biology takes over. Biology takes over in basically the same fashion as it does when the child metabolizes protein after eating. He uses the proteins but not in ready-made form. They are broken down into polypeptides and amino acids and reassembled according to built-in purposes, purposes embodied in the genetic codes that determine the directions of protein synthesis and serve the needs of his maturing body.

A very close parallel, amounting to far more than a convenient analogy, exists between such reactions and the acquisition of language. The child needs language for survival just as he needs food. The information he receives from us may be regarded as raw material of a sort. It passes via auditory channels into the central nervous system, where it is "absorbed," broken down into its elements, and resynthesized in the achievement of varied and complex language skills. The critical question, of course, is how this processing is accomplished, and at this stage of our ignorance we have clues and hunches rather than answers.

The course of language development somehow seems to be related to a unique characteristic of the human species. Man is born "premature" in a sense that holds true for no other primate. He comes into the world more helpless and remains helpless longer than any other member of the primate order. The weight of his brain at birth is only about a fourth of its adult weight, which means that maturational processes go on long after birth—and that the brain retains some of its "plasticity," its capacity for change and growth, long after birth. There is reason to believe that one of the primary selective values of prolonged cerebral immaturity may be to make language possible.

Milestones in Motor and Language Development

12 Weeks

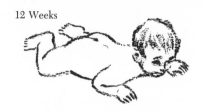

16 Weeks

Baby supports head when in prone position; weight is on elbows; no grasp reflex is present. Crying has diminished, vowel-like cooing has begun and is sometimes sustained for 15 to 20 seconds.

Head is self-supported, and baby can shake rattle; tonic neck reflex is subsiding. Response to human sounds is more definite; eyes seem to search for speaker. Occasional chuckling sounds are made.

20 Weeks

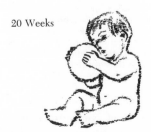

6 Months

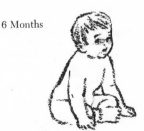

Child can sit with props. Consonantal sounds are beginning to be interspersed with the vowel-like cooing. Acoustically, however, all vocalizations are very different from sounds of mature language.

Baby bends forward and uses hands for support while sitting; reaching is unilateral. Cooing is changing into babbling with resemblance to single syllables. Most common sounds are ma, mu, da, di.

8 Months

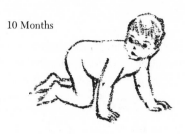

10 Months

Baby stands holding on and can grasp with thumb apposition. Repetitions of sounds are becoming frequent, intonation patterns distinct, and utterances begin to be used to signal emphasis and emotions.

Creeping is efficient, and child can take side steps holding on, pull self to standing position. Vocalizations are mixed with sound play like gurgling or bubble-blowing; baby tries to imitate sounds, begins to respond differentially to words heard.

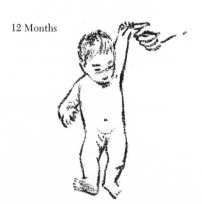

12 Months

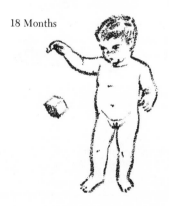

18 Months

Child walks when held by one hand, or walks on feet and hands with knees in air, and can seat self on floor. Identical sound sequences are repeated more often, and words (mamma or dadda) are emerging. Definite signs of understanding appear in responses to simple commands.

Grasp, prehension, and release are fully developed; gait is still stiff. Child can creep downstairs backward. Word repertoire is more than three, less than 50; understanding is progressing rapidly but joining of word units into spontaneous two-word phrases is uncommon.

In this connection the end of resonance may also have special evolutionary significance. Nature must make some sort of compromise between maintaining cerebral plasticity as long as possible and the need for stability, for a kind of "freezing" of developmental possibilities, upon which unvarying adult communication and social cohesion depend. The human group is by far the most complex and demanding that has yet evolved, and language is essential to enable the individual to play his roles in a social context. So it makes sense both that there be ample time for language development and that the process be completed by the age of puberty, when the individual must begin to play his social roles most actively.

As we have already pointed out, language acquisition begins at about the age of two, when the brain has reached some 60% of full maturity. This is also a time of rapid progress in walking and other motor skills; indeed, a notable feature of human development is the close synchronization of milestones in the acquisition of such skills and language. Among the most obvious cerebral changes is the increasing involvement of the left hemisphere in language function, which usually becomes well established before the age of 10. The precise significance of cerebral dominance remains unknown. But in general it represents one aspect of prolonged and continuing maturation, reflecting the fact that different parts of the brain are committed at different times in line with programs perhaps specified in genetic codes.

The earliest commitments, and in many ways the most elusive and significant, actually precede the appearance of natural-language features. Infants indicate that they understand some words and simple commands as early as the 12th month, although they may not utter words for another half year or more, and understanding continues to outrun speech production throughout life. I had an opportunity to study an extreme example of this phenomenon in a boy suffering from a congenital neurological deficit of speech articulation, probably due to fetal anoxia. Nine years old when last seen, he was essentially with-

The Inheritance of Language Disorders

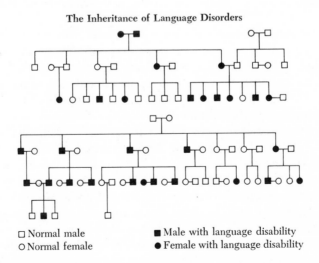

☐ Normal male   ■ Male with language disability
○ Normal female   ● Female with language disability

out productive speech. Yet many tests have shown beyond doubt the boy has a full comprehension of spoken language. For example, he follows such instructions as "take the block and put it in the bottle" and answers questions based on stories he has just heard, including questions designed to eliminate visual and other extralinguistic clues.

This case demonstrates the important principle that understanding may not only come before speaking, but that it is in some way simpler and more basic. In other words there is something distinct from speaking, which we may call a knowledge of language—and which takes shape very early in life.

The newborn infant is immersed in sensation, including a rich variety of sounds, and his job is to make sense of them. Perhaps the first and most obvious step is to make a provisional distinction between meaningful sounds that must be heeded and analyzed further, and meaningless sounds that may be ignored. But this is only the beginning of a long series of more and more sophisticated distinctions. For example, as the Harvard linguist Roman Jakobson was the first to point out some 25 years ago, the primitive phonemes uttered between the sixth and the 12th months of life are not really clean-cut individual acoustic items. They actually consist of large groups of closely related sounds. In other words, the infant is recognizing and reproducing increasingly subtle acoustic patterns and further subdividing the world of meaningful sounds into classes that will ultimately become what we know as mature phonemes.

This process is also at work during the naming stage. Many of the name-words in early vocabularies have not yet acquired their full "status," their precise adult meanings. Strictly speaking, they are often overgeneralized, standing for groups of objects rather than for particular objects. At one stage all the large deep-voiced objects that enter the infant's field of vision are lumped under the single heading "daddy"; he learns later that the term applies to only one of the objects. Similarly, "truck" may stand for all vehicles, and "bye-bye" for all exits and everything related to them.

Again, it is a matter of recognizing patterns and making increasingly refined distinctions. The process of dividing and subdividing represents a kind of differentiation, and in the last analysis it turns out to be identical to biological differentiation itself—to the complex of stage-by-stage chain reactions whereby a single cell gives rise to hundreds of types or classes of cells. The significance of classifying, creating categories, in language development has been emphasized in basic mathematical studies by Noam Chomsky of the Massachusetts Institute of Technology. Indeed, his research has stirred the imagination of investigators at many laboratories and helped bring about an increase in experimental as well as theoretical studies of language.

One of the major effects of this work has been to stimulate new interest in the truly formidable problem of bringing language to congenitally deaf children. The biological or developmental approach offers considerable encouragement to these patients and to their dedicated teachers. In the first place it is highly probable that their cognitive ability is not defective or inferior to that of hearing children. They may have very little language or none at all by the time they enter a school for the deaf at the age of five or six, but there is every reason to assume that their capacity for reasoning and forming nonverbal concepts has not been adversely affected.

Furthermore, there is reason to believe that the central mechanisms concerned with the essentially automatic development of cognition and language are intact—and that in most cases of sensory deprivation the brain readily accepts information entering through substitute sensory channels. The main qualification here is that the deprivation involve only a single sensory modality. Animal experiments and clinical observations indicate that the loss of two modalities results in severe behavioral disturbances, while the loss of one may have relatively minor central effects. So we may proceed on the basis that as far as the biological apparatus for cognition is concerned, deaf and hearing pre-schoolers have equal underlying capacities for language development.

A warning is in order here. It is important to point out that this situation apparently holds for a limited period only, the critical period during which the state of resonance exists. While in about three out of four cases a relevant family history or one of the well-known antecedents for congenital deafness (rubella during the first trimester, erythroblastosis fetalis, meningitis, bilateral ear infection, and so on) will alert the parents to the possibility of deafness, in other cases they have no advance warning. An experienced observer can detect deafness as early as the sixth month or so, because the babbling of the affected infant is less varied than that of the hearing infant, and his intonation patterns tend to be inferior. But very commonly the condition is not detected until the end of the first year, and often not until the 18th to 24th month. This is by no means too late, although in general the earlier we recognize the problem the better.

When it comes to special training, prospects are bright for achieving appreciable improvements simply by applying more fully the knowledge we already possess. Schools for the deaf have made notable progress in oral education, in a variety of drills and exercises designed to develop speech as far as possible by promoting proper breathing, lip and tongue articulation, and so on. But there has been a tendency to discourage certain other measures, such as the use of graphics (writing and pictures), partly on the grounds that they might interfere with the achievement of vocal skills.

It so happens that all the available evidence suggests that precisely the opposite is the case. The odds are that graphics will actively facilitate rather than hinder vocal communication. We have emphasized that knowledge of language precedes speech and may exist without speech—and it is this fundamental capacity, rather than subsidiary skills, which must be the primary focus of our educational efforts, which must be fostered and given complete scope for development. That means providing as much language as possible and making the fullest possible use of the visual modality, an especially important point when we consider the limited value of lip-reading. (Hearing adults without formal training do at least as well in lip-reading tests as deaf adults who have been trained for years.)

I am convinced that much can be gained by a more extensive application of graphic techniques. For one thing, the vast majority of deaf individuals cannot produce a page of writing without making at least one grammatical or stylistic mistake, and it seems likely that this difficulty could be eliminated. On a broader scale, the free use of graphics such as notes may be expected to make possible richer, more rapid, and less self-conscious communication with hearing persons.

It may be helpful to consider another serious communication problem, the wide gap between the teacher of the deaf and the physician. The teacher is apt to be isolated from the mainstream of medical investigation and so is not as aware as he might be of recent findings and thinking that could make his work still more productive. On the other hand, the physician, who devotes considerable attention to education for nurses, is often reluctant to take corresponding pains in the case of speech teachers—largely because he does not realize how difficult it is to help deaf children. Part of the solution to this problem calls for a greater involvement of the medical profession and the hospital. Teachers should be included regularly in appropriate seminars and offered more systematic training by physicians in a hospital setting.

From a research standpoint the big task for the future is to understand the detailed anatomy and physiology of language. The task might be less formidable if gross structures of the brain were involved, if language had a reasonably straightforward connection with relative or absolute brain size, for example. Unfortunately this is definitely not

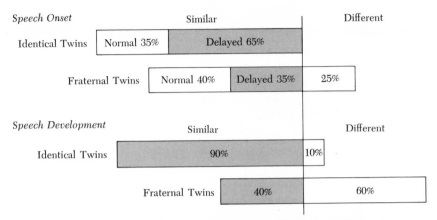

Twin Studies and Language Development

Speech Onset — Similar / Different

Identical Twins: Normal 35% | Delayed 65%

Fraternal Twins: Normal 40% | Delayed 35% | 25%

Speech Development — Similar / Different

Identical Twins: 90% | 10%

Fraternal Twins: 40% | 60%

Role of genetic (i.e., biological) factors in speech is further under-scored by studies in twins, who may be assumed to share identical environments. Identical twins show far more synchronous history than fraternal twins, in both onset and growth of speech.

the case, a conclusion supported by observations of a rare recessive disease known as nanocephalic dwarfism. Individuals suffering from the condition have normal skeletal proportions, a height of often no more than 2½ feet, and a brain weighing an estimated 400 gm, or about a third of the weight of the normal adult brain. Although these dwarfs are intellectually retarded, they all master the rudiments of language and speak and understand at least as well as a five-year-old child.

It would be difficult indeed to present more striking evidence for the notion that our capacity for language has little to do with the mass or quantity of nervous tissue, with sheer numbers of neurons—and everything to do with how neurons are organized and interact with one another. At this level we know nothing about the shaping or use of language, about the biology of pattern recognition and category formation and naming, but our knowledge of neurophysiology broadly indicates what must be going on.

The brain is a machine where the dynamic changes of developmental processes produce changes of living rhythms. Neurons are not passive receiver-transmitters that "speak only when spoken to," responding only when stimulated. They are constantly on the go, producing spontaneous rhythms. And all our experiences, linguistic and otherwise, are reflected in enduring changes of those rhythms, perhaps analogous to frequency modulation. This process in turn may reflect underlying structural changes on a molecular level, and here, again, we are ignorant.

Relevant biochemical studies are a long way off. We must learn more concerning the basic workings of the brain, the nature of cerebral plasticity and neural coding, and the capacity for categorizing in lower animals, before we become sufficiently sophisticated to conduct research specifically on the neurophysiology of language. Then we shall be coming to grips with the most human thing about human beings, the quality that distinguishes man from all other species.

GEORGE MILLER

The Psycholinguists

INTRODUCTION

Miller feels that the central task of psycholinguistics is "to describe the psychological processes that go on when people use sentences." In this essay he narrows the question to a consideration of the processes that we may suppose the listener performs on a spoken utterance. Miller recognizes six levels of activity: (1) hearing, (2) matching, (3) accepting, (4) interpreting, (5) understanding, and (6) believing. This is an ascending scale of abstraction ranging from "the superficial to the inscrutable."

The first level, hearing, is the simplest activity. Even an unknown language can be heard. However, the second level, matching, involves the hearer's ability to impose a *phonological* interpretation upon what is heard; that is, the hearer breaks the stream of sound into recognizable syllables and words. The third level, accepting, involves the ability to impose a *grammatical* interpretation upon the utterance; that is, the hearer can accept or reject the sentence as a grammatical sentence in his language and can also offer grammatical paraphrases of the sentence. The fourth level, interpreting, involves the hearer's ability to understand what the sentence means; that is, he can impose a *semantic* interpretation upon the sentence. The

Reprinted by permission of the author, from *Encounter,* Vol. 23, No. 1 (July 1964), pp. 29–37.

fifth level, understanding, involves the hearer's ability to grasp the contextual significance of the sentence, for example, the speaker's intention. The last level, believing, involves the hearer's ability to judge the truth of the sentence.

Miller next explores the concept of "matching" in greater detail. He suggests that a hearer is able to recognize an utterance by virtue of his ability to generate an utterance of his own that has the same phonological properties as the utterance heard and that would also be appropriate to the occasion.

One difficulty with this theory of matching is that the number of possible sentences that the hearer might be called upon to match is unlimited. Obviously the capacity of the human brain is not so great that it can store all possible English sentences in its memory. Instead, Miller argues, the brain must have the capacity to generate and interpret (match) new sentences as it needs them. All human language (as opposed to nonhuman languages such as logical languages) are basically alike in that they are capable of being generated by man's unique linguistic capacity.

To demonstrate that man's linguistic capacity is innate and not learned, Miller compares the way a child acquires language with the difficulties that a computer would have if given the same data as the child. The child learns the language of his environment without instruction or motivation. The computer, however, cannot, even in theory, discover what kind of organization to look for. Miller concludes that children are born predisposed to learn language, or as Miller puts it, "Human language must be such that a child can acquire it."

The final part of the essay draws a distinction between the speaker's linguistic competence and his actual performance. There are many limitations on performance that have nothing to do with competence, and Miller illustrates this by presenting three versions of the same sentence. One of the three versions is almost completely beyond our ability to understand, even though it is basically the same as the other two versions. In this case the form of the sentence, even though it is grammatical, imposes an impossible burden on our memory.

Psychologists have long recognized that human minds feed on linguistic symbols. Linguists have always admitted that some kind of psycho-social motor must move the machinery of grammar and lexicon. Sooner or later they were certain to examine their intersection self-consciously. Perhaps it was also inevitable that the result would be called "psycholinguistics."

In fact, although the enterprise itself has slowly been gathering strength at least since the invention of the telephone, the name, in its unhyphenated form, is only about ten years old. Few seem pleased with the term, but the field has grown so rapidly and stirred so much interest in recent years that some way of referring to it is urgently needed. *Psycholinguistics* is as descriptive a term as any, and shorter than most.

Among psychologists it was principally the behaviourists who wished to take a closer look at language. Behaviourists generally try to replace anything subjective by its most tangible, physical manifestation, so they have had a long tradition of confusing thought with speech—or with "verbal behaviour," as many prefer to call it. Among linguists it was principally those with an anthropological sideline who were most willing to collaborate, perhaps because as anthropologists they were sensitive to all those social and psychological processes that support our linguistic practices. By working together they managed to call attention to an important field of scientific research and to integrate it, or at least to acquaint its various parts with one another, under this new rubric.*

Interest in psycholinguistics, however, is not confined to psychologists and linguists. Many people have been stirred by splendid visions of its practical possibilities. One thinks of medical applications to the diagnosis and treatment of a heterogeneous variety of language disorders ranging from simple stammering to the overwhelming complexities of aphasia.† One thinks too of pedagogical applications, of potential improvements in our methods for teaching reading and writing, or for teaching second languages. If psycholinguistic principles were made sufficiently explicit, they could be imparted to those technological miracles of the twentieth century, the computing machines, which would bring into view a whole spectrum of cybernetic possibilities.‡ We could exploit our electrical channels for voice communications more efficiently. We might improve and automate our dictionaries, using them for mechanical translation from one language to another. Perhaps computers could print what we say, or even say what we print, thus making speech visible for the deaf and printing

---

* A representative sample of research papers in this field can be found in *Psycholinguistics: A Book of Readings*, edited by S. Saporta (Holt, Rinehart and Winston, New York, 1962). R. Brown provides a readable survey from a psychologist's point of view in *Words and Things* (Free Press, Glencoe, Illinois, 1957).

† The CIBA Foundation Symposium, *Disorders of Language* (J. & A. Churchill, London, 1964), provides an excellent sample of the current status of medical psycholinguistics.

‡ *Natural Language and the Computer*, edited by P. L. Garvin (McGraw-Hill, New York, 1963).

audible for the blind. We might, in short, learn to adapt computers to dozens of our human purposes if only they could interpret our languages. Little wonder that assorted physicians, educators, philosophers, logicians, and engineers have been intrigued by this new adventure.

Of course, the realisation of practical benefits must await the success of the scientific effort; there is some danger that enthusiasm may colour our estimate of what can be accomplished. Not a few sceptics remain unconvinced; some can even be found who argue that success is impossible in principle. "Science," they say, "can go only so far. . . ."

The integration of psycholinguistic studies has occurred so recently that there is still some confusion concerning its scope and purpose; efforts to clarify it necessarily have something of the character of personal opinions.§ In my own version, the central task of this new science is to describe the psychological processes that go on when people use sentences. The real crux of the psycholinguistic problem does not appear until one tries to deal with sentences, for only then does the importance of productivity become completely obvious. It is true that productivity can also appear with individual words, but there it is not overwhelming. With sentences, productivity is literally unlimited.

Before considering this somewhat technical problem, however, it might be well to illustrate the variety of processes that psycholinguists hope to explain. This can best be done if we ask what a listener can do about a spoken utterance, and consider his alternatives in order from the superficial to the inscrutable.

The simplest thing one can do in the presence of a spoken utterance is to listen. Even if the language is incomprehensible, one can still *hear* an utterance as an auditory stimulus and respond to it in terms of some discriminative set: how loud, how fast, how long, from which direction, etc.

Given that an utterance is heard, the next level involves *matching* it as a phonemic pattern in terms of phonological skills acquired as a user of the language. The ability to match an input can be tested in psychological experiments by asking listeners to echo what they hear; a wide variety of experimental situations—experiments on the perception of speech and on the rote memorisation of verbal materials—can

§ My own opinions have been strongly influenced by Noam Chomsky. A rather technical exposition of this work can be found in Chapters 11–13 of the second volume of the *Handbook of Mathematical Psychology*, edited by R. D. Luce, R. R. Bush, and E. Galanter (Wiley, New York, 1963), from which many of the ideas discussed here have been drawn.

be summarised as tests of a person's ability to repeat the speech he hears under various conditions of audibility or delay.

If a listener can hear and match an utterance, the next question to ask is whether he will *accept* it as a sentence in terms of his knowledge of grammar. At this level we encounter processes difficult to study experimentally, and one is forced to rely most heavily on linguistic analyses of the structure of sentences. Some experiments are possible, however, for we can measure how much a listener's ability to accept the utterance as a sentence facilitates his ability to hear and match it; grammatical sentences are much easier to hear, utter or remember than are ungrammatical strings of words, and even nonsense (*pirot, karol, elat*, etc.) is easier to deal with if it looks grammatical (*pirots karolise elatically*, etc.).‖ Needless to say, the grammatical knowledge we wish to study does not concern those explicit rules drilled into us by teachers of traditional grammar, but rather the implicit generative knowledge that we all must acquire in order to use a language appropriately.

Beyond grammatical acceptance comes semantic interpretation: we can ask how listeners *interpret* an utterance as meaningful in terms of their semantic system. Interpretation is not merely a matter of assigning meanings to individual words; we must also consider how these component meanings combine in grammatical sentences. Compare the sentences: *Healthy young babies sleep soundly* and *Colourless green ideas sleep furiously.* Although they are syntactically similar, the second is far harder to perceive and remember correctly—because it cannot be interpreted by the usual semantic rules for combining the senses of adjacent English words.＃ The interpretation of each word is affected by the company it keeps; a central problem is to systematise the interactions of words and phrases with their linguistic contexts. The lexicographer makes his major contribution at this point, but psychological studies of our ability to paraphrase an utterance also have their place.

At the next level it seems essential to make some distinction between interpreting an utterance and understanding it, for understanding frequently goes well beyond the linguistic context provided by the utterance itself. A husband greeted at the door by "I bought some electric light bulbs to-day" must do more than interpret its literal reference; he must understand that he should go to the kitchen and replace that

‖ W. Epstein, "The Influence of Syntactical Structure on Learning," *American Journal of Psychology* (1961), vol. 74, pp. 80–85.
＃ G. A. Miller and S. Isard, "Some Perceptual Consequences of Linguistic Rules," *Journal of Verbal Learning and Verbal Behavior* (1963), vol. 2, pp. 217–228. J. J. Katz and J. A. Fodor have recently contributed a thoughtful discussion of "The Structure of Semantic Theory," *Language* (1963), vol. 39, pp. 170–210.

burned-out lamp. Such contextual information lies well outside any grammar or lexicon. The listener can *understand* the function of an utterance in terms of contextual knowledge of the most diverse sort.

Finally, at a level now almost invisible through the clouds, a listener may *believe* that an utterance is valid in terms of its relevance to his own conduct. The child who says "I saw five lions in the garden" may be heard, matched, accepted, interpreted, and understood, but in few parts of the world will he be believed.

The boundaries between successive levels are not sharp and distinct. One shades off gradually into the next. Still the hierarchy is real enough and important to keep in mind. Simpler types of psycholinguistic processes can be studied rather intensively; already we know much about hearing and matching. Accepting and interpreting are just now coming into scientific focus. Understanding is still over the horizon, and pragmatic questions involving belief systems are presently so vague as to be hardly worth asking. But the whole range of processes must be included in any adequate definition of psycholinguistics.

I phrased the description of these various psycholinguistic processes in terms of a listener; the question inevitably arises as to whether a different hierarchy is required to describe the speaker. One problem a psycholinguist faces is to decide whether speaking and listening are two separate abilities, co-ordinate but distinct, or whether they are merely different manifestations of a single linguistic faculty.

The mouth and ear are different organs; at the simplest levels we must distinguish hearing and matching from vocalising and speaking. At more complex levels it is less easy to decide whether the two abilities are distinct. At some point they must converge, if only to explain why it is so difficult to speak and listen simultaneously. The question is where.

It is easy to demonstrate how important to a speaker is the sound of his own voice. If his speech is delayed a fifth of a second, amplified, and fed back into his own ears, the voice-ear asynchrony can be devastating to the motor skills of articulate speech. It is more difficult, however, to demonstrate that the same linguistic competence required for speaking is also involved in processing the speech of others.

Recently Morris Halle and Kenneth Stevens of the Massachusetts Institute of Technology revived a suggestion made by Wilhelm von Humboldt over a century ago.** Suppose we accept the notion that a listener recognises what he hears by comparing it with some internal

** M. Halle and K. N. Stevens, "Speech Recognition: A Model and a Program for Research," *IRE Transactions on Information Theory* (1962), vol. ɪᴛ-8, pp. 155–159.

representation. To the extent that a match can be obtained, the input is accepted and interpreted. One trouble with this hypothesis, however, is that a listener must be ready to recognise any one of an enormous number of different sentences. It is inconceivable that a separate internal representation for each of them could be stored in his memory in advance. Halle and Stevens suggest that these internal representations must be generated as they are needed by following the same generative rules that are normally used in producing speech. In this way the rules of the language are incorporated into the theory only once, in a generative form; they need not be learned once by the ear and again by the tongue. This is a theory of a language-user, not of a speaker or a listener alone.

The listener begins with a guess about the input. On that basis he generates an internal matching signal. The first attempt will probably be in error; if so, the mismatch is reported and used as a basis for a next guess, which should be closer. This cycle repeats (unconsciously, almost certainly) until a satisfactory (not necessarily a correct) match is obtained, at which point the next segment of speech is scanned and matched, etc. The output is not a transformed version of the input; it is the programme that was followed to generate the matching representation.

The perceptual categories available to such a system are defined by the generative rules at its disposal. It is also reasonably obvious that its efficiency is critically dependent on the quality of the initial guess. If this guess is close, an iterative process can converge rapidly; if not, the listener will be unable to keep pace with the rapid flow of conversational speech.

A listener's first guess probably derives in part from syntactic markers in the form of intonation, inflection, suffixes, etc., and in part from his general knowledge of the semantic and situational context. Syntactic cues indicate how the input is to be grouped and which words function together; semantic and contextual contributions are more difficult to characterise, but must somehow enable him to limit the range of possible words that he can expect to hear.

How he is able to do this is an utter mystery, but the fact that he can do it is easily demonstrated.

The English psychologist David Bruce recorded a set of ordinary sentences and played them in the presence of noise so intense that the voice was just audible, but not intelligible.†† He told his listeners that these were sentences on some general topic—sports, say—and asked

†† "Effects of Context upon the Intelligibility of Heard Speech," in *Information Theory,* edited by Colin Cherry (Butterworths, London, 1956, pp. 245–252).

them to repeat what they heard. He then told them they would hear more sentences on a different topic, which they were also to repeat. This was done several times. Each time the listeners repeated sentences appropriate to the topic announced in advance. When at the end of the experiment Bruce told them they had heard the same recording every time—all he had changed was the topic they were given—most listeners were unable to believe it.

With an advance hypothesis about what the message will be we can tune our perceptual system to favour certain interpretations and reject others. This fact is no proof of a generative process in speech perception, but it does emphasise the important role of context. For most theories of speech perception the facilitation provided by context is merely a fortunate though rather complicated fact. For a generative theory it is essential.

Note that generative theories do not assume that a listener must be able to articulate the sounds he recognises, but merely that he be able to generate some internal representation to match the input. In this respect a generative theory differs from a motor theory (such as that of Sir Richard Paget) which assumes that we can identify only those utterances we are capable of producing ourselves. There is some rather compelling evidence against a motor theory. The American psychologist Eric Lenneberg has described the case of an eight-year-old boy with congenital anarthria; despite his complete inability to speak, the boy acquired an excellent ability to understand language.[‡‡] Moreover, it is a common observation that utterances can be understood by young children before they are able to produce them. A motor theory of speech-perception draws too close a parallel between our two capacities as users of language. Even so, the two are more closely integrated than most people realise.

I have already offered the opinion that productivity sets the central problem for the psycholinguist and have even referred to it indirectly by arguing that we can produce too many different sentences to store them all in memory. The issue can be postponed no longer.

To make the problem plain, consider an example on the level of individual words. For several days I carried in my pocket a small white card on which was typed UNDERSTANDER. On suitable occasions I would hand it to someone. "How do you pronounce this?" I asked.

He pronounced it.

"Is it an English word?"

‡‡ "Understanding Language without Ability to Speak: A Case Report," *Journal of Abnormal and Social Psychology* (1962), vol. 65, pp. 419–425.

He hesitated. "I haven't seen it used very much. I'm not sure."

"Do you know what it means?"

"I suppose it means 'one who understands.'"

I thanked him and changed the subject.

Of course, understander *is* an English word, but to find it you must look in a large dictionary where you will probably read that it is "now rare." Rare enough, I think, for none of my respondents to have seen it before. Nevertheless, they all answered in the same way. Nobody seemed surprised. Nobody wondered how he could understand and pronounce a word without knowing whether it was a word. Everybody put the main stress on the third syllable and constructed a meaning from the verb "to understand" and the agentive suffix "*er*." Familiar morphological rules of English were applied as a matter of course, even though the combination was completely novel.

Probably no one but a psycholinguist captured by the ingenuous behaviouristic theory that words are vocal responses conditioned to occur in the presence of appropriate stimuli would find anything exceptional in this. Since none of my friends had seen the word before, and so could not have been "conditioned" to give the responses they did, how would this theory account for their "verbal behaviour"? Advocates of a conditioning theory of meaning—and there are several distinguished scientists among them—would probably explain linguistic productivity in terms of "conditioned generalisations."§§ They could argue that my respondents had been conditioned to the word understand and to the suffix—*er*; responses to their union could conceivably be counted as instances of stimulus generalisation. In this way, novel responses could occur without special training.

Although a surprising amount of psychological ingenuity has been invested in this kind of argument, it is difficult to estimate its value. No one has carried the theory through for all the related combinations that must be explained simultaneously. One can speculate, however, that there would have to be many different kinds of generalisation, each with a carefully defined range of applicability. For example, it would be necessary to explain why "understander" is acceptable, whereas "erunderstand" is not. Worked out in detail, such a theory would become a sort of Pavlovian paraphrase of a linguistic description. Of course, if one believes there is some essential difference between behaviour governed by conditioned habits and behaviour

§§ A dog conditioned to salivate at the sound of a tone will also salivate, though less copiously, at the sound of similar tones, the magnitude declining as the new tones become less similar to the original. This phenomenon is called "stimulus generalisation."

governed by rules, the paraphrase could never be more than a vast intellectual pun.

Original combinations of elements are the life blood of language. It is our ability to produce and comprehend such novelties that makes language so ubiquitously useful. As psychologists have become more seriously interested in the cognitive processes that language entails, they have been forced to recognise that the fundamental puzzle is not our ability to associate vocal noises with perceptual objects, but rather our combinatorial productivity—our ability to understand an unlimited diversity of utterances never heard before and to produce an equal variety of utterances similarly intelligible to other members of our speech community. Faced with this problem, concepts borrowed from conditioning theory seem not so much invalid as totally inadequate.

Some idea of the relative magnitudes of what we might call the productive as opposed to the reproductive components of any psycholinguistic theory is provided by statistical studies of language. A few numbers can reinforce the point. If you interrupt a speaker at some randomly chosen instant, there will be, on the average, about ten words that form grammatical and meaningful continuations. Often only one word is admissible and sometimes there are thousands, but on the average it works out to about ten. (If you think this estimate too low, I will not object; larger estimates strengthen the argument.) A simple English sentence can easily run to a length of twenty words, so elementary arithmetic tells us that there must be at least 10^{20} such sentences that a person who knows English must know how to deal with.[1] Compare this productive potential with the 10^4 or 10^5 individual words we know—the reproductive component of our theory—and the discrepancy is dramatically illustrated. Putting it differently, it would take 100,000,000,000 centuries (one thousand times the estimated age of the earth) to utter all the admissible twenty-word sentences of English. Thus, the probability that you might have heard any particular twenty-word sentence before is negligible. Unless it is a cliché, every sentence must come to you as a novel combination of morphemes. Yet you can interpret it at once if you know the English language.

With these facts in mind it is impossible to argue that we learn to understand sentences from teachers who have pronounced each one and explained what it meant. What we have learned are not particular strings of words, but *rules* for generating admissible strings of words.

Consider what it means to follow a rule; this consideration shifts the discussion of psycholinguistics into very difficult territory. The nature of rules has been a central concern of modern philosophy and perhaps no analysis has been more influential than Ludwig Wittgenstein's. Wittgenstein remarked that the most characteristic thing we can say about "rule-governed behavior" is that the person who knows the rules knows whether he is proceeding correctly or incorrectly. Although he may not be able to formulate the rules explicitly, he knows what it is to make a mistake. If this remark is accepted, we must ask ourselves whether an animal that has been conditioned is privy to any such knowledge about the correctness of what he is doing. Perhaps such a degree of insight could be achieved by the great apes, but surely not by all the various species that can acquire conditioned reflexes. On this basis alone it would seem necessary to preserve a distinction between conditioning and learning rules.

As psychologists have learned to appreciate the complexities of language, the prospect of reducing it to the laws of behaviour so carefully studied in lower animals has grown increasingly remote. We have been forced more and more into a position that non-psychologists probably take for granted, namely, that language is rule-governed behaviour characterised by enormous flexibility and freedom of choice.

Obvious as this conclusion may seem, it has important implications for any scientific theory of language. If rules involve the concepts of right and wrong, they introduce a normative aspect that has always been avoided in the natural sciences. One hears repeatedly that the scientist's ability to suppress normative judgments about his subject-matter enables him to see the world objectively, as it really is. To admit that language follows rules seems to put it outside the range of phenomena accessible to scientific investigation.[2]

At this point a psycholinguist who wishes to preserve his standing as a natural scientist faces an old but always difficult decision. Should he withdraw and leave the study of language to others? Or should he give up all pretence of being a "natural scientist," searching for causal explanations, and embrace a more phenomenological approach? Or should he push blindly ahead with his empirical methods, hoping to find a causal basis for normative practices, but running the risk that all his efforts will be wasted because rule-governed behaviour in principle lies beyond the scope of natural science?

To withdraw means to abandon hope of understanding scientifically all those human mental processes that involve language in any important degree. To persevere means to face the enormously difficult, if not actually impossible task of finding a place for normative rules in a descriptive science.

Difficult, yes. Still one wonders whether these alternatives are really as mutually exclusive as they seem.

The first thing we notice when we survey the languages of the world is how few we can understand and how diverse they all seem. Not until one looks for some time does an even more significant observation emerge concerning the pervasive similarities in the midst of all this diversity.

Every human group that anthropologists have studied has spoken a language. The language always has a lexicon and a grammar. The lexicon is not a haphazard collection of vocalisations, but is highly organised; it always has pronouns, means for dealing with time, space, and number, words to represent true and false, the basic concepts necessary for propositional logic. The grammar has distinguishable levels of structure, some phonological, some syntactic. The phonology always contains both vowels and consonants, and the phonemes can always be described in terms of distinctive features drawn from a limited set of possibilities. The syntax always specifies rules for grouping elements sequentially into phrases and sentences, rules governing normal intonation, rules for transforming some types of sentences into other types.

The nature and importance of these common properties, called "linguistic universals," are only beginning to emerge as our knowledge of the world's languages grows more systematic.‖ ‖ These universals appear even in languages that developed with a minimum of interaction. One is forced to assume, therefore, either that (a) no other kind of linguistic practices are conceivable, or that (b) something in the biological makeup of human beings favours languages having these similarities. Only a moment's reflection is needed to reject (a). When one considers the variety of artificial languages developed in mathematics, in the communication sciences, in the use of computers, in symbolic logic, and elsewhere, it soon becomes apparent that the universal features of natural languages are not the only ones possible. Natural languages are, in fact, rather special and often seem unnecessarily complicated.

A popular belief regards human language as a more or less free creation of the human intellect, as if its elements were chosen arbitrarily and could be combined into meaningful utterances by any rules that strike our collective fancy. The assumption is implicit, for example, in Wittgenstein's well-known conception of "the language game." This

‖ ‖ *Universals of Language,* edited by J. Greenberg (M.I.T. Technology Press, Cambridge, Mass., 1963).

metaphor, which casts valuable light on many aspects of language, can, if followed blindly, lead one to think that all linguistic rules are just as arbitrary as, say, the rules of chess or football. As Lenneberg has pointed out, however, it makes a great deal of sense to inquire into the biological basis for language, but very little to ask about the biological foundations of card games.##

Man is the only animal to have a combinatorially productive language. In the jargon of biology, language is "a species-specific form of behaviour." Other animals have signalling systems of various kinds and for various purposes—but only man has evolved this particular and highly improbable form of communication. Those who think of language as a free and spontaneous intellectual invention are also likely to believe that any animal with a brain sufficiently large to support a high level of intelligence can acquire a language. This assumption is demonstrably false. The human brain is not just an ape brain enlarged; its extra size is less important than its different structure. Moreover, Lenneberg has pointed out that nanocephalic dwarfs, with brains half the normal size but grown on the human blueprint, can use language reasonably well, and even mongoloids, not intelligent enough to perform the simplest functions for themselves, can acquire the rudiments.*** Talking and understanding language do not depend on being intelligent or having a large brain. They depend on "being human."

Serious attempts have been made to teach animals to speak. If words were conditioned responses, animals as intelligent as chimpanzees or porpoises should be able to learn them. These attempts have uniformly failed in the past and, if the argument here is correct, they will always fail in the future—for just the same reason that attempts to teach fish to walk or dogs to fly would fail. Such efforts misconstrue the basis for our linguistic competence: they fly in the face of biological facts.†††

E. Lenneberg, "Language, Evolution, and Purposive Behavior," in *Culture in History: Essays in Honor of Paul Radin* (Columbia University Press, New York, 1960).

*** E. Lenneberg, I. A. Nichols, and E. R. Rosenberger, "Primitive Stages of Language Development in Mongolism," in the *Proceedings* of the 42nd. Annual Meeting (1962) of the *Association for Research in Nervous and Mental Diseases.*

††† The belief that animals have, or could have, languages is as old as man's interest in the evolution of his special talent, but the truth of the matter has long been known. Listen, for example, to Max Müller (*Three Lectures on the Science of Language*) in 1889: "It is easy enough to show that animals communicate, but this is a fact which has never been doubted. Dogs who growl and bark leave no doubt in the minds of other dogs or cats, or even of man, of what they mean, but growling and barking are not language, nor do they even contain the elements of language."

Unfortunately, Müller's authority, great as it was, did not suffice, and in 1890 we hear Samuel Butler ("Thought and Language," in his *Collected Essays*) reply

Human language must be such that a child can acquire it. He acquires it, moreover, from parents who have no idea how to explain it to him. No careful schedule of rewards for correct or punishments for incorrect utterances is necessary. It is sufficient that the child be allowed to grow up naturally in an environment where language is used.

The child's achievement seems all the more remarkable when we recall the speed with which he accomplishes it and the limitations of his intelligence in other respects. It is difficult to avoid an impression that infants are little machines specially designed by nature to perform this particular learning task.

I believe this analogy with machines is worth pursuing. If we could imagine what a language-learning automaton would have to do, it would dramatise—and perhaps even clarify—what a child can do. The linguist and logician Noam Chomsky has argued that the description of such an automaton would comprise our hypothesis about the child's innate ability to learn languages or (to borrow a term from Ferdinand de Saussure) his innate *faculté de langage*.[‡‡‡]

Consider what information a language-learning automaton would be given to work with. Inputs to the machine would include a finite set of sentences, a finite set of non-sentences accompanied by some signal that they were incorrect, some way to indicate that one item is a repetition or elaboration or transformation of another, and some access to a universe of perceptual objects and events associated with the sentences. Inside the machine there would be a computer so programmed as to extract from these inputs the nature of the language, *i.e.*, the particular syntactic rules by which sentences are generated, and the rules that associate with each syntactic structure a particular phonetic representation and semantic interpretation. The important question, of course, is what programme of instructions would have to be given to the computer.

---

that although "growling and barking cannot be called very highly specialised language," still there is "a sayer, a sayee, and a covenanted symbol designedly applied. Our own speech is vertebrated and articulated by means of nouns, verbs, and the rules of grammar. A dog's speech is invertebrate, but I do not see how it is possible to deny that it possesses all the essential elements of language."

Müller and Butler did not argue about the facts of animal behaviour which Darwin had described. Their disagreement arose more directly from differences of opinion about the correct definition of the term "language." To-day our definitions of human language are more precise, so we can say with correspondingly more precision why Butler was wrong.

[‡‡‡] N. Chomsky, "Explanatory Models in Linguistics," in *Logic, Methodology, and Philosophy of Science*, edited by E. Wagel, P. Suppes, and A. Tarski (Stanford University Press, Stanford, 1962, pp. 528–550).

We could instruct the computer to discover any imaginable set of rules that might, in some formal sense of the term, constitute a grammar. This approach—the natural one if we believe that human languages can be infinitely diverse and various—is doomed from the start. The computer would have to evaluate an infinitude of possible grammars; with only a finite corpus of evidence it would be impossible, even if sufficient time were available for computation, to arrive at any unique solution.[3]

A language-learning automaton could not possibly discover a suitable grammar unless some strong *a priori* assumptions were built into it from the start. These assumptions would limit the alternatives that the automaton considered—limit them presumably to the range defined by linguistic universals. The automaton would test various grammars of the appropriate form to see if they would generate all of the sentences and none of the non-sentences. Certain aspects would be tested before others; those found acceptable would be preserved for further evaluation. If we wished the automaton to replicate a child's performance, the order in which these aspects would be evaluated could only be decided after careful analysis of the successive stages of language acquisition in human children.

The actual construction of such an automaton is, of course, far beyond our reach at the present time. That is not the point. The lesson to learn from such speculations is that the whole project would be impossible unless the automaton— and so, presumably, a child—knew in advance to look for particular kinds of regularities and correspondences, to discover rules of a rather special kind uniquely characteristic of human language in general.

The features that human infants are prepared to notice sharply limit the structure of any human language. Even if one imagines creating by decree a Newspeak in which this generalisation were false, within one generation it would have become true again.[4]

Psycholinguistics does not deal with social practices determined arbitrarily either by caprice or intelligent design, but with practices that grow organically out of the biological nature of man and the linguistic capacities of human infants. To that extent, at least, it is possible to define an area of empirical fact well within the reach of our scientific methods.

Another line of scientific investigation is opened up by the observation that we do not always follow our own rules. If this were not so, of course, we would not speak of rules, but of the laws of language. The fact that we make mistakes, and that we can know we made mistakes, is central to the psycholinguistic problem. Before we can see the empirical issue this entails, however, we should first draw a crucial distinction between theories of language and theories of the users of language.

There is nothing in the linguistic description of a language to indicate what mistakes will occur. Mistakes result from the psychological limitations of people who use the language, not from the language itself. It would be meaningless to state rules for making mistakes.

A formal characterisation of a natural language in terms of a set of elements and rules for combining those elements must inevitably generate an infinitude of possible sentences that will never occur in actual use. Most of these sentences are too complicated for us. There is nothing mysterious about this. It is very similar to the situation in arithmetic where a student may understand perfectly the rules for multiplication, yet find that some multiplication problems are too difficult for him to do "in his head," *i.e.*, without extending his memory capacity by the use of pencil and paper.

There is no longest grammatical sentence. There is no limit to the number of different grammatical sentences. Moreover, since the number of elements and rules is finite, there must be some rules and elements that can recur any number of times in a grammatical sentence. Chomsky has even managed to pinpoint a kind of recursive operation in language that, in principle, lies beyond the power of any finite device to perform indefinitely often. Compare these sentences:

(R) Remarkable is the rapidity of the motion of the wing of the hummingbird.
(L) The hummingbird's wing's motion's rapidity is remarkable.
(E) The rapidity that the motion that the wing that the hummingbird has has has is remarkable.

When you parse these sentences you find that the phrase structure of (R) dangles off to the right; each prepositional phrase hangs to the noun in the prepositional phrase preceding it. In (R), therefore, we see a type of recurring construction that has been called right-branching. Sentence (L), on the other hand, is left-branching; each possessive modifies the possessive immediately following. Finally, (E) is an onion; it grows by embedding sentences within sentences.[5] Inside "The rapidity is remarkable" we first insert "the motion is rapid" by a syntactic transformation that permits us to construct relative clauses, and so we obtain "The rapidity that the motion has is remarkable." Then we repeat the transformation, this time inserting "the wing has motion" to obtain "The rapidity that the motion that the wing has has is remarkable." Repeating the transformation once more gives (E).

It is intuitively obvious that, of these three types of recursive operations, self-embedding (E) is psychologically the most difficult. Although they seem grammatical by any reasonable standard of grammar, such sentences never occur in ordinary usage because they exceed our cognitive capacities. Chomsky's achievement was to prove rigorously that any language that does *not* restrict this kind of recursive embedding contains sentences that cannot be spoken or understood by devices, human or mechanical, with finite memories. Any device that uses these rules must remember each left portion until it can be related to its corresponding right portion; if the memory of the user is limited, but the number of admissible left portions is not, it is inevitable that some admissible sentences will exceed the capacity of the user to process them correctly.§§§

It is necessary, therefore, to distinguish between a description of the language in terms of the rules that a person *knows* and uses and a description of that person's *performance* as a user of the rules. The distinction is sometimes criticised as "psycholatry" by strict adherents of behaviourism; "knowing" is considered too mentalistic and subjective, therefore unscientific. The objection cannot be taken seriously. Our conception of the rules that a language-user knows is indeed a hypothetical construct, not something observed directly in his behaviour. But if such hypotheses were to be forbidden, science in general would become an empty pursuit.

Given a reasonable hypothesis about the rules that a language-user knows, the exploration of his limitations in following those rules is proper work for an experimental psychologist. "Psychology should assist us," a great linguist once said, "in understanding what is going on in the mind of speakers, and more particularly how they are led to deviate from previously existing rules in consequence of conflicting tendencies." Otto Jespersen made this request of psychology in 1924; now at last the work is beginning.‖ ‖ ‖

One example. Stephen Isard and I asked Harvard undergraduates to memorise several sentences that differed in degree of self-embedding. For instance, the twenty-two words in the right-branching sentence, "We cheered the football squad that played the team that brought the mascot that chased the girls that were in the park," can be re-arranged to give one, two, three, or four self-embeddings; with four it becomes, "The girls (that the mascot (that the team (that the football squad (that we cheered) played) brought) chased) were in the park." One

§§§ N. Chomsky, *Syntactic Structures* (Mouton, The Hague, 1957).
‖ ‖ ‖ *The Philosophy of Grammar* (Allen and Unwin, London, 1924, p. 344).

self-embedding caused no difficulty; it was almost as easy to memorise as the sentence with none. Three or four embeddings were most difficult. When the sentence had two self-embeddings—"The team (that the football squad (that we cheered) played) brought the mascot that chased the girls that were in the park"—some subjects found it as easy to memorise as sentences with zero or one embedding, others found it as difficult as sentences with three or four. That is to say, everybody can manage one embedding, some people can manage two, but everybody has trouble with three or more.

Records of eye movements while people are reading such sentences show that the trouble begins with the long string of verbs, "cheered played brought," at which point all grasp of the sentence structure crumbles and they are left with a random list of verbs. This is just what would be expected from a computer executing a programme that did not make provision for a sub-routine to refer to itself, *i.e.*, that was not recursive. If our ability to handle this type of self-embedded recursion is really as limited as the experiment indicates, it places a strong limitation on the kinds of theories we can propose to explain our human capacities for processing information.

On the simpler levels of our psycholinguistic hierarchy the pessimists are wrong; much remains there to be explored and systematised by scientific methods. How far these methods can carry us remains an open question. Although syntax seems well within our grasp and techniques for studying semantic systems are now beginning to emerge, understanding and belief raise problems well beyond the scope of linguistics. Perhaps it is there that scientific progress will be forced to halt.

No psychological process is more important or difficult to understand than understanding, and nowhere has scientific psychology proved more disappointing to those who have turned to it for help. The complaint is as old as scientific psychology itself. It was probably first seen clearly by Wilhelm Dilthey, who called for a new kind of psychology— a kind to which Karl Jaspers later gave the name *"verstehende Psychologie"*—and in one form or another the division has plagued psychologists ever since. Obviously a tremendous gulf separates the interpretation of a sentence from the understanding of a personality, a society, historical epoch. But the gap is narrowing. Indeed, one can even pretend to see certain similarities between the generative theory of speech perception discussed above and the reconstructive intellectual processes that have been labelled *verstehende*. The analogy may some day prove helpful, but how optimistic one dares feel at the present time is not easily decided.

Meanwhile, the psycholinguists will undoubtedly continue to advance as far as they can. It should prove interesting to see how far that will be.

NOTES ON "THE PSYCHOLINGUISTS"

1. 10^{20} means 1 followed by 20 zeros (or 10 to the twentieth power). According to Miller, the average substitutability for a word in English is 10. That means if we take a two-word sentence, the number of possible combinations is 100; each of the 10 possible substitutes for the first word with each of the 10 substitutes for the second word (10×10). If we take a three-word sentence, the number of combinations is $10 \times 10 \times 10$, and so on.

2. Miller is concerned that the introduction of *rules* into scientific investigation implies that the scientist is regulating behavior, not just observing it. Nothing could be farther from the case. A rule is a statement of a convention. For instance, a rule of written English is that a sentence begins with a capital letter. A linguist does not say that a writer should or should not follow the convention, he would merely observe that the convention exists. Furthermore, he can predict that any sentence that violates a convention will call attention to itself. Whether the violation was inadvertent (as in the case of a child) or intentional (as in the case of e. e. cummings) is another matter. Similarly, the grammar of English is the set of conventions that speakers of the language follow. If one of the conventions is violated, the sentence will sound "funny." For instance, the following two sentences violate the conventions governing the use of the progressive tense:

   a. I am knowing what to do.
   b. He is thinking that this is the right answer.

3. In any limited corpus (no matter how big) there would be a large number of patterns that we would never notice because they are irrelevant to the way that we know human languages work. For instance, in a given corpus it might be the case that every sentence that begins with the letter *t* has an odd number of words, or that every seventh sentence has three prepositions in it. A computer would have no way of knowing that these patterns are accidental. Miller's point is that since the number of patterns in any given corpus is infinite, a human language learner must know what to look for in advance.

4. Newspeak is the language employed by the government in George Orwell's novel *1984*. Miller's point is that even if it were possible to legislate a made-up language, the next generation would learn it just as though it were a natural language.

5.   The right branching version might be represented:

Remarkable is the rapidity
                           of the motion
                                       of the wing
                                                   of the hummingbird.

   Left branching might be represented:
                                   rapidity is remarkable.
                           motion's
                       wing's
The hummingbird's
   Embedding might be represented:
The rapidity   is remarkable.
           that the motion   has
                   that the wing   has
                       that the hummingbird has

NOAM CHOMSKY

Formal Discussion of "The Development of Grammar in Child Language" by Wick Miller and Susan Ervin

INTRODUCTION

In this essay Chomsky makes an important distinction between the description of a speaker's linguistic competence and his actual performance. Chomsky illustrates this distinction by an example drawn from arithmetic. The fact that a person has grasped the rules of multiplication (competence) does not thereby automatically guarantee that he can do complicated problems in his head or that his answers are always correct (performance). Conversely, the fact that a child says that 2 times 2 is 4 does not automatically demonstrate that he understands the basic concepts of multiplication. In the same manner, the fact that a speaker has a linguistic competence that enables him to produce an infinite number of sentences does not guarantee that those sentences are free from mistakes and slips of all kinds. Chomsky is claiming, in effect, that a study of a speaker's actual performance (or put another way, the study of forms in a corpus) is almost useless for gaining any insight into the nature of the speaker's linguistic competence.

The essay then comments on four fallacies which result from not making the proper distinction between competence and performance:

Reprinted by permission of the author and the Society for Research in Child Development, Inc. from *The Acquisition of Language*. ed. by Ursula Bellugi and Roger Brown, 1964, pp. 35–39.

1. The relation between competence and performance is probabilistic. That is, there is some connection between frequency of occurrence and grammaticality. Chomsky rejects the position on the grounds that the probability of predicting *any* sentence is effectively zero.

2. The speaker and the hearer must use separate grammars. Chomsky argues that linguistic competence is basic to the processes of speaking and hearing and therefore is neutral between them.

3. There is a clear separation between "lexical items" (nouns, verbs, adjectives, and adverbs) on the one hand and "function words" (prepositions, conjunctions, interrogatives, noun determiners, and auxiliaries) on the other. The former have "referential" meaning while the latter have a grammatical or "relational" meaning. Chomsky argues against this distinction between lexical and grammatical words. He points out that words like "useful" and "expect" have little referential meaning, and that words that do appear to have referential meaning, such as "table" and "green" may be atypical.

4. A speaker's phonemic system (that is, what the speaker perceives to be the sounds of his language) can be discovered by a classification of his phonetic system (that is, the range of variation of actually produced sounds). Chomsky rejects this theory without going into any detail. His position assumes that the speaker of a language has a set of abstract rules which allow him to impose an interpretation upon the infinitely varied phonetic signal.

Chomsky concludes that attempts to investigate children's linguistic competence by direct description of their performance are hopeless. He does, however, suggest more indirect ways in which competence might be investigated. He closes the essay by presenting evidence that the child's linguistic competence is much more developed than his actual performance might suggest.

My initial reaction to this paper was one of surprise that so much success could be attained in dealing with this question. It seems that the attempt to write a grammar for a child raises all of the unsolved problems of constructing a grammar for adult speech, multiplied by some rather large factor. To mention just the most obvious difficulty, since the language is constantly changing rather dramatically, it is impossible to use the one "method" available to linguists who attempt to go beyond surface description, namely, learning the language oneself. Clearly the general problem is at least as difficult, and, in fact, much more difficult than the problem of discovering the grammar of the language of a mature speaker, and this, I think, is a problem of much greater difficulty than is often realized. In fact, the only remarks I would like to make reflect an impression that underlying these descriptions of children's speech, laudible and interesting as they are, there is a somewhat oversimplified conception of the character of grammatical description, not unrelated, perhaps, to a similarly oversimplified view that is typical of much recent work on language in psychology and linguistics.

For one thing, it should be clearly recognized that a grammar is not a description of the performance of the speaker, but rather of his linguistic competence, and that a description of competence and a description of performance are different things. To illustrate, consider a trivial example where one would want to distinguish between a description of competence and a description of performance. Suppose that we were to attempt to give an account of how a child learns to multiply (rather than how he acquires his language). A child who has succeeded in learning this has acquired a certain competence, and he will perform in certain ways that are clearly at variance with this competence. Once he has learned to multiply, the correct description of his competence is a statement, in one or another form, of some of the rules of arithmetic—i.e., a specification of the set of triples (x, y, z) such that z is the product of x and y.[1] On the other hand, a description of the performance of either an adult or a child (or a real computer) would be something quite different. It might, for example, be a specification of a set of quadruples (x, y, z, w) such that w is the probability that, given x and y, the person will compute the product as z.[2] This set of quadruples would incorporate information about memory span, characteristic errors, lapses of attention, etc., information which is relevant to a performance table but not, clearly, to an account of what the person has learned—what is the basic competence that he has acquired. A person might memorize the performance table and perform on various simple-minded tests exactly as the person who knows the rules of arithmetic, but this would not, of course, show that he knows these rules. It seems clear that the description which is of greatest psychological relevance is the account of competence, not that of performance, both in the case of arithmetic and the case of language. The deeper question concerns the kinds of structures the person has succeeded in mastering and internalizing, whether or not he utilizes them, in practice, without interference from the many other factors that play a role in actual behavior. For anyone concerned with intellectual processes, or any question that goes beyond mere data arranging, it is the question of competence that is fundamental. Obviously one can find out about competence only by studying performance, but this study must be carried out in devious and clever ways, if any serious result is to be obtained.

These rather obvious comments apply directly to study of language, child or adult. Thus it is absurd to attempt to construct a grammar that describes observed linguistic behavior directly. The tape recordings of this conference give a totally false picture of the conceptions of linguistic structure of the various speakers. Nor is this in the least bit surprising. The speaker has represented in his brain a grammar that gives an ideal account of the structure of the sentences of his language, but, when actually faced with the task of speaking or "understanding," many other factors act upon his underlying linguistic competence to produce actual performance. He may be confused or have several things in mind, change his plans in midstream, etc. Since this is obviously the condition of most actual linguistic performance, a direct record—an actual corpus—is almost useless, as it stands, for linguistic analysis of any but the most superficial kind.

Similarly, it seems to me that, if anything far-reaching and real is to be discovered about the actual grammar of the child, then rather devious kinds of observations of his performance, his abilities, and his comprehension in many different kinds of circumstance will have to be obtained, so that a variety of evidence may be brought to bear on the attempt to determine what is in fact his underlying linguistic competence at each stage of development. Direct description of the child's actual verbal output is no more likely to provide an account of the real underlying competence in the case of child language than in the case of adult language, ability to multiply, or any other nontrivial rule-governed behavior. Not that one shouldn't start here, perhaps, but surely one shouldn't end here, or take too seriously the results obtained by one or another sort of manipulation of data of texts produced under normal conditions.

It is suggested in this paper—and this is a view shared by many psychologists and linguists—that the relation between competence and performance is somehow a probabilistic one. That is, somehow the higher probabilities in actual output converge towards the actual underlying grammar, or something of the sort. I have never seen a coherent presentation of this position, but, even as a vague idea, it seems to me entirely implausible. In particular, it surely cannot be maintained that the child forms his conception of grammatical structure by just assuming that high probabilities correspond to "rules" and that low probabilities can be disregarded, in some manner. Most of what the child actually produces and hears (and this is true for the adult as well) is of extremely low probability. In fact, in the case of sentence structure, the notion of probability loses all meaning. Except for a ridiculously small number (e.g., conventionalized greetings, etc., which, in fact, often do not even observe grammatical rules), all actual sentences are of a probability so low as to be effectively zero, and the same is true of structures (if, by the "structure" of a sentence, we mean the sequence of categories to which its successive words or morphemes belong). In actual speech, the highest probability must be assigned to broken and interrupted fragments of sentences or to sentences which begin in one way and end in a different, totally incompatible way (surely the tapes of this meeting would be sufficient to demonstrate this). From such evidence it would be absurd to conclude that this represents in any sense the linguistic consciousness of the speakers, as have been noted above. In general, it is a mistake to assume that—past the very earliest stages—much of what the child acquires is acquired by imitation. This could not be true on the level of sentence formation, since most of what the child hears is new and most of what he produces, past the very earliest stages, is new.

In the papers that have been presented here—and again, this is not unrepresentative of psychology and linguistics—there has been talk about grammars for the decoder and grammars for the encoder. Again, there are several undemonstrated (and, to me, quite implausible) assumptions underlying the view that the speaker's behavior should be modeled by one sort of system, and the hearer's by another. I have never seen a precise characterization of a "grammar for the encoder" or a "grammar for the decoder" that was not convertible, by a notational change, into the other. Furthermore, this is not surprising. The grammars that linguists construct are, in fact, quite neutral as between speaker and hearer. The problems of constructing models of performance, for the speaker and hearer, incorporating these grammars, are rather similar. This of course bears again on the question of relation between competence and performance. That is, the grammar that represents the speaker's competence is, of course, involved in both his speaking and interpreting of speech, and there seems no reason to assume that there are two different underlying systems, one involved in speaking, one in "understanding." To gain some insight into this underlying system, studies of the speaker's actual output, as well as of his ability to understand and interpret, are essential. But again, it cannot be too strongly emphasized that the data obtained in such studies can only serve as the grounds for inference about what constitutes the linguistic consciousness that provides the basis for language use.

A few other minor remarks of this sort might be made to indicate areas in which experimental methods that go far beyond mere observation of speech in normal situations will be needed to shed some light on underlying competence. To take just one example, it is often remarked, and, in particular, it is remarked in this paper, that in the case of lexical items (as distinct from "function words," so-called) it is generally possible to assign referential meaning rather easily. Of course, as clearly stated in the paper, this is in part a matter of degree. However, I think that the notion that it is generally a straightforward matter in the case of lexical items is a faulty conclusion derived from concentration on atypical examples. Perhaps in the case of "green," "table," etc., it is not difficult to determine what is the "referential meaning." But consider, on the other hand, such words as "useful," where the meaning is clearly "relational"—the things in the world cannot be divided into those that are useful and those that are not. In fact, the meaning of "useful," like that of a function word, in some respects, must be described in partly relational terms. Or, to take a more complicated example, consider a word like "expect." A brief attempt to prescribe the behaviors or situations that make application of this word appropriate will quickly convince one that this is entirely the wrong approach and that "referential meaning" is simply the wrong concept in this case. I don't think that such examples are at all exotic. It may be that such atypical examples as "table" and "green" are relatively more frequent in the early stages of language learning (though this remains to be shown, just as it remains to be shown that determination of referential meaning in such cases is in some sense "primitive"), and, if true, this may be important. However, this is clearly not going to carry one very far.

Consider now a rather comparable phonetic example. One of the problems to be faced is that of characterizing the child's phonemic system. Phonemes are often defined by linguists as constituting a family of mutually exclusive classes of phones, and this is the definition adopted in this paper. If this were true, there would be, in this case, a fairly simple relation between performance (i.e., a sequence of phones) and the underlying abstract system (i.e., the phonemic representation of this sequence). One might hope that by some simple classification technique one might determine the phonemic system from the phonetic record or the phonemic constitution of an utterance from the sequence of its phones. There is, however, extremely strong evidence (so it seems to me, at least) that phonemes cannot be defined as classes of sounds at all (and certainly not as mutually exclusive classes) and that the relation between a phonemic system and the phonetic record (just as the relation between a phonemic representation of an utterance and its actual sound) is much more remote and complex. I do not want to try to give the evidence here; it is being presented elsewhere in fair detail. But I would like to reiterate, for what it is worth, my conviction that the evidence is extremely strong.

These two examples are randomly chosen illustrations of a general tendency to oversimplify drastically the facts of linguistic structure and to assume that the determination of competence can be derived from description of a corpus by some sort of sufficiently developed data-processing techniques. My feeling is that this is hopeless and that only experimentation of a fairly indirect and ingenious sort can provide evidence that is at all critical for formulating a true account of the child's grammar (as in the case of investigation of any other real system). Consequently, I would hope that some of the research in this area would be diverted from recording of texts towards attempting to tap the child's underlying abilities to use and comprehend sentences, to detect deviance and compensate for it, to apply rules in new situations, to form highly specific concepts from scattered bits of evidence, and so on. There are, after all, many ways in which such study can be approached. Thus, for example, the child's ability to repeat sentences and nonsentences, phonologically possible sequences and phonologically impossible ones, etc., might provide some evidence as to the underlying system that he is using. There is surely no doubt that the child's achievements in systematizing linguistic data, at every stage, go well beyond what he actually produces in normal speech. Thus it is striking that advances are generally "across the board." A child who does not produce initial s + consonant clusters may begin to produce them all, at approximately the same time, thus distinguishing for the first time between "cool" and "school," etc.—but characteristically will do this in just the right words, indicating that the correct phonemic representation of these words was present to the mind even at the stage where it did not appear in speech. Similarly, some of the data of Brown and Fraser seem to suggest that interrogatives, negatives, and other syntactically related forms appear and are distinguished from declaratives at approximately the same time, for some children. If so, this suggests that what has actually happened is that the hitherto latent system of verbal auxiliaries is now no longer suppressed in actual speech, as previously. Again, this can be investigated directly. Thus a child producing speech in a "telegraphic style" can be shown to have an underlying, fuller conception of sentence structure (unrealized in his speech, but actively involved in comprehension) if misplacement of the elements he does not produce leads to difficulties of comprehension, inability to repeat, etc., while correct placement gives utterances intelligible to him, and so on.

I would, finally, like to say that I don't intend these remarks as criticism of the present work, as it stands. It is clear from what has been presented already that quite a bit can be learned from observation of the spoken record. I make these remarks only to indicate a difficulty which I think is looming rather large and to which some serious attention will have to be given fairly soon.

OPEN DISCUSSION

The group focused on the distinction between receptive control of grammar (comprehension) and productive control (speech). The research work of Miller and Ervin and also that of Brown, Fraser, and Bellugi had concentrated on the analysis of obtained speech, and so the papers of these investigators were concerned almost exclusively with productive control. The linguists judged it to be very important, even for a proper understanding of production, to make a parallel study of comprehension.

1. How is the study of sentence comprehension relevant to an appropriate description of sentence production? One of the linguists had noticed that in the papers reporting data on child speech there was evidence of a rather abrupt shift from speech completely free of auxiliaries (such as *to be, have, can, will*) to speech manifesting the full auxiliary system. Such a shift—if it is in fact relatively complete and abrupt—would suggest that the auxiliary system had been built up internally before being utilized in production. In addition, there is some evidence from common observation that children understand the use of auxiliaries even when they do not produce them. For example, auxiliaries are used by adults to form interrogatives "Will you play now?" "Are you hungry yet?" and children do seem to distinguish questions from declaratives.

Suppose that we distinguish between the "computation" of a sentence and its "print out." Computation may include both the grammatical analysis of sentences fed in, which is a part of comprehension, and also the planning or programming of sentences to be spoken or "printed out." It is also conceivable that the analysis of input and programming of output are accomplished separately. In any case, it may be incorrect to say that a child who produces no auxiliaries does not possess the auxiliary system. He may have the system on the computational-comprehension level. With greater maturity, when it is possible to increase the length or span of the "print out," a rule is added to his programming operation which directs: "Produce the auxiliaries." Alternatively, it might be appropriate to say that, until a certain age, the computational level has included a rule: "Delete the auxiliaries in printing out." This latter rule would then be dropped with increasing age.

2. It was pointed out that the kind of description given above credits the child with much more grammatical competence than he is manifesting in speech, and we ought not to do that without good evidence. One kind of evidence could be obtained from production itself: if both the declarative and interrogative uses of auxiliaries emerge together, that argues that the system has existed prior to production. In addition, however, there would have to be evidence of comprehension itself.

It is a familiar generalization from diary studies of child speech that comprehension is always more advanced than production. The same kind of thing is said of second-language learning: the comprehension performance is generally more impressive than the production performance. But the evidence for comprehension in the natural situation of a child at home leaves much to be desired.

Suppose a parent says: "Are you hungry yet?" and a child responds: "Yes." There may have been a rising interrogative intonation on the question, and it may be *that* feature that governs the child's response. He might have reacted in the same way to such other forms as: "You hungry?" or "Hungry?" It is not clear in the ordinary case that he needs to grasp the use of the auxiliary. Parents, even those who keep diaries, do not ordinarily test for the range of variations in a sentence that will produce the same response from a child. A linguist suggested that one might experimentally interchange articles and auxiliaries or simply delete auxiliaries to see whether children were "computing" them internally.

A monograph by Kahane, Kahane, and Saporta (1958) has, from the evidence of diary studies, concluded that children first do not code a distinction they can comprehend, while later on they do so. However, the authors of this monograph have often simply assumed that since an adult would have understood a certain distinction in a given situation a child must also have understood it. A child may use the present tense in cases when an adult would use either the future or past. The authors of the monograph would be inclined to credit him with understanding the difference but not yet coding it. Ervin and Brown and their collaborators would be more inclined to say that he does not have the future or past tenses but only the present. What is badly needed is evidence independent of tense production that the child either does or does not understand the past and future.

3. Chomsky in his discussion had said that comprehension competence seems generally to be in advance of production competence; he pointed out that, while most of us can understand a play by George Bernard Shaw, none of us can write one. A psychologist pointed out that the performance standard shifts in this comparison; if we ask how

many of us can understand a Shaw play *as Shaw understood it,* the answer is unknown. The difficulty is that behavioral criteria of comprehension are less clear than criteria of production. We do not even know how to find out whether someone fully understands a Shaw play. Evidence for comprehension has usually been little more than the child's correct pointing to or approach to a named referent or his performance of a verbalized command. This evidence does not demonstrate grammatical comprehension since it is quite likely that the substantive words alone—the noun naming a referent or the verb naming an action to be performed—would suffice to produce the appropriate reaction.

A linguist noted that, while the psychological investigation of production seems easier than the investigation of comprehension because the utterance output can be recorded, when it comes to formulating the internal process it is comprehension that is the more easily handled. The sentence of another person is the input, and we can suggest that some data-processing device utilizes the information in the comprehending person's grammar to analyze the sentence—yielding as output a structural description of the sentence that is part of understanding. No one knows how this is done, but at least the problem can be phrased. However, if we ask the comparable problem—how the grammar in the brain operates to generate sentences—it is difficult even to pose the problem. What are the inputs that select sentences? They are not often referents, since we seldom name objects or describe the immediate scene. What, for example, is the input for a person who says: "I would like a cup of coffee."?

NOTES ON "FORMAL DISCUSSION OF 'THE DEVELOPMENT OF GRAMMAR IN CHILD LANGUAGE' BY WICK MILLER AND SUSAN ERVIN"

1. Chomsky defines multiplication as involving three elements: x, y, and z. The two numbers being multipled are x and y (x is the first number, y is the second), and z is the result. For example, 15 times 3 equals 45 would be written as the set of triples (15,3,45).
2. The x, y, and z are the same as in note 1. w is the probability that z will be the correct answer for any given x and y. For most problems the w would be 99.999+. For multiplying two-million digit numbers together, the w for most of us would be rather low. The point, however, is that in *any* actual performance, except the possibility of error or distraction, there is also a limit on the performance that has nothing intrinsically to do with competence—memory limitations, for example.

NOAM CHOMSKY

Linguistic Theory

INTRODUCTION

Chomsky's essay is directed specifically to foreign language teachers, but virtually all of what he says is equally applicable to English teachers. Throughout the essay Chomsky cautions the teacher against over reliance on the "fundamental disciplines" of linguistics and psychology. Both fields are undergoing sweeping changes and have considerably retrenched their claims of pedagogical utility. Chomsky feels that this loss of confidence is "both healthy and realistic."

The main subject matter of the essay is an exploration of the two main current theories of learning and the close connection between them and the two main current schools of linguistics. The two learning theories might be termed "empiricist" and "rule governed." Structural linguistics is closely associated with the "empiricist" school while transformational linguistics is associated with the "rule-governed" school.

From the empiricist point of view, a language is learned as a set of habits. These habits are acquired by reinforcement, association, and generalization. Chomsky argues that this theory is inadequate to account for

Reprinted by permission of the author from *Northeast Conference on the Teaching of Foreign Languages* (1966) Working Committee Reports, ed. by Robert C. Mead, Jr., pp. 43–49.

one of the most basic facts about language—its "creativity." That is, virtually every sentence a speaker of a language hears, says, reads, or writes is new to him. (A simple demonstration of the creativity of language is to open a book and select a sentence at random. Barring intentional quotation, the odds are almost incalculably remote that you will never see that exact sentence again.) Chomsky argues that if, for all practical purposes, each sentence we encounter is unique, the empiricist claim that language is learned as a set of habits seems inadequate.

From the rule-governed point of view, a language is learned through the formation of a set of rules of great generality that are used to generate and interpret new sentences. Chomsky terms this internal rule system the speaker's "linguistic competence." A linguist's rule system—a generative grammar—is a model of the speaker's linguistic competence.

Investigation of generative grammars has shown that in order for the rules to be sufficiently general they must be very abstract. By abstract, Chomsky means that they are often many steps removed from any kind of physical fact. Chomsky then poses the question as to whether rules of this abstraction are learned or inherent. His conclusion is that the human mind has an "intrinsic intellectual organization" which is inherently predisposed to make linguistic abstractions of great generality. Chomsky feels that the primary goal of both linguistic and psychological investigation of language is the determination and characterization of man's innate capacity for language.

I should like to make it clear from the outset that I am participating in this conference not as an expert on any aspect of the teaching of languages, but rather as someone whose primary concern is with the structure of language and, more generally, the nature of cognitive processes. Furthermore, I am, frankly, rather skeptical about the significance, for the teaching of languages, of such insights and understanding as have been attained in linguistics and psychology. Surely the teacher of language would do well to keep informed of progress and discussion in these fields, and the efforts of linguists and psychologists to approach the problems of language teaching from a principled point of view are extremely worthwhile, from an intellectual as well as a social point of view. Still, it is difficult to believe that either linguistics or psychology has achieved a level of theoretical understanding that might enable it to support a "technology" of language teaching. Both fields have made significant progress in recent decades, and, furthermore, both draw on centuries of careful thought and study. These disciplines are, at present, in a state of flux and agitation. What seemed to be well-established doctrine a few years ago may now be the subject of extensive debate. Although it would be difficult to document this generalization, it seems to me that there has been a significant decline, over the past ten or fifteen years, in the degree of confidence in the scope and security of foundations in both psychology and linguistics. I personally feel that this decline in confidence is both healthy and realistic. But it should serve as a warning to teachers that suggestions from the "fundamental disciplines" must be viewed with caution and skepticism.

Within psychology, there are now many who would question the view that the basic principles of learning are well understood. Long accepted principles of association and reinforcement, gestalt principles, the theory of concept formation as it has emerged in modern investigation, all of these have been sharply challenged in theoretical as well as experimental work. To me it seems that these principles are not merely inadequate but probably misconceived—that they deal with marginal aspects of acquisition of knowledge and leave the central core of the problem untouched.[1] In particular, it seems to me impossible to accept the view that linguistic behavior is a matter of habit, that it is slowly acquired by reinforcement, association, and generalization, or that linguistic concepts can be specified in terms of a space of elementary, physically defined "criterial attributes."[2] Language is not a "habit structure." Ordinary linguistic behavior characteristically involves innovation, formation of new sentences and new patterns in accordance with rules of great abstractness and intricacy. This is true both of the speaker, who constructs new utterances appropriate to the occasion, and of the hearer who must analyze and interpret these novel structures. There are no known principles of association or reinforcement, and no known sense of "generalization" that can begin to account for this characteristic "creative" aspect of normal language use. The new utterances that are produced and interpreted in the daily use of language are "similar" to those that constitute the past experience of speaker and hearer only in that they are determined, in their form and interpretation, by the same system of abstract underlying rules. There is no theory of association or generalization capable of accounting for this fact, and it would, I think, be a fundamental misunderstanding to seek such a theory, since the explanation very likely lies along different lines. The simple concepts of ordinary language (such concepts as "human being" or "knife" or "useful," etc., or, for that matter, the concept "grammatical sentence") cannot be specified in terms of a space of physical attributes, as in the concept formation paradigm. There is, correspondingly, no obvious analogy between the experimental results obtained in studies of concept formation and the actual processes that seem to underlie language learning.

Evidently, such an evaluation of the relevance of psychological theory to language acquisition requires justification, and it is far from uncontroversial. Nor will I attempt, within the framework of this paper, to supply any such justification. My point simply is that the relevance of psychological theory to acquisition of language is a highly dubious and questionable matter, subject to much controversy and plagued with uncertainties of all sorts. The applied psychologist and the teacher must certainly draw what suggestions and hints they can from psychological research, but they would be well-advised to do so with the constant realization of how fragile and tentative are the principles of the underlying discipline.

Turning to linguistics, we find much the same situation. Linguists have had their share in perpetuating the myth that linguistic behavior is "habitual" and that a fixed stock of "patterns" is acquired through practice and used as the basis for "analogy." These views could be maintained only as long as grammatical description was sufficiently vague and imprecise. As soon as an attempt is made to give a careful and precise account of the rules of sentence formation, the rules of phonetic organization, or the rules of sound-meaning correspondence in a language, the inadequacy of such an approach becomes apparent. What is more, the fundamental concepts of linguistic description have been subjected to serious critique. The principles of phonemic analysis, for example, have recently been called into question, and the status of the concept "phoneme" is very much in doubt. For that matter, there are basic unsolved problems concerning even the phonetic representations used as a basis for analysis of form in structural linguistics. Whereas a decade ago it would have been almost universally assumed that a phonetic representation is simply a record of physical fact, there is now considerable evidence that what the linguist takes to be a phonetic transcription is determined, in nontrivial ways, by the syntactic structure of the language, and that it is, to this extent, independent of the physical signal. I think there are by now very few linguists who believe that it is possible to arrive at the phonological or syntactic structure of a language by systematic application of "analytic procedures" of segmentation and classification, although fifteen or twenty years ago such a view was not only widely accepted but was also supported by significant results and quite plausible argument.

I would like to emphasize again that this questioning of fundamental principles is a very healthy phenomenon that has led to important advances and will undoubtedly continue to do so. It is, in fact, characteristic of any living subject. But it must be recognized that well-established theory, in fields like psychology and linguistics, is extremely limited in scope. The applications of physics to engineering may not be seriously affected by even the most deep-seated revolution in the foundations of physics, but the applications of psychology or linguistics to language teaching, such as they are, may be gravely affected by changing conceptions in these fields, since the body of theory that resists substantial modification is fairly small.

In general, the willingness to rely on "experts" is a frightening aspect of contemporary political and social life. Teachers, in particular, have a responsibility to make sure that ideas and proposals are evaluated on their merits, and not passively accepted on grounds of authority, real or presumed. The field of language teaching is no exception. It is possible—even likely—that principles of psychology and linguistics, and research in these disciplines, may supply insights useful to the language teacher. But this must be demonstrated, and cannot be presumed. It is the language teacher himself who must validate or refute any specific proposal. There is very little in psychology or linguistics that he can accept on faith.

I will not try to develop any specific proposals relating to the teaching of languages—as I mentioned before, because I am not competent to do so. But there are certain tendencies and developments within linguistics and psychology that may have some potential impact on the teaching of language. I think these can be usefully summarized under four main headings: the "creative" aspect of language use; the abstractness of linguistic representation; the universality of underlying linguistic structure; the role of intrinsic organization in cognitive processes. I would like to say just a few words about each of these topics.

The most obvious and characteristic property of normal linguistic behavior is that it is stimulus-free and innovative. Repetition of fixed phrases is a rarity; it is only under exceptional and quite uninteresting circumstances that one can seriously consider how "situational context" determines what is said, even in probabilistic terms. The notion that linguistic behavior consists of "responses" to "stimuli" is as much a myth as the idea that it is a matter of habit and generalization. To maintain such assumptions in the face of the actual facts, we must deprive the terms "stimulus" and "response" (similarly "habit" and "generalization") of any technical or precise meaning. This property of being innovative and stimulus-free is what I refer to by the term "creative aspect of language use." It is a property of language that was

described in the seventeenth century and that serves as one corner-
stone for classical linguistic theory, but that has gradually been for-
gotten in the development of modern linguistics, much to its detriment.
Any theory of language must come to grips with this fundamental
property of normal language use. A necessary but not sufficient step
towards dealing with this problem is to recognize that the native
speaker of a language has internalized a "generative grammar"—a
system of rules that can be used in new and untried combinations to
form new sentences and to assign semantic interpretations to new
sentences. Once this fact has become clear, the immediate task of the
linguist is likewise clarified. He must try to discover the rules of this
generative grammar and the underlying principles on the basis of
which it is organized.

The native speaker of a language has internalized a generative
grammar in the sense just described, but he obviously has no awareness of this fact or of the properties of this grammar. The problem
facing the linguist is to discover what constitutes unconscious, latent
knowledge—to bring to light what is now sometimes called the
speaker's intrinsic "linguistic competence." A generative grammar of
a language is a theory of the speaker's competence. If correct, it
expresses the principles that determine the intrinsic correlation of
sound and meaning in the language in question. It thus serves as one
component of a theory that can accommodate the characteristic creative aspect of language use.

When we try to construct explicit, generative grammars and investigate their properties, we discover at once many inadequacies in traditional and modern linguistic descriptions. It is often said that no
complete generative grammar has ever been written for any language,
the implication being that this "new-fangled" approach suffers in comparison with older and well-established approaches to language description, in this respect. The statement concerning generative grammar is quite accurate; the conclusion, if intended, reveals a serious
misunderstanding. Even the small fragments of generative grammars
that now exist are incomparably greater in explicit coverage than
traditional or structuralist descriptions, and it is important to be aware
of this fact. A generative grammar is simply one that gives explicit
rules that determine the structure of sentences, their phonetic form,
and their semantic interpretation. The limitations of generative grammar are the limitations of our knowledge, in these areas. Where traditional or structuralist descriptions are correct, they can immediately
be incorporated into generative grammars. Insofar as these descriptions merely list examples of various kinds and make remarks (which

may be interesting and suggestive) about them, then they cannot be directly incorporated into generative grammars. In other words, a traditional or structuralist description can be immediately incorporated into a generative grammar to the extent that it is correct and does not rely on the "intelligence of the reader" and his "linguistic intuition."[3] The limitations of generative grammar, then, are a direct reflection of the limitations of correctness and explicitness in earlier linguistic work.

A serious investigation of generative grammars quickly shows that the rules that determine the form of sentences and their interpretations are not only intricate but also quite abstract, in the sense that the structures they manipulate are related to physical fact only in a remote way, by a long chain of interpretative rules. This is as true on the level of phonology as it is on the level of syntax and semantics, and it is this fact that has led to the questioning both of structuralist principles and of the tacitly assumed psychological theory that underlies them. It is because of the abstractness of linguistic representations that one is forced, in my opinion, to reject not only the analytic procedures of modern linguistics, with their reliance on segmentation and classification, but also principles of association and generalization that have been discussed and studied in empiricist psychology. Although such phenomena as association and generalization, in the sense of psychological theory and philosophical speculation, may indeed exist, it is difficult to see how they have any bearing on the acquisition or use of language. If our current conceptions of generative grammar are at all accurate, then the structures manipulated and the principles operating in these grammars are not related to given sensory phenomena in any way describable in the terms that empiricist psychology offers, and what principles it suggests simply have no relation to the facts that demand explanation.[4]

If it is correct that the underlying principles of generative grammars cannot be acquired through experience and training, then they must be part of the intellectual organization which is a prerequisite for language acquisition. They must, therefore, be universal properties, properties of any generative grammar. These are, then, two distinct ways of approaching what is clearly the most fundamental question of linguistic science, namely, the question of linguistic universals. One way is by an investigation of a wide range of languages. Any hypothesis as to the nature of linguistic universals must meet the empirical condition that it is not falsified by any natural language, any language acquired and used by humans in the normal way. But there is also another and, for the time being, somewhat more promising way of studying the problem of universals. This is by deep investigation of a particular language, investigation directed towards establishing underlying principles of organization of great abstractness in this language. Where such principles can be established, we must account for their existence. One plausible hypothesis is that they are innate, therefore, universal. Another plausible hypothesis is that they are acquired through experience and training. Either hypothesis can be made precise; each will then be meaningful and worthy of attention. We can refute the former by showing that other aspects of this language or properties of other languages are inconsistent with it. We can refute the latter by showing that it does not yield the structures that we must presuppose to account for linguistic competence. In general, it seems to me quite impossible to account for many deep-seated aspects of language on the basis of training or experience, and that therefore one must search for an explanation for them in terms of intrinsic intellectual organization. An almost superstitious refusal to consider this proposal seriously has, in my opinion, enormously set back both linguistics and psychology. For the present, it seems to me that there is no more reason for assuming that the basic principles of grammar are learned than there is for making a comparable assumption about, let us say, visual perception. There is, in short, no more reason to suppose that a person learns that English has a generative grammar of a very special and quite explicitly definable sort than there is to suppose that the same person learns to analyze the visual field in terms of line, angle, motion, solidity, persons with faces, etc.[5]

Turning then to the last of the four topics mentioned above, I think that one of the most important current developments in psychology and neurophysiology is the investigation of intrinsic organization in cognition. In the particular case of language, there is good reason to believe that even the identification of the phonetic form of a sentence presupposes at least a partial syntactic analysis, so that the rules of the generative grammar may be brought into play even in identifying the signal. This view is opposed to the hypothesis that phonetic representation is determined by the signal completely, and that the perceptual analysis proceeds from formal signals to interpretation, a hypothesis which, I understand, has been widely quoted in discussion of language teaching. The role of the generative grammar in perception is paralleled by the role of the universal grammar—the system of invariant underlying principles of linguistic organization—in acquisition of language. In each case, it seems to me that the significance of the intrinsic organization is very great indeed, and that the primary goal of linguistic and psychological investigation of language must be to determine and characterize it.

I am not sure that this very brief discussion of some of the leading ideas of much current research has been sufficiently clear to be either informative or convincing. Once again, I would like to stress that the implications of these ideas for language teaching are far from clear to me. It is a rather dubious undertaking to try to predict the course of development of any field, but, for what it is worth, it seems to me likely that questions of this sort will dominate research in the coming years, and, to hazard a further guess, that this research will show that certain highly abstract structures and highly specific principles of organization are characteristic of all human languages, are intrinsic rather than acquired, play a central role in perception as well as in production of sentences, and provide the basis for the creative aspect of language use.

NOTES ON "LINGUISTIC THEORY"

1.   Chomsky draws a distinction between "marginal" and "central" aspects of the acquisition of knowledge. By marginal Chomsky means the work of empiricist psychologists who have investigated learning theory in terms of measuring behavior that an organism is *not* inherently built to do, for instance, training pigeons to perform tricks on command. Chomsky complains that such investigation sheds little light on the central question of how an organism learns to perform behavior that it is built to do, for instance, how humans learn language. For a detailed discussion see Chomsky's "A Review of B. F. Skinner's *Verbal Behavior*" in *Language*, Vol. 35, pp. 26–58.
2.   Here and in the next to last sentence of the paragraph, Chomsky refers to a "space" of attributes. I take this to be a reference to a way of charting relationships developed in psychology. See especially C. E. Osgood, G. J. Suci, and P. H. Tannbaum: *The Measurement of Meaning*, University of Illinois Press (1957). Chomsky's point is that linguistic concepts are so tied to the nature of the mind that they cannot be completely described as combinations of elementary concepts.
3.   Chomsky says that the grammatical description of a language cannot *rely* on the "intelligence of the reader" of the grammar or upon his "linguistic intuition" to fill in the assumptions and implications of the description. The description is based completely on the speaker's intuition, but the description can only be *tested* to the degree that the claims of the description are made clear and precise.
4.   To illustrate this point from the area of syntax, compare these two sentences (from Chomsky's *Syntactic Theory*):

> a. *I heard the shooting of the hunters.*
> b. *I heard the growling of the lions.*

Every speaker of English knows that (a) is ambiguous in a way that (b) is not. This is a fact that an adequate grammar must account for. However, there is no physically observable signal that marks the ambiguity of (a) or the lack of ambiguity of (b). Chomsky's point, of course, is that any theory of language that starts with only the information in the signal cannot possibly account for the difference between (a) and (b).

5.   Put another way, our ability to use language is not dependent on the study of grammar any more than our ability to see is dependent on the study of visual perception. This distinction is sometimes termed the difference between "knowledge of" and "knowledge about." Every speaker of a language has a knowledge *of* that language which enables him to speak it, but unless he has been schooled on the subject, he has little knowledge *about* the language, for example, its history, and its phonological and grammatical structure.

ERIC H. LENNEBERG

The Capacity for Language Acquisition

INTRODUCTION

In this essay Lenneberg draws a distinction between biologically determined and culturally determined behavior. Biologically determined behavior is innate within the species, while culturally determined behavior is learned. Lenneberg argues that language and language acquisition, in certain key respects, are instances of biologically determined behavior.

Lenneberg proposes four criteria which distinguish biologically determined activity from culturally determined, and uses the activity of walking to illustrate the former and writing to illustrate the latter.

1. *Variation within species.* Where there is no significant variation within the species, the behavior is common to all members of the species and thus innate.

Reprinted by permission of the author, Prentice-Hall, Inc., and Columbia University Press from *The Structure of Language: Readings in the Philosophy of Language*, ed. by Jerry A. Fodor and Jerrold J. Katz, 1964. pp. 579–603.

An extended version of an article, written while its author was Career Investigator, National Institute of Mental Health, and published under the title "Language, Evolution, and Purposive Behavior" in S. Diamond, ed., *Culture in History: Essays in Honor of Paul Radin* (New York: Columbia University Press, 1960), pp. 869–893. Revised and reprinted by permission.

2. *History within species.* If an activity were innate, there could be no record of a change in the activity from past to present. Consequently, a biologically determined behavior has no history.

3. *Evidence for inherited predisposition.* A biologically determined behavior is one that takes place spontaneously, that is, the behavior is not dependent upon motivation or reward within the environment.

4. *Presumption of specific organic correlates.* Lenneberg divides this criterion into two sections:

   a. *Onset and fixed developmental history.* An inherent activity appears in an individual member of the species at a predictable point of maturity and goes through a specific course of development.

   b. *Dependence upon environment.* All activity, innate or learned, is dependent upon the environment for some kind of stimulus. The difference between an innate activity and a learned activity is that the former activity may be said to be *programmed* into the organism—the environment serves only as a trigger of "innate releasing mechanism." A culturally determined activity, on the other hand, is nearly completely dependent upon the environment for its structure and sequence.

Lenneberg then examines language and language acquisition in light of these four criteria in order to demonstrate that they are biologically determined activities.

1. *Variation with species.* While the amount of linguistic diversity in the languages of the world is great, all languages share certain fundamental properties: (1a) all have a phonology based on contrasting sounds, (2b) all languages string the individual units of the language together into larger concatenated sequences called phrases, sentences or discourses, and (3c) all languages have a grammar. Lenneberg concludes from these generalizations that all human languages are the same in terms of their formal properties and consequently these similarities must reflect some innate property of man himself.

2. *History within species.* It is apparently natural for all languages to change, but the change does not involve any kind of evolution: linguists are totally unable to trace the development of language back to some primitive stage.

3. *Evidence for inherited predisposition.* Lenneberg points out that while no man inherits a predisposition to learn a specific language, he does inherit a propensity for language learning which is so powerful that it is manifested even in physically and mentally handicapped children who are cut off from a normal linguistic environment.

4. *Presumption of specific organic correlates.*

   a. *Onset and fixed developmental history.* The development of speech

in children begins at a predictable age and seems to follow a
specific maturational pattern.
b. *Dependence upon environment.* The question here is whether or
not a child is "trained" to speak. Lenneberg argues that speech
activity requires enormous creativity: children create linguistic
forms that they have never heard before, that, in fact, do not exist
in the adult model. Consequently, a child must possess some
innate linguistic capability beyond what the mechanism of imitation could account for.

Lenneberg concludes the essay by sketching the model of language
acquisition that is presented in behavioral psychology and then raises five
problems that seem to be beyond the capacity of the model:

1. Even simple imitation of a sound requires the child to make generalizations and abstractions since no two sounds are ever acoustically
   identical.
2. Children "imitate" in a highly characteristic way: they do not appear
   to be striving to gain control over the motor skills of articulation,
   rather the goal seems to be the much more abstract skill of *naming*.
3. The noises that animals make seem related to some biological function such as courting, danger signals, anger, and the like. It is
   apparently impossible to train an animal to switch noises, that is, to
   use a noise in one situation that would normally be used in another.
   Humans, however, seem to be able to separate noise from emotion
   as part of their normal language development.
4. Children, without any special training, seem to automatically pay
   attention to language cues.
5. The great apes have the physical capacity to produce speech sounds,
   yet no primate has been able to learn to manipulate the vocal mechanism with anything approaching the level of skill that every child
   ordinarily displays.

There is a tendency among social scientists to regard language as a
wholly learned and cultural phenomenon, an ingeniously devised in-
strument, purposefully introduced to subserve social functions, the
artificial shaping of an amorphous, general capacity called *intelligence*.
We scarcely entertain the notion that man may be equipped with
highly specialized, biological propensities that favor and, indeed, shape
the development of speech in the child and that roots of language may
be as deeply grounded in our natural constitution as, for instance, our

predisposition to use our hands. To demonstrate the logical possibility —if not probability—of such a situation is the purpose of this paper. It is maintained that clarity on the problem of the biological foundation of language is of utmost importance in formulating both questions and hypotheses regarding the function, mechanism, and history of language.

The heuristic method to be employed here will be analogous to procedures employed in studying processes too slow and inert to be amenable to laboratory experimentation, notably biological evolution. The reasoning of our argument may gain by a few general statements on this type of theory construction and by a review of the basic, modern principles evoked in current discussions of evolution.

In many scientific endeavors we are faced with the problem of reconstructing a sequence of events from scattered, static evidence. The writing of geological, phylogenetic, and cultural histories is alike in this respect. But our treatment of geological and phylogenetic history differs from cultural history when it comes to "explaining" the causal relationships that hold between the events.

In geology we may trace cycles of elevation of the continent: subsequent leveling by erosion, followed by sedimentation at the bottom of the sea, and then recurrent elevation of the once submerged land, far above the level of the sea, resulting again in erosion and so forth. We cannot *explain* these sequences in terms of purpose, for purpose assumes a planned action, a pre-established end. Erosion, for instance, serves no more the *purpose* of establishing a balance than the eruption of a volcano serves the purpose of making erosion possible. It is appropriate to speak about disturbed and re-established equilibria; but the use of the word *purpose* has the common connotation of striving toward a goal, and, therefore, ought to be reserved for pieces of behavior that do indeed aim at a pre-established end without, however, being bound by nature to reach such ends by pre-established means.

In our discussions of phylogeny we must be as careful to avoid teleological explanations as in the case of geological history. Yet, many a time we seem to have no small difficulty in living up to this ideal. It seems so reasonable to say that the *purpose* of man's increased cranial vault is to house a large brain; and that the *purpose* of a large brain is the perfection of intelligence. We must take exception to this formulation because it implies finality in evolution or, at least, the assumption of a pre-established direction and end.* The geneticist

* For a philosophical treatment of this point, see H. Feigl, "Notes on Causality" in H. Feigl and M. Brodbeck, Eds., *Readings in the Philosophy of Science* (New

looks at evolution as the interplay between a *random* process and certain constraining factors. The random process is the blind generation of inheritable characteristics, i.e., mutations, while all the constraining factors have to do with viability of the individual or the species as a whole. Of the many new traits that may chance to appear, the great majority will have a lethal effect under given environmental conditions and are thus of no consequence for evolution. But occasionally there is one that *is* compatible with life and will thus result in perpetuation, at least over a limited period of time.

Attempts have been made to discover whether specific types of mutation could be regarded as adaptive responses of the germ plasm to environmental necessities, but I believe it is fair to say that so far results are not sufficient to conclude that there is a generally adaptive directionality in mutations. Dobzhansky states: "Genetics . . . asserts that the organism is not endowed with providential ability to respond to the requirements of the environment by producing mutations adapted to these requirements."[†]

If it is conceded that variability of inheritable traits due to mutation does not reflect direct responses to *needs*, it is quite conceivable that we may find characteristics that are compatible with life under prevailing conditions but that have no heightened adaptive value and can therefore not be explained in terms of utility to the organism.[‡] The differentiating characteristics of human races may be cases in point. The shape of skulls or the textures of hair cannot be rated by usefulness; nor can those mutations that have resulted in new species without extermination or limitation of the older forms.

The problem is more complicated when we observe a long and linear evolutionary trend, for instance the more or less steady increase in the body size of a species. When such a linear development occurs, we say that the evolved trait is *useful* to the species. I would like to stress, however, that the word *useful* (or reference to utility) must be employed with great care in this context and not without careful

---

York, Appleton-Century-Crofts, Inc. 1953), pp. 408–418, and E. Nagel, "Teleological Explanations and Teleological Systems," in S. Ratner, Ed., *Vision and Action: Essays in Honor of Horace Kallen* (New Brunswick, N.J.: Rutgers University Press, 1953). For a biotheoretical view see L. V. Bertalanffy, *Theoretische Biologie* (Berlin: Borntrager, 1932), vol. I. For the geneticist's position see J. B. S. Haldane, *Causes of Evolution* (New York: Harper & Row, Publishers, Inc., 1932).

† T. Dobzhansky, *Genetics and the Origin of Species* (3d ed.; New York: Columbia University Press, 1951) p. 51. See also the same author's broad survey of the entire field, *Evolution, Genetics, and Man* (New York: John Wiley and Sons, Inc., 1955).

‡ Cf. H. J. Muller, "Human Values in Relation to Evolution," *Science,* **127** (1958), 625f.

definition lest it be confused with purposiveness. In case of gradually increasing body size (take for instance the history of the horse), an individual animal stays alive if it is of a certain size, whereas an individual may perish if it falls short of the size that is critical at the time it is born. Since the individual cannot alter its inherited size, it also cannot change its fate of starving or being killed before maturation. Thus, no matter how *useful* it may be to be large, this state of affairs cannot be reached by purposeful striving of individual animals. Much less can we conceive of a super-individual entity (such as the species as a whole), making *use* of this or that trait in order to "insure the continuation" of the species. Something can become useful after it has come into being by a random process; but to make systematic use of a trait, such as size, seems to imply foresight and providence not usually accorded to the driving forces of genetics.

The situation is quite different when we come to a discussion of cultural history. Here, explanations in terms of long-range purpose and utility often are in order because man, indeed, does have final ends in view which he strives to achieve by this or that means. Frequently there are even explicit criteria for usefulness in reaching a goal, such as reduction of physical effort, maximizing gratification, or introducing order and manageability into a certain situation. In the development of coin money, for instance, there may have been some trial and error in the course of history, but many changes were introduced by fiat with the explicit purpose of facilitating economic intercourse. In other words, the development of coin money is the direct result of a certain property of human behavior, namely purposiveness. Or, more generally, it may be said that the phenomenon of *culture per se* is the outgrowth of this characteristic trait. But this should not obscure the fact that man and his abilities are also the product of biological evolution and that many of his traits are genetically determined and as such their existence must not be explained in terms of purpose. For instance the alternations between sleep and wakefulness, the shedding of tears, the closure of the epiglottis in swallowing, or any other unconditioned responses cannot be considered as the outcome of rational invention, as the end product of a purposeful striving just as any other genetic phenomena must not be accounted for in this way.

It is well to remember that purposiveness is a trait that is itself the result of evolutionary history, of phylogenetic development. Rudimentary forms of short-term purpose are observable as far back as the invertebrates. It is the ability to strive toward a goal (say nest building) by more than a single rigid action pattern. It is an ability to take advantage of specific environmental conditions in the accomplishment of certain tasks. For instance, birds are not confined to one specific type of material in the construction of their nests; the use of tiny shreds of newspaper incorporated in these structures is not an uncommon finding. Purposiveness requires anticipation or expectancy together with a flexibility in the choice of routes that lead to the goal.[§]

The purposiveness displayed in man's activities differs from that seen in lower animals not so much in quality as in degree. No other animal seems capable of performing actions with such long-range purpose as is seen in our socio-cultural activities. Not even such activities as nest building in birds which may last for days and weeks are the result of long-range purpose. This has been described by Tinbergen and commented on by Thorpe.[||] The nest is merely the end result of a very long series of individual tasks where each accomplishment seems to trigger off a striving for the fulfillment of the next task, and there is evidence that purposiveness, as defined above, does not actually extend over the entire plan; each task has its own characteristic, short-term purposiveness.

Our objective now is to examine language and to decide in which of its aspects we must assume it to be a genetically determined trait and in which of its aspects it might be the result of cultural activity. Insofar as it is revealed to be a biologically determined affair, we cannot explain it as the result of a purposefully devised system; we may not claim that *the reason* a child learns it is the inherent possibility of providing pleasure, security, or usefulness; or that language has this or that property because this was found in pre-historic times to serve best the purpose of communication. Any hedonistic or utilitarian explanation of language is tantamount to claim that speech as such is a cultural phenomenon or, at least, that it is the product of purposive behavior. Whereas, a demonstration that language is at least partly determined by innate predispositions would put serious constraints on utilitarian explanations of language and would instead focus our attention on physiological, anatomical, and genetic factors underlying verbal behavior.

Before embarking on the actual argument, a brief warning may be in place. The distinction between genetically determined and purposive behavior is *not* the same as the distinction between behavior that does or does not depend upon environmental conditions. The

§ W. H. Thorpe, *Learning and Instinct in Animals* (Cambridge, Mass.: Harvard University Press, 1956). This is the most scholarly source on the subject of innate and acquired behavior. My entire article has been thoroughly influenced by this book.

|| Thorpe, *op. cit.*, Chap. 2; N. Tinbergen, "Specialists in Nest Building," *Country Life,* **30** (January 1953), 270–271.

following example based on work by B. F. Riess will illustrate this point; the quotation is due to Beach.

> The maternal behavior of primiparous female rats reared in isolation is indistinguishable from that of multiparous individuals. Animals with no maternal experience build nests before the first litter is born. However, pregnant rats that have been reared in cages containing nothing that can be picked up and transported do not build nests when material is made available. They simply heap their young in a pile in a corner of the cage. Other females that have been reared under conditions preventing them from licking and grooming their own bodies fail to clean their young at the time of parturition.#

From this example it is obvious that innate behavior may be intimately related to or dependent upon the organism's interaction with its environment, yet the action *sequence* as a whole (first carrying things in an unorganized way; then, when pregnant, carrying things in an organized way so that the end product is a nest) is innately given. In other words, it would not be reasonable to claim that the young female rat carries things around because she is planning to build a nest if she should be pregnant and that she is purposefully training herself in carrying around material to be better prepared for the eventualities in store for her.

On the other hand, *purposive* behavior may only be very indirectly related to environmental conditions and thus give the impression of completely spontaneous creation; the composition of the Jupiter Symphony is an example.

In our discussion of language, we shall proceed in the following way. We shall juxtapose two types of human activities, one of which we have good reasons to believe to be biologically given, i.e., walking, while the other one we can safely assume to be the result of cultural achievement and thus a product of purposiveness, namely, writing. By comparing these two types of activities, it will be shown that there are at least four good criteria which distinguish in man biologically determined from culturally determined behavior. When these criteria are applied to language, it will be seen that verbal behavior in many important respects resembles the biological type, while in other respects it bears the sign of cultural and purposive activity. Since the culturally determined features in language are widely noted, the discussion will emphasize innate factors more than cultural ones.

F. A. Beach, "The Descent of Instinct," *Psychological Review*, **62** (1955), 401–410. Since writing this article H. L. Teuber has drawn my attention to contrary evidence: I. Eibl-Eibesfeld, "Angeborenes und Erworbenes im Nestbauverhalten der Wanderratte," *Naturwissenschaft*, **42** (1955), 633:34.

Bipedal Gait	Writing

CRITERION 1

No intraspecies variations: The species has only one type of loco-motion; it is universal to all men. (This is a special case of the more general point that inherited traits have poor correlations—if any— with social groupings: cf. black hair or protruding zygoma.)

Intraspecies variations correlated with social organizations: A num-ber of very different successful writing systems have co-existed. The geographical distribution of writing systems follows cultural and social lines of demarcation.

CRITERION 2

No history within species: We cannot trace the development of bipedal gait from a primitive to a complex stage throughout the history of human *cultures.* There are no geographical foci from which cultural diffusion of the trait seems to have emanated at earlier times. All human races have the same basic skeletal foot pattern. For significant variations in gait, we have to go back to fossil forms that represent a predecessor of modern man.

Only history within species: There are cultures where even the most primitive writing system is com-pletely absent. We can follow the development of writing histori-cally just as we can study the dis-tribution of writing geographi-cally. We can make good guesses as to the area of invention and development and trace the cul-tural diffusion over the surface of the globe and throughout the last few millenia of history. The emergence of writing is a rela-tively recent event.

CRITERION 3

Evidence for inherited predisposi-tion: Permanent and customary gait cannot be taught or learned by practice if the animal is not biologically constituted for this type of locomotion.

No evidence for inherited predis-position: Illiteracy in non-Western societies is not ordinarily a sign of mental deficiency but of defi-ciency in training. The condition can be quickly corrected by ap-propriate practice.

CRITERION 4

Presumption of specific organic correlates: In the case of gait, we do not have to *presume* organic correlates; we *know* them. However, behavioral traits that are regarded as the product of evolution (instincts) are also thought to be based on organic predispositions, in this case, on the grounds of circumstantial evidence and often in the absence of anatomical and physiological knowledge.

No assumption of specific organic correlates: We do, of course, assume a biological capacity for writing, but there is no evidence for innate predisposition for this activity.** A child's contact with written documents or with pencil and paper does not ordinarily result in automatic acquisition of the trait. Nor do we suppose that the people in a society that has evolved no writing system to be genetically different from those of a writing society. It is axiomatic in anthropology that any normal infant can acquire all cultural traits of any society given the specific cultural upbringing.

BIOLOGICAL AND SOCIO-CULTURAL FACTORS IN LANGUAGE

Let us now view language in the light of the four criteria discussed above in order to see to what extent language is part of our biological heritage.

1. First Criterion: Variation within Species. One of the major contributions of modern linguistics was the dispelling of the eighteenth-century notion of a *universal grammar* which, at that time, was based on the assumption of a universal logic. In America it was particularly the descriptivist school initiated by Franz Boas that has been most active during the last thirty years in demonstrating the truly amazing variety of phonological, grammatical, and semantic systems in the languages of the world. These workers have shown how the traditional method of describing languages in terms of logic must be abandoned for more objective, formal, and unprejudiced analyses; they have shown that lexicons of different languages are never strictly comparable; in fact, they have made us aware of the difficulty inherent in such notions as *word, tense,* or *parts of speech.* Thus, today anyone

** Cf. A. L. Drew, "A Neurological Appraisal of Familial Congenital Word-Blindness," *Brain,* **76** (1956), 440–460.

interested in language and speech is keenly aware of the great diversi-
fication of linguistic form in the languages of the world, and it is commonly acknowledged that their histories cannot be traced back to a
common "*ur-language*." In the light of this realization, it is very remarkable to note that in some respects all languages are alike and that this
similarity is by no means a *logical* necessity. Following are three points
in which languages are identical; they are, however, not the only
similarities.

1.1 *Phonology*. Speech is without exception a vocal affair, and,
more important, the vocalizations heard in the languages of the world
are always within fairly narrow limits of the total range of sounds that
man can produce. For instance, we can faithfully imitate the noises of
many mammals, the songs of a number of birds, the crying noises of
an infant; yet, these direct imitations never seem to be incorporated in
vocabularies. There is onomatopoeia, to be sure; but onomatopoetic
words are never faithful imitations but phonemicized expressions. This
is precisely the point: all languages have phonemic systems; that is,
the morphemes of all languages can be further segmented into smaller,
meaningless, components of functionally similar sounds. Words and
morphemes are constituted in all languages by a sequence of phonemes.
This is not a matter of definition or a methodological artifact. One can
visualize a very complex language in which the symbol for *cat* is a
perfect imitation of that animal's noise (and so on for other mammals),
for *baby* the infant's characteristic cries, for a *shrew* scolding yells; the
size of objects could be represented by sound intensity, *vertical direction* by pitch, *color* by vowel quality, *hunger* by roaring, *sex* by caress-
ing whimpers, and so on. In such a language we would have morphemes or words that could not be segmented into common, concatenated sound elements. Most words and perhaps all morphemes
would constitute a sound-Gestalt *sui generis* much the way pictograms
and idiograms cannot be analyzed into a small set of letters.

It would be interesting to see whether parrots speak in phonemes or
not; if they do not speak in phonemes (as I would assume), we would
have an empirical demonstration that the phonemic phenomenon is
neither a methodological artifact nor a logical necessity. One could,
for instance, take a parrot who was raised in Brazil and who has
acquired a good repertoire of Portuguese phrases and words, and
suddenly transplant him to an English-speaking environment where
he would add English bits to his stock of exclamations. If the first few
words are pronounced with a heavy Portuguese accent, we would have
evidence that the bird generalizes his Portuguese habits, that is, that
he has actually learned Portuguese phonemes which he now uses in

the production of English words. However, if his English acquisitions sound at once *native*, it would appear that the parrot merely has an ability for imitating sounds without deriving from it a generalized habit for the production of speech.

Whether this experiment is practically possible, I do not know. It is related here rather to highlight the problem at stake. It also suggests some empirical research on human subjects. If foreign accents are a proof for the existence of phonemes and if the child at three is said to speak phonemically (which every linguist would have to affirm), we would expect him to have an English accent if he is suddenly asked to pronounce say a simple German word—provided he has never heard German before. This is a project that could be done quite easily and objectively and which would be very revealing. (We are not speaking here of the young child's ability quickly to learn foreign languages, i.e., learn more than a single phonemic system. This is a different problem that will be discussed in greater detail.)

1.2 *Concatenation.* This term denotes the phenomenon of stringing up morphemes or words into a complex sequence called *phrases, sentences,* or *discourse.* No speech community has ever been described where communication is restricted to single-word discourse, where the customary utterance would be something like "water!" or "go," or "bird"; where it would be impossible, for example, to give geographical directions by means of concatenated, independent forms. Man everywhere talks in what appears to be a "blue streak."

1.3 *Syntactic structure.* We know of no language that concatenates randomly, that is, where any word may be followed by any other. There are contingencies between words (or, languages have typical statistical structures)[††] but this in itself does not constitute grammars.[‡‡] We can program stochastic processes into machines such that they generate symbols (e.g., words) with the same statistical properties as that noted for languages; yet these machines will not "speak grammatically," at least not insofar as they generate new sentences. It is generally assumed by linguists—and there are compelling reasons for this—that there must be a finite set of rules that defines all grammatical operations for any given language. Any native speaker will generate

[††] G. A. Miller, *Language and Communication* (New York: McGraw-Hill Book Company, 1951), Chap. 10.

[‡‡] N. A. Chomsky, *Syntactic Structures* (The Hague: Mouton, 1957), and N. A. Chomsky, "Three Models for the Description of Language," *IRE Transactions on Information Theory,* IT-2, 3 (no date), 113–124. I am also indebted to Chomsky for reading an earlier version of this article and for making valuable suggestions. See also G. A. Miller, E. Galanter, K. H. Pribram, *Plans and the Structure of Behavior* (New York: Holt, Rinehart and Winston, Inc., 1960), pp. 139–158.

sentences that conform to these grammatical rules, and any speaker of the speech community will recognize such sentences as grammatical. We are dealing here with an extremely complex mechanism and one that has never been fully described in purely formal terms for any language (if it had, we could program computers that can "speak" grammatically); and yet, we know that the mechanism must exist for the simple reason that every speaker knows and generally agrees with fellow speakers whether a sentence is grammatical or not. (This has nothing to do with familiarity or meaning of an utterance. One may easily demonstrate this by comparing Chomsky's two sentences, "colorless green ideas sleep furiously" and "furiously sleep ideas green colorless," where neither of the sentences are likely to have occurred prior to Chomsky's illustration, yet one is recognized as grammatical and the other not.) Note that types of sentence structures are as variable as speech sounds among languages of the world, but the phenomenon of grammar as such is absolutely universal.

1.4 *Conclusion.* The importance of the universality of phonematization (evidenced by the universality of small and finite phoneme stocks), of the universality of concatenation, and of the ubiquitous presence of grammar cannot be overestimated. Consider the vast differences in the forms and semantics of languages (making a common and focal origin of language most unlikely); consider the geographical separation of some human societies that must have persisted for thousands of years; consider the physical differentiation into a number of different stocks and races. Yet, everywhere man communicates in a strikingly similar pattern. There are only two kinds of conclusion that can be drawn from this situation. Either the similarities are due to the fact that, by happenstance, identical principles of communication have developed completely independently over and over, hundreds of times—an extremely improbable supposition, or the universal phenomena reflect some trait that is related to the genetic mutation that has constituted the speciation of *homo sapiens* and are, therefore, of a venerable age. I should like to take the latter view, and I feel strengthened in this position by the evidence that follows.

Perhaps someone would like to argue that a third explanation *is* possible, namely, that languages are alike because everywhere it was discovered that there is an "optimal way of oral communication" and that languages as we find them simply reflect optimization of conditions. This statement is either false or else it turns out to be simply a different formulation of my second alternative. It is objectively not true that languages are the most efficient communication systems possible. From an information-theoretical point of view, they are very redundant; as far as their grammars are concerned, they seem to be "unnecessarily complicated" (the simplicity of English grammar as against, say, Navaho is certain to be an illusion); in semantic efficiency they leave much to be desired. They can only be said to be ideally efficient if we add "given man's articulatory, perceptual, and intellectual capacity." But with this concession we have admitted that man's pattern of speech is determined by his biological equipment, a point that will be further expanded in connection with the fourth criterion.

2. **Second Criterion: History within Species.** Languages, like fashions, have histories, but nowhere does the historical evidence take us back to a stage where the phonemic mode of vocalization was in its infancy: we have no records testifying to an absence of grammar; we have no reason to believe that there are places or times where or when concatenation had not been developed. Perhaps this ought to be attributed to the rather recent development of written records. Yet, a lingering doubt remains: writing can be traced back some five thousand years, and, while the earliest written records give us few clues about the language they represent, some of our linguistic reconstructions reach back to about the same era. This is a time span that comprises about one tenth of the age of the earliest evidence of Levalloiso-Mousterian culture (some 50,000 years ago) and the appearance of fossil forms that may be considered to be the direct ancestors of modern man. Thus, the oldest documented history of languages may be short when compared with palaeontological history; but it would not be too short to demonstrate trends in the development of, for instance, phonematization if this phenomenon *did have a cultural history.* We might expect that historical phonemic changes follow a general pattern, namely, from a supposedly *primitive* stage to one that could be called *advanced.* But the phonemic changes that we actually find—and they occur rapidly (within periods of 10 to 15 generations), frequently, and continuously—seem to follow no universal line and have, by and large, a random directionality; we cannot make predictions as to the qualitative changes that will occur in English 300 years hence.

The concatenating phenomenon is, historically, completely static. Throughout the documented history there is evidence that concatenation must have existed in its present complex and universal form for at least some five thousand years and most likely considerably longer.

The history of syntax is the same as that of phonemes. Our oldest linguistic reconstructions are based on reliable evidence that there was *order* in the concatenation of forms, that there were rules and regularities governing the sequences of morphemes which from a formal point of view cannot have been much different from grammatical processes of modern languages. We are not speaking here of specific grammars, but merely of the grammatical phenomenon as such. Syntax changes as rapidly and widely as phonemic structures, but, again, we cannot discern any constant and linear direction. At the most, there is a certain cyclicity, one grammatical type perhaps alternating with another. The so-called "analytical languages," such as Chinese and English, were preceded by synthetic types; and there is reasonable evidence, at least for Indo-European, that the grammatical *synthesis* as seen in ancient Greek was preceded by a more analytic stage (inflectional endings having been derived from once independent words). We cannot be sure, however, whether synthesis *generally* alternates with analysis; indeed, the very polarity expressed by these two terms is not very well defined in grammatical theory. It is widely agreed today that no typology of modern grammars reflects stages of absolute, nonrecurring grammatical development. Nor do we have any means for judging one grammatical system as more primitive than another.

Contrast to this situation the forms found in the animal kingdom. Species *can* be ordered in terms of anatomical simplicity (which we equate with primitivity) so that an arrangement from low to high forms results; and since phylogenetic stages are assumed to be unique and nonrecurring, we can construct phylogenetic history merely from taxonomy. But this reasoning may not be extended to linguistics. No classification of languages in terms of structural type (such as *synthetic, analytic* or *agglutinative*) provides us with a theory for a universal development of language.[1]

There can be no question today that we are unable to trace languages back to an ungrammatical, aphonemic, or simple imitative stage; and there is, indeed, no cogent reason to believe that such a stage has ever existed. This does not imply a nineteenth-century assumption of an instinct, particularly not an instinct for specific languages. Obviously, the child's acquisition of Chinese consists in the acquisition of certain culturally evolved traits. But a phenomenon such as phonematization *per se* need not be thought of as a cultural achievement, need not constitute the summation of inventions, need not have resulted from a long series of trial and error learning in communication.

To put my point more bluntly: the absolutely unexceptional universality of phonemes, concatenation, and syntax and the absence of historical evidence for the slow cultural evolvement of these phenomena lead me to suppose that we have here the reflection of a biological matrix or Anlage which forces speech to be of one and no other basic type.

3. Third Criterion: Evidence for Inherited Predisposition. The obvious experiments for testing the question, to what degree language is inherited, cannot be performed: we may not control the verbal stimulus input of the young child. However, pathology occasionally performs some quasi-experiments, and, while anomaly frequently introduces untoward nuisance variables, it gives us, nevertheless, some glimpses into the immensely intricate relation between man's nature and his verbal behavior.

Just as we can say with assurance that no man inherits a propensity for French, we can also and with equal confidence say that all men are endowed with an innate propensity for a type of behavior that develops automatically into language and that this propensity is so deeply ingrained that language-like behavior develops even under the most unfavorable conditions of peripheral and even central nervous system impairment.

Language development, or its substitute, is relatively independent of the infant's babbling, or of his ability to hear. The congenitally deaf who will usually fail to develop an intelligible vocal communication system, who either do not babble or to whom babbling is of no avail (the facts have not been reliably reported), will nevertheless learn the intricacies of language and learn to communicate efficiently through writing. Apparently, even under these reduced circumstances of stimulation the miracle of the development of a feeling for grammar takes place.

There is another important observation to be mentioned in connection with the deaf. Recently I had occasion to visit for half a year a public school for the congenitally deaf. At this school the children were not taught sign language on the theory that they must learn to make an adjustment to a speaking world and that absence of sign language would encourage the practice of lip-reading and attempts at vocalization. It was interesting to see that all children, without exception, communicated behind the teacher's back by means of "self-made" signs. I had the privilege of witnessing the admission of a new student, eight years old, who had recently been *discovered* by a social worker who was doing relief work in a slum area. This boy had never had any training and had, as far as I know, never met with other deaf children. This newcomer began to "talk" sign language with his contemporaries almost immediately upon arrival. The existence of an innate impulse for symbolic communication can hardly be questioned.

The case history of another handicapped child[§§] gives an illustration

[§§] See my article "Understanding Language Without Ability to Speak: A Case Report," *Journal of Abnormal and Social Psychology,* **65** (1962), 419–425.

that true organic muteness in the presence of good hearing is no hindrance for the development of a speech comprehension that is ever so much more detailed than, for instance, a dog's capacity to "understand" his master. This was a five-year-old boy who, as a consequence of fetal anoxia, had sustained moderate injury to the brain pre-natally, resulting in an inability to vocalize upon command. When completely relaxed and absorbed in play he was heard to make inarticulate sounds which at times appeared to express satisfaction, joy, or disappointment (when a tall tower of blocks would tumble to the floor). But the boy has never said a single word, nor has he ever used his voice to call someone's attention. I was once able, after considerable coaxing and promises of candy, to make him say "ah" into a microphone of a tape recorder. The tape recorder had a voltmeter with a large pointer that would make excursions with each sound picked up by the microphone. The child had been fascinated by this and had learned to make the pointer go through an excursion by clapping his hands. After his first production of the sound "ah" he was able to repeat the sound immediately afterwards, but when he came back the next day, he tried in vain to say "ah," despite the fact that he seemed to be giving himself all the prompting that he could think of, like holding the microphone in both hands and approaching it with his mouth as if to say "ah." A series of examinations revealed that this boy had a remarkable understanding of spoken English; he could execute such complex commands as "take a pencil and cross out all A's in this book," "look behind the tape-recorder and find a surprise" (this was a tape-recorded instruction delivered in the absence of the experimenter), "point at all pictures of things to eat." He was able to distinguish pronouns ("touch my nose; touch your nose"), to show one, two, three, four, or five fingers; he could distinguish between a question and a declarative statement by nodding a yes-or-no answer to the question but not to the declarative sentence. He would even nod yes or no correctly when asked about situations that were spatially and temporally removed. This is discrimination learning but on a plane that requires a much more intricate understanding and sensory organization than the simple association of an object and a sign.

These examples do not *prove* that language is an inherited phenomenon. But they do point to the degree of man's preparedness for speech, a preparedness which seems to be responsible for the universality of the speech phenomenon.

4. Fourth Criterion: Presumption of Specific Organic Correlates. From the title of this section it should not be inferred that we wish to draw a sharp line between behavior with and without organic basis.

Thought and emotion have no less an organic basis than breathing or the tonic neck reflex. Yet there is a difference between the former and the latter types which can be described in empirical terms. In drawing the distinction we must not forget that we are dealing with a difference of degree, not quality.

4.1 *Onset and fixed developmental history.* Any innate reflex activity and sensory irritability appears at a characteristic moment in an individual's pre- or post-natal maturational process and follows a typical natural history throughout life. For instance, rudiments of the tonic neck reflex have been observed in a 20-week-old embryo; during the second half of fetal life this reflex seems to be well established, and it is strongest during the first eight post-natal weeks, with a peak of activity during the fourth week. At 12 weeks the reflex is less conspicuous and it is normally absent by the twentieth week. If the tonic neck reflex is observed at a later period, it is usually a sign of neurological disorder or pathognomonic retardation. Another example is manual dexterity: our hands become increasingly skillful throughout infancy, greatest control being achieved during young adulthood after which time there is a steady decrease which is accelerated about the fifth decade. Also the acuity of sensory perception follows characteristic age curves. Sensitivity to a number of acoustic stimuli is very low at birth, rapidly reaches a peak during the second decade and then steadily declines throughout the rest of life.‖ ‖

In the case of human behavior it is not always easy to rid ourselves of our pervasive and often quite irrational belief that all of our activities are the result of training. For instance, in the case of walking on two feet it is popularly believed that this is the result of the social environment. People who hold this view earnestly propose that the healthy child learns to walk between its 12th and 18th month because this is the time during which the mother is expected to teach her child this accomplishment. Speculation is often carried to the extreme where it is assumed that children brought up in social isolation would probably be seen with different modes of locomotion than is actually observed. That this need not even be regarded seriously as a possible hypothesis may be seen from the developmental events alone. Gesell and associates write:

> Although incipient stepping movements occur during the first week
> [after delivery!], they are more marked and appear with greater

‖ ‖ Cf. A. Gesell "The Ontogenesis of Infant Behavior" in L. Carmichael, Ed., *Manual of Child Psychology* (New York: John Wiley and Sons, Inc., 1946). For data on hearing see J. Sataloff, *Industrial Deafness, Hearing Testing, and Noise Measurement* (New York: McGraw-Hill, 1957), pp. 248 ff.

frequency at about 16 weeks. At this time also the infant pushes
against pressure applied to the soles of the feet. At 28 weeks he makes
dancing and bouncing reactions when held in the upright [N.B.]
position. Flexion and extension of the legs are accompanied by raising
the arms. At 48 weeks the infant cruises or walks, using support.##

We get a flavor here of how deeply walking is based on reflexes that
must, under all circumstances, be called *innate*. Also, walking is not
an isolated event in the child's developmental history. It is merely one
aspect of his total development of motor activity and posture. Compare the same authors' description of the development of the upright
position:

> [Stiffening of] the knees occurs before full extension of the legs at the
> hips. At 40 weeks the infant can pull himself to his knees. He can also
> stand, holding onto support. At 48 weeks he can lift one foot while he
> supports his weight on the other, an immature anticipation of a three-
> year-old ability to stand on one foot with momentary balance. At this
> age he can also pull himself to standing by holding onto the side rails
> of the crib. In standing he supports his weight on the entire sole
> surface.***

Anyone who has observed a child during the second half of his first
year knows that there is continuous activity and exercise, so to speak,
and that most accomplishments occur spontaneously and not as a
response to specific training (for instance, climbing out of the playpen).
The most suggestive (even though not conclusive) evidence for this
point comes from animal experiments. Thorpe††† reports on an experiment by Grohmann in which young pigeons were reared in narrow
tubes which prevented them from moving their wings. He writes:

> Thus they could not carry out the incipient flights which would natu-
> rally be regarded as in the nature of practice. When Grohmann's
> control birds, which were allowed free practice flights every day, had
> progressed to a certain point, both groups were tested for flying
> ability, but no difference was found between them. In other words,
> the instinctive behavior pattern of flight had been maturing at a
> steady rate, quite irrespective of the birds' opportunity of exercising it.
> Those that had been kept in tubes had reached just the same stage of
> development as those that had what appeared to be the advantage

A. Gesell, *The First Five Years of Life; A Guide to the Study of the Pre-
school Child* (New York: Harper & Row, Inc., 1940). p. 70.
*** Gesell, *op. cit.,* p. 68.
††† Thorpe, *op. cit.,* p. 51.

of practice. There is little reasonable doubt that at a later stage further skill in the fine adjustment of flight is acquired as a result of practice . . . ; [Grohmann's] work . . . suffices to show how cautious one must be in interpreting what appears to be the learning behavior of young birds.

Coghill‡‡‡ has shown how the primary neural mechanism of swimming and walking in Amblystoma is laid down before the animal can at all respond to its environment. Also, it is common knowledge that neonate colts or calves can stand immediately after birth and that most quadrupeds can either take a few steps or at least go through walking motions within the first few hours of life. If locomotion is innate in such a great variety of vertebrates, why should man be an exception?

The developmental history is not always perfectly synchronized with the advance of chronological age so that we often have the impression that individual maturational phenomena, such as control over equilibrium in stance or the onset of menstruation, occur more or less randomly within a given period. This is probably an erroneous notion arising from our lack of information on other concomitant developmental aspects. If we had complete and accurate longitudinal case histories (instead of dealing with data gathered in cross-sectional surveys), developmental histories would probably reveal fairly constant sequences of events.

Contrast now the appearance and history of acquired behavior. A child waves goodbye when he is taught to do so. Some children may learn it before they can speak; some may learn it only in school; and in some cultures, it may never be practiced at all. Another characteristic of acquired habits or skills is that they may be lost at any time during the individual's life so that neither onset nor disappearance of the phenomenon fits into an established place of the life cycle.

When the development of speech is considered in this light, it appears to follow *maturational* development. Cultural differences seem to have no effect on the age of onset and mastery of speech. Unfortunately, completely reliable data on cross-cultural comparison of language development are still a desideratum, but a check through pertinent literature in anthropology and child development have revealed no contradictory evidence. Nor have the author's personal experience with two North American Indian tribes (Zuni and Navaho) or his inquiries from natives of non-English speaking countries cast the slightest doubt on perfect chronological commensurability of language

‡‡‡ G. E. Coghill, *Anatomy and the Problem of Behavior* (Cambridge, England: Cambridge University Press, 1929).

development throughout the world. This is also congruent with our present belief that a normal child will learn any language with the same degree of ease, whereas a child who has failed to learn the language of his native land by the time he is six, also could not learn a foreign *simpler* language without trouble. We have to conclude from this that natural languages differ little in terms of complexity when regarded from a developmental point of view.

Compare this situation with writing. Writing does not develop automatically at a specific age and it also seems that various cultures have developed writing systems of varying degrees of difficulty. For instance, the *petroglyphs* left behind by the North American Indians of the South West can be roughly interpreted even today by the naïve observer. The picture of a woman, an infant, and two feet in a certain direction is most likely a message involving a mother, child, and walking. Narrowing down the meaning of this inscription is easier than one written in Runes. Knowledge of Chinese characters requires greater study than that of the Roman alphabet. I have also made some clinical observations that deserve mention in this connection.

Neuro-psychiatrists are familiar with a condition that is referred to in the American medical literature as *specific reading disability*. It consists of a marked congenital difficulty in learning to write. Intensive drill will sometimes correct this deficit but cases have been reported (see reference in 7n for bibliography) where writing was never acquired despite a normal IQ as measured by the usual tests. I have examined eight such cases (who were seen in a neuro-medical outpatient department) in order to find out whether these patients had learned some more primitive type of graphic representation. It appeared that none of them had the slightest difficulty in understanding such symbols as arrows pointing in certain directions, simple representations of stars, hearts, or crosses; nor was there any difficulty in interpreting simple action sequences represented by three very schematic stick-men designs:

("man walking   he enters a house   he is sitting down")

Each of these three pictures was understood when presented individually as well as in conjunction.

Presumably, these subjects have difficulty with some aspects of English orthography but not with visual pattern recognition or the interpretation of graphic symbols. The condition, therefore, is not actually a general *reading difficulty* but merely a difficulty with certain, at present unidentified, associative processes involved in *our* type of writing system. It would be interesting to know whether other countries have the same incidence and types of "specific reading disability" as encountered in England and the United States.

Let us now take a closer look at the longitudinal development of language acquisition. Unfortunately, we only have data gathered within our own culture; but even this much will be instructive, and there is, indeed, very little reason to believe that the main phenomena should differ significantly in nonEnglish speaking communities.

All children go through identical phases in the process of acquiring speech. First, they have a few words or phrases, never longer than three syllables, that refer to objects, persons, or complex situations. At this stage they may have a repertoire of fifty short utterances that are somewhat stereotyped and are never combined one with the other. All attempts to make the child string up the words that he is known to use singly will fail until he reaches a certain stage of maturation. When this is attained, the combining of words seems to be quite automatic, that is, he will surprise the parents by suddenly putting two words together that may not have been given him for repetition, in fact, that may often sound queer enough to make it quite unlikely that anyone in the child's environment has ever spoken these words in just that sequence. "Eat cup" may mean "the dog is eating out of the cup" or "is the dog eating the cup?" and so on. Whatever was meant by this utterance (which was actually heard), it is a sequence of words that nobody had used in the particular situation in which the words were spoken. As the child grows older, longer phrases are composed of individual vocabulary items which had been in the child's repertoire for many months, sometimes years.

Other aspects of language exhibit a similar developmental constancy. There are certain sentence structures that are virtually never heard during the first three years of life (for instance, conditionals or subjunctives). The frequency of occurrence of words shows certain characteristic constancies for child language, which, interestingly enough, are somewhat different from the frequency of occurrences of adult speech. In English, the most frequently occurring words are the articles *a* and *the*; yet, the child's first words never include these. (There is an active process of selection going on that must not be confused with mechanical parroting.) There is also a fairly constant semantic development. Children seem to begin speech with very characteristic semantic generalizations. The word *car* may be extended at first to all vehicles (a child of my acquaintance once pointed to a plane and said car); *dog* to all animals; *daddy* to all people or all men. But there is already an ordering activity apparent that is characteristic of speech as a whole.

Also, the usage of words have a characteristic history. All observers of longitudinal child-language development have reported a difficulty in naming colors correctly at an early stage.§§§ The curriculum of many public Kindergartens includes special training in color naming. This characteristic difficulty for the child at 2½ to 3½ years of age is the more interesting as color words are among the most frequently occurring words in English, and it is hard to see that their correct use should have smaller reinforcement value than words such as *big* and *small, hot* and *cold,* or *heavy* and *light, wet* and *dry,* all of which are words used correctly before color words. Of course, we do not take this observation to mean that something like a special structure has to mature which is particularly involved in color naming. The point here is that naming is a complex process which presents varying degrees of difficulty or, in other words, which depends upon a number of skills that develop at a slow rate. All we can say at our present state of knowledge is that on his second birthday the child does not ordinarily have the capacity to learn to name four basic colors consistently and correctly, whereas he develops this capacity within the next two or three years. (To make a distinction between *concrete* and *abstract* names is of little help since we only have *post hoc* definitions of these terms.)

Another line of evidence that would support the thesis that language-learning follows a maturational course is the phenomenon of foreign accents; it seems as if the degree of accent correlates fairly well with the age during which a second language is acquired. The following case will illustrate the point: Mr. R. W., whose major interest is the study of language, is a middle-aged graduate of one of this country's universities. He was born and lived in Germany until he was twelve years old when his family emigrated from Germany to a Portuguese-speaking country where he spent the next ten years. Within two years after his arrival in the new country he had such a perfect command over the second language that his foreign background was never suspected when he spoke to natives. At the age of 22 he came to the United States where he was at once obliged to speak English exclusively. From then on he had no further opportunity to speak Portuguese, and only occasionally (never more than a few hours at a time)

§§§ For theory and experimental work on this problem, see my paper: "A Probabilistic Approach to Language Learning" *Behavioral Science,* 2 (1957), 1–13.

has he spoken German since his arrival in this country. The result is interesting. His ability to speak English has completely displaced his facility in Portuguese and even the availability of his German vocabulary seems to have suffered in the course of the years. Yet, his pronunciation of English is marked by a gross and virtually insuperable foreign accent while his German continues to sound like that of a native and his Portuguese, as evidenced in the pronunciation of isolated words, continues to have the phonological characteristics of perfect Portuguese. (Yet, this person has heard and spoken more English during his life than either German or Portuguese.)

Here again it would be important to verify empirically the plasticity for the acquisition of languages throughout an individual's life history. Systematic research on immigrant families and their progress in learning English as a function of the age of the learner would seem to be a quite feasible and interesting study.

Before leaving the subject of fixed developmental histories in language learning, we must briefly consider those cases where language does not develop normally. Speech disturbances are among the most common complaints of the pediatric patient with neurologic disorders. It is precisely the area of speech disorders in childhood, which can shed the most light on the nature of language development; yet, despite a very prolific literature, the most elementary observations have either not yet been made or the reports cannot be used reliably. This is primarily due to the imprecise terminology common in these studies, to a predilection for subjective interpretation, to the complete absence of complete and accurate case reports of longitudinal descriptions (instead of the now fashionable cross-sectional studies of many hundreds of subjects), poor categories for classification, and similar other shortcomings. The only aspect in which little or no further spade-work needs to be done in this respect is the establishment of norms for speech development. We have little trouble today in deciding whether or not a patient's speech is normal for his age.

If speech disturbances were viewed as nature's own experiments on the development of speech, a wide variety of observational research projects could be formulated details of which need not be gone into here. Suffice it to point out that research could easily be conducted that would constitute direct verification of (or means for refining) the view that language development follows a characteristic, natural history. It would be very revealing, for instance, to know exactly under what circumstances the present practice of speech "therapy" (which is strictly speaking a training procedure) is successful. This would include detailed description of the patient's condition before and after treatment, perfectly objective evaluation of his improvement, and an accurate assessment of the role that specific speech therapy played in the course of the condition. In reporting on the patient's condition, it is not enough to mention one or another type of speech defect, but a complete inventory of the subject's speech facility ought to be given in addition to a complete and accurate report of his clinical and developmental status. Speech is so complicated a matter that we must not be surprised that a full case report is meaningful only after collecting most meticulous data on hours of patient testing and observations. A few scattered clinical notes, a random collection of psychological test results and a global statement of "improvement" is meaningless in this field. Among the most important objectives of a "log" of a long course of speech therapy is the determination whether language must be taught and learned in terms of a hierarchy of levels of complexity, whether it is essential that one set of skills precedes another, or whether almost anything can be taught and learned in a wide variety of orders. If there *is* a hierarchy of complexity, what are the linguistic correlates, what are the factors that make some linguistic aspects "easy," and what makes them "difficult"? Answers to these questions would be major contributions to our present state of knowledge.

In conclusion, I would like to suggest (subject to further verification) that the development of speech does not proceed randomly; there are certain regularities that characterize speech at certain stages of development, but empirical work still needs to be done on the individual differences that may also be observed. Moreover, we know that language development, viewed cross-culturally, has never been said to deviate essentially from development in Western cultures, and if we accept temporarily and subject to further work this indirect evidence, it would be more reasonable to assume that the acquisition of language is controlled by a biologically determined set of factors and not by intentional training, considering that cultures differ radically in their educational procedures.

4.2 *Dependence upon Environment.* Thorpe[1] describes the behavior of a hand-reared Tawny Owl "which, after being fed, would act as if pouncing upon living prey although it had never had the experience of dealing with a living mouse." This is not an isolated instance. Ethologists are familiar with this and similar types of action patterns that are usually triggered by so-called "innate releasing

[1] W. H. Thorpe, "The Modern Concept of Instinctive Behavior" *Bulletin Animal Behavior*, 1, 7, (1948), 12f.

mechanisms." Thorpe[###] notes that for every action pattern there is an ideal training stimulus such that every time it acts upon the animal, the latter will go through the entire action pattern. However, it is said that if the animal has not encountered the ideal stimulus in his environment for some time, the threshold for the release of the action pattern is lowered so that a stimulus that ordinarily does not evoke the patterned response is now capable of so doing. In the complete and continuing absence of suitable stimuli for the release of the mechanical action pattern, the threshold is lowered to a zero point, that is, the action pattern will go off in the complete absence of any environmental stimulus. This is the significance of the behavior of Thorpe's hand-reared Tawny Owl. But the absence of environmental stimuli does not imply absence of stimulation. Just as there is no effect without a cause, so there is no biological activity without a stimulus. In the owl's case, the stimuli must be assumed to be within the organism, i.e., be reducible to chemico-physical events. Again, this is nothing that is peculiar to innate action patterns because the behavior of pigeons that learn to pick at certain spots is also the direct result of chemico-physical reactions that take place within the bird's body. But differences there are. Compare the owl's pouncing behavior with Skinner's rat that learned to "purchase" a token which it would drop into a food-dispensing machine.[****] In the case of the rat, various bits of spontaneous rat behavior have been artificially (from the rat's point of view, *randomly*) chained so that the *sequence* of rat-behavior-bits has a *perfect* correspondence to a sequence of environmental events. Or, in other words, every individual bit of behavior making up the food-purchasing sequence was at one time preceded by a distinct environmental stimulus or at least linked to a reinforcing event. The only reason the total food-purchasing behavior appears in the sequence that it does, is that environmental stimuli and reinforcements have been arbitrarily arranged in a particular order. But the owl's pouncing behavior, which may not be as complex an affair as the purchase of food but still is elaborate enough and may last for as long a time as it takes the rat to purchase food, cannot be decomposed into bits of individual behavior components that can be rearranged into any combination and sequence. The sequence is completely fixed. This is a very important point. These days of electronic computers have made it fashionable to use electronic metaphors. We may say that innate behavior, such as the owl's pouncing is *programmed* into the organism. Environmental conditions may trigger the sequence (or perhaps forcefully prevent it),

[###] Thorpe, *Learning and Instinct in Animals, op. cit.,* introductory chapters.
[****] B. F. Skinner, *The Behavior of Organisms: An Experimental Analysis* (New York: Appleton-Century-Crofts, Inc., 1938).

but once it goes off it follows a prescribed course. It hardly needs to be pointed out that food purchasing is different.

If we were asked whether instinctive behavior, such as the predisposition for nest-building, or the pouncing of the owl, is primarily based on organic factors, we could hardly fail to answer in the affirmative. Since the environment alone is either insufficient for producing the behavior (dogs are not stimulated to build nests), or in some cases quite unnecessary, the action pattern must have an internal cause. This statement must be true even if we shall never discover the neuroanatomical basis of the behavior.

Let us now consider how language development fits into this scheme. The purpose of the following discussion will be to show that the rat who learns to press a lever or to purchase food gives us no more insight into the process of language acquisition than, for instance, thorough observations on the nest building habit of the rat or the acquisition of flight in the bird.

The constancy in language developmental histories is merely an indirect cue for the deep-seated nature of language predispositions in the child. Much stronger arguments can be marshalled.

First of all, in the case of the food purchasing rat, the sequence of behavior is pre-planned by the trainer and in that sense it has a rational aim. But language "training" and acquisition cannot possibly be the result of rational pre-planning because no adult "knows" how he generates new grammatical sentences. This fact cannot be appreciated except by sophisticated analysis of the principles of language. In the current explanations of language-learning we hear a good deal of how the supposedly random babbling of the infant is gradually shaped into words by the trainer's waiting for the accidental appearance of certain sounds which can then be reinforced, and thereby elicited with greater frequency, and how from this procedure the infant learns to imitate in general. This conception of speech acquisition is unsatisfactory from many viewpoints; for the time being, we merely point out that *imitation* (whatever psychological processes this term might cover) may be part of language-learning but by no means its most important aspects. Speech activity is virtually never a mechanical play-back device. This is most readily seen on the morphological level, where children will automatically extend inflexional suffixes both to nonsense words[††††] and to words that have irregular forms such as *good-gooder, go-goed, foot-foots*. Not quite so obvious, but in a sense

[††††] J. Berko, "The Child's Learning of English Morphology," *Word*, 14 (1958) 150–177. Compare also D. L. Wolfle, "The Relation between Linguistic Structure and Associative Interference in Artificial Linguistic Material," *Language Monograph*, 11 (1932) 1–55.

much more striking, is the generalization that takes place in syntactic matters. Here it becomes quite clear that there must be a second process in addition to imitation, for the language of children is not confined to stereotyped sentences. Children ask questions that have never been asked before ("What does blue look like from in back?"), make statements that have never been stated before (" I buyed a fire dog for a grillion dollars!"), and in general apply grammatical rules that only few adults could make explicit ("I didn't hit Billy; Billy hit me!").

The phenomenon of morphological generalization puts great strains on a simple referent-symbol association theory of language. The -*s* suffix of the third person singular ("he go[e]*s*") has no demonstrable referent taking this word in its literal meaning; nor the *s* of plurality, the *ed* of the past tense, the -*er* of the comparative. The referent of the "small" words such as *the, is, will* is completely nebulous, and neither training nor learning can possibly be the result of any kind of referent-symbol contiguity, that is, the proximity of the words *the* and *man* welds them into a unit. As long as ten years ago, Lashley[‡‡‡‡] thoroughly demonstrated the impossibility of explaining syntax on the grounds of temporal contiguity association, and he has pointed to the generality of his observations on language with respect to other motor behavior. Lashley's argument is so compelling that little can be added to it. More recently, Chomsky[§§§§] has demonstrated from a purely formal approach that grammatical sentences cannot be the product of stochastic processes in which the probability of occurrence of an element (morpheme or word) is entirely determined by preceding elements, and Miller[‖‖‖‖] and Chomsky[####] have discussed the psychological implications of this observation. We have neither a good theoretical model nor any practical insights into how we could teach an organism to respond to plurality, third-person-ness, past-ness, let alone how we could train him to use these responses in the correct order and verbal contexts within original sentence constructions. Con-

[‡‡‡‡] K. S. Lashley, "The Problem of Serial Order in Behavior" in L. A. Jeffress, Ed., *Cerebral Mechanisms in Behavior, The Hixon Symposium* (New York: John Wiley and Sons, Inc., 1951).

[§§§§] Chomsky, "Three Models for the Description of Language," *op. cit.*

[‖‖‖‖] N. Chomsky, G. A. Miller, "Introduction to the Formal Analysis of Natural Languages" in R. D. Luce, R. R. Bush, E. Galanter, Eds., *Handbook of Mathematical Psychology* (New York: John Wiley and Sons, Inc., 1963). N. Chomsky, G. A. Miller, "Finitary Models of Language Users," in R. D. Luce, R. R. Bush, E. Galanter, *op. cit.*

[####] J. S. Bruner, "Mechanisms Riding High," *Contemporary Psychology*, 2 (1957) 155–157.

sequently, both the teaching and learning of language cannot simply be explained by extrapolating from rat and pigeon experiments where all learning follows an explicit program.

All that we have said about production of speech is equally valid for the understanding of speech. The baby can repeat new words with great ease and be satisfied with his own baby-talk replica of the adult prototype, because he seems to perceive adult words not like a tape recorder but like a "phoneme-analyzer." He recognizes the functional similarity between phones and between his own reproduction of the adult speech sounds, and this enables him to disregard the very marked, objective, physical differences between a baby's voice and a middle-aged man's voice. Chomsky and Miller regard the child at three as a machine that can make syntactic analysis of the input speech. Obviously, children are not given rules which they can apply. They are merely exposed to a great number of examples of how the syntax works, and from these examples they completely automatically acquire principles with which new sentences can be formed that will conform to the universally recognized rules of the game. (We must not be disturbed by the fact that a transcription of a child's speech— or adult's speech for that matter—would be quite unpolished stylistically. There might be incomplete sentences and every now and then ungrammatical constructions resulting primarily from beginning a sentence one way and finishing it another. The important point here is that words are neither randomly arranged nor confined to unchangeable, stereotyped sequences. At every stage there is a characteristic structure.)

A word on the problem of motivation is in place. Animals are not passive objects upon which the environment acts. Their peripheral sensitivities are centrally controlled to the extent that, for instance, a certain odor may at one time have an arousing effect upon an individual animal but at another time (say after consuming a satiating meal) leave it inert. Moreover, *ability to stimulate* is not an objective physical property such as weight or temperature. It can only be defined with reference to a given animal species. A tree might stimulate a monkey to do some acrobatics, a beaver to start gnawing, and a grandmother to rest in its shade (where the latter is merely a subspecies). Motivation for action resides in the physiological state of the organism and in some instances can be immediately correlated with clear-cut states of deprivation, say of food or sex. Ordinarily it is false to assume that the environment *produces* a given type of behavior; it merely triggers it. There are many ways of chasing and eating a rabbit, and even though all of its predators may be motivated by the same physiological drive, hunger, the mode of catching and consuming the rabbit will bear the characteristic stamp of the predator's species.

In view of this, it seems reasonable to assert that there are certain propensities built into animals and man to utilize the environment in a fairly species-specific way. Sometimes this is obscured (a) because of individual differences in behavior traits and (b) because behavior is also affected, within limits, by environmental variations (such as availability *either* of little sticks, *or* of leaves, *or* of rags for the building of nests; analogously, because a child may grow up *either* in a Chinese, *or* in a German, *or* in a Navaho speaking environment).

The appearance of language may be thought to be due to an innately mapped-in *program* for behavior, the exact realization of the program being dependent upon the peculiarities of the (speech) environment. As long as the child is surrounded at all by a speaking environment, speech will develop in an automatic way, with a rigid developmental history, a highly specific mode for generalization behavior, and a relative dependence upon the maturational history of the child.

It may seem as if we were begging the question here: If speech develops automatically provided a speech environment is given, how did the speech environment come about originally? Actually, we are in no greater logical trouble than is encountered by explanations of any social phenomenon in biology, for instance, communal life as the evolution of herds, flocks, or schools. Compare also the colonial life of ants, the family formation of badgers, the social stratification of chickens. Nor is human language the only form of communication that has evolved in the animal kingdom. Bees and many species of birds have communication systems, and in none of these cases do we find ourselves forced to argue either that these communication systems (or the social phenomena) are the result of purposeful invention or that an individual of the species undergoes a purposeful training program to acquire the trait. If in the case of lower animals we assume without compunction that the communicating trait is the result of an *innate predisposition elicited by environmental circumstances*, we have no reason to assume *a priori* that the language trait of man is purely acquired behavior (not pre-determined by innate predispositions). We are making no stronger a claim here than what is expressed by Dobzhansky's words:

> The genetic equipment of our species was molded by natural selection; it conferred upon our ancestors the capacity to develop language and culture. This capacity was decisive in the biological success of

man as a species; . . . man . . . has become specialized to live in a man-made environment.*****

CONSEQUENCES FOR THEORY AND RESEARCH

The great achievement of contemporary psychology was the replacement of mentalistic explanations by mechanistic ones and the simultaneous insistence upon empirical testability of hypothesized laws. In the search for laws of behavior it seemed at once desirable to discover the most universal laws since this alone, it was thought, could give our theoretical edifice insurance against *ad hoc* explanations. Many behaviorists have explicitly renounced interest in those aspects of behavior that are specific to one species and consequently, confine themselves, by program, to what is universal to the behavior of *all* organisms. This attitude has cost the science of behavior a price: it has made it difficult to recognize the very intimate connection between the behavior repertoire of a species and its biologically defined constitution, that is, its anatomy and physiology.

The treatment of language by behaviorists is an excellent example of this situation. The literature, including experimental reports, in the area of verbal behavior is very voluminous and cannot be reviewed here. In general it may be characterized as a gigantic attempt to prove that general principles of association, reinforcement, and generalization are at work also in this type of behavior. The basic process of language acquisition is roughly pictured as follows: The child associates the sounds of the human voice with need-satisfying circumstances; when he hears his own random babbling, these sounds are recognized to be similar to those uttered by the adults so that the pleasure or anticipation of pleasure associated with mother's voice is now transferred to his own vocalizations. Thus, hearing his own sounds becomes a pleasurable experience in itself, the more so as mother tends to reinforce these sounds, particularly if they by chance resemble a word such as *Dada*. This induces a quantitative increase in the infant's vocal output. Soon he will learn that approximating adult speech patterns, i.e., imitating, is generally reinforced, and this is thought to put him on his way toward adult forms of language. Admittedly, this account is a gross simplification of what has been published on the subject, but the basic mechanisms postulated are not violated. Many psychologists have noted that the concept of imitation is not satisfactory in an ex-

***** T. Dobzhansky, "Evolution at Work" *Science,* **122** (1958) 1091–1098.

planation because it is precisely the process that needs to be accounted for. I am in agreement with this objection but would add to the current views on the problem of language acquisition that there is a host of other questions that have not even been recognized, let alone *answered*. A few illustrations follow.

1. The perception of similarities is a general psychological problem closely related to the problem of generalization which, however, in the perception of speech sounds plays a particularly prominent role. Acoustically, the sounds of a two-month-old infant are totally different from those of the mother; how then can it become aware of similarities between his and his mother's voices? There is also great random variation in the acoustic nature of phonemes. The identical physical sound is in one context assignable to one phoneme and in another context to another phoneme. This is even true for the speech of one individual. Thus, phoneme identification is dependent upon analysis of larger language units thus calling for a sound-Gestalt perception which may well be based on highly specialized sensory skills. We cannot be sure, for instance, whether a dog that has learned to respond to some twenty spoken commands responds to these words phonemically or whether he responds to secondary extralinguistic cues such as its master's movements. (This is an empirical question and the evidence so far is in favor of the latter.)

2. Even if we agree that we do not know how the process of imitation works, everyone has to admit that in some way the child learns to behave like those around him, that is, to imitate. Bracketing the problem of imitation *per se*, there is a still more primitive problem: why does the child begin to "imitate" in as highly characteristic a way as he does? His first goal does not appear to be a replication of the motor skill—he does not at first simply parrot—but his first accomplishment is to *name* objects; in fact, the motor skill lags significantly behind the naming. There is nothing necessary or obvious about this. Talking birds do the exact opposite—if they learn to name at all, for which there is, again, no good evidence. Reinforcement theory does not explain this; to the contrary, from the common psychological accounts of the beginning of verbal behavior the perfection of the motor skill intuitively ought to have preference over the more abstract naming skill in the infant's learning agenda. The naming of objects, that is, to learn that there is a general class of objects called *cup* is notoriously difficult for animals.

3. Most terrestial vertebrates make noises, and in mammals these are produced through the larynx and oro-pharyngeal cavity. Without exception these acoustic signals serve some biological function which,

in their homologous form in man, would relate to emotions. Examples are courting, territoriality, warnings and danger signals, anger, care for the young. It is extremely difficult and, for many species, reportedly impossible to train animals to use these vocal signals for instrumental conditioning. It is not possible, to my knowledge, to teach a dog to howl in order to obtain a morsel of food; a tomcat to make courting noises to avoid shock; a rat to squeal in order to have doors opened in a maze. There are many indications that human vocalization is phylogenetically also related to the expression of emotions; yet, in the course of normal development a child begins to make use of his vocal apparatus independently from his emotions. Why is this so?

4. The general problem of attention has haunted practically every research in psychology, and so we are not surprised to encounter it also in connection with language acquisition. The apes that were raised in human homes failed to develop speech partly, it was thought, because they could not be induced to pay attention to the relevant cues in their environment. But why do all children without any special training automatically attend to these cues?

5. It is well known that there is a nearly perfect homology of muscles and bones in the head and neck of mammals and the geometry of the oral cavity of the great apes is sufficiently similar to that of man to make it potentially and physically possible to produce speech sounds. Except for a report on a single chimpanzee, who could whisper a few "words" in heavy and, to the outside, incomprehensible chimpanzee accent,[†††††] no chimpanzee or other primate has been able to learn to coordinate respiration, laryngeal, and oral mechanism with the speed, precision, and endurance that every child displays. What is the extraordinary skill due to? Does it merely depend on practice, or are there physiological predispositions?

Many more questions of this kind could be asked. They are all essential to our understanding of language and speech yet we have no answers to any one of them. Present-day psychology tends to brush these problems aside by simply admitting that it is in the biological nature of man to behave in this way and not in that and that biological aspects of behavior may be disregarded in the psychological treatment of it. But such a position endangers the discovery value which a psychological description of behavior may have. It threatens many a conclusion to boil down to the triviality that children learn to speak

[†††††] K. J. Hayes and C. Hayes, "A Home-Raised Chimpanzee" in R. G. Kuhlen and G. G. Thompson, eds., *Psychological Studies of Human Development* (New York: Appleton-Century-Crofts, Inc., 1952), p. 117.

because they are children and that all children learn to speak provided they are healthy and live in a normal environment.

If, on the other hand, the study of speech and language is from the outset seen as a study in biology (including the study of the inter-action between heredity and environment), we can hope to combine research on questions such as those posed above with those that are customarily asked in psychology and thus to obtain new insights into the nature of man. It is true that this approach will not allow us to generalize our findings to all species or to speak about "the organism" in general. But I see no reason why the difference between species and their behavior should be less interesting or pertinent to a general science than the similarities.

SUMMARY AND CONCLUSION

The behavior repertoire of many animals depends upon certain biological predispositions. On the one hand, the animal may be con-stitutionally pre-destined or have an Anlage for the exercise of given behavior patterns, or, on the other hand, it is innately tuned to react to specific environmental stimuli in a species-characteristic fashion. In a sense, all of man's activities are a consequence of his inherited en-dowments including his capacity for culture and social structure. But some of his behavior patterns, for instance, bipedal gait, are based upon very specific anatomical and physiological predispositions, where-as other patterns, such as writing, are based on more general capacities of motor coordination, perception, and cognitive processes. In the present article, criteria were developed to distinguish behavior patterns based on specific predispositions from those based on general ones. When these criteria are applied to language, one discovers that it falls between these two poles, though considerably closer to the side of special predispositions than to its opposite.

Since it is proper to speak of language as species-specific behavior, we are implicitly postulating a biological matrix for the development of speech and language. This is tantamount to an assumption that the general morphology characteristic of the order *primates* and/or uni-versal physiological processes such as *respiration* and *motor-coordina-tion* have undergone specialized adaptations, making the exercise of this behavior possible. At present, there is scanty evidence for this because proper questions that might lead to decisive answers—either for or against the hypothesis—have not been asked. Let us hope that the present formulations help us to ask such novel questions.

NOTES ON "THE CAPACITY FOR LANGUAGE ACQUISITION"

1. The terms *analytical, synthetic,* and *agglutinative* were used by historical linguists to describe the morphology of different language types. Leonard Bloomfield, in his book *Language*, cites several examples of schemes for classifying the morphological structure of world languages:

> One such scheme distinguishes analytic *languages, which use few bound forms, from* synthetic, *which use many. At one extreme is a completely analytic language, like modern Chinese, where each word is a one-syllable morpheme or a compound word or phrase-word; at the other, a highly synthetic language like Eskimo, which unites long strings of bound forms into single words, such as* [a:wlisa-ut-iss? ar-si-niarpu-ŋa] *"I am looking for something suitable for a fish-line."* . . . *Another scheme of this sort divided languages into four morphologic types,* isolating, agglutinative, polysynthetic, *and* inflecting. *Isolating languages were those which, like Chinese, used no bound forms; in agglutinative languages the bound forms were supposed merely to follow one another, Turkish being the stock example; polysynthetic languages expressed semantically important elements, such as verbal goals, by means of bound forms, as does Eskimo; inflectional languages showed a merging of semantically distinct features either in a single bound form or in closely united bound forms. (Holt, Rinehart and Winston, Inc., New York, 1933, 207–208)*

ALASDAIR MACINTYRE

Noam Chomsky's View of Language

INTRODUCTION

This article is somewhat different from all the others in this anthology in both format and subject matter. It is an interview rather than an essay, and the subject matter often ranges into philosophy. For readers without a background in philosophy, the subject matter will probably make this article the most difficult in the anthology. However, in many ways it is perhaps the most important.

The subject matter of the interview is a topic fundamental to all teaching: "How do we learn things?" The discussion revolves around two competing theories of learning: the empiricist and the rationalist. Chomsky points out that the debate which began in the Age of Reason between these two fundamentally opposed theories has continued to the present day, and tries to place his own views of language and language learning within the historical context of the debate.

Alasdair MacIntyre supplies a clear and thorough abstract of the main ideas developed in the discussion and gives some general background information. If the reader will go through MacIntyre's introduction carefully, he will find the interview quite approachable and well worth the effort.

Reprinted by permission of the author from *The Listener*, Vol. 79, No. 2044 (May 30), 1968, pp. 686–691.

*

At a purely technical level, the work of Chomsky could only be
assessed by an expert in linguistics. But Chomsky's achievement is in
part to have made linguistics more important for workers in many
disciplines. Even metaphysical questions have been revivified by what
he has done. Can we understand man simply as a product of his
environment? Is there something distinctive about human nature—
apart from its complexity—which sets men apart from the rest of
nature?

The 17th- and 18th-century philosophical debate on these questions
partly centred on the relationship between the human mind and its
sense-experience. Nothing is in the mind which was not first in the
senses: so ran the empiricist slogan. Nothing is in the mind which was
not first in the senses—except the mind itself: so the rationalists reply,
with the contention that there are innate ideas, as Descartes called
them, principles native to the human mind which we utilise in grasp-
ing sense-experience, but not derived from it. The empiricist standpoint has often been presented as if it were the obvious one for the
tough-minded and scientific to hold. This may be because the empiricists have in modern times had more heirs than the rationalists.
A good deal of psychology, and especially of learning theory, has been
simply a slightly sophisticated re-edition of 18th-century empiricism.
What the 18th-century philosophers said *must* happen in human
learning—the building up by a conditioning process of a network of
associations and habits—is what 20th-century experimental psychologists have said *does as a matter of fact happen*. Yet the nature of language was always a stumbling-block for the classical empiricist. Some,
like Hobbes, give wildly implausible accounts of how language is
learnt. Others, like Hume, feel able to discuss the resemblances and
differences between men and animals without mentioning language
at all. Their modern successors have been bolder, and in a book like
B. F. Skinner's *Verbal Behaviour* we find a determined attempt to treat
the use of language as a series of learned responses to stimuli. We owe
it to Chomsky that we have strong grounds for believing that no such
attempt can succeed.

Consider one of the simplest facts whose importance Chomsky has
pointed out. Take the sentence: "Language never gives bilious ele-
phants food for thought." We repeatedly hear and understand sentences such as this which we have never heard before; we continually
utter such sentences ourselves, and we do so from the very early age
at which we first become language-users. This creative ability must

escape explanation in terms of habit, association and conditioning. We are somehow able in our use of language to go beyond all our previous experience. How?

Chomsky has posed this problem in terms of the contrast between the relatively meagre data which are offered to the child, the things said and shown to him by those who "teach" him to speak, and the relatively rich linguistic abilities which every normal child comes to display so readily. How is so meagre an input transformed into so rich an output? Chomsky looks for an answer by first examining the structure of language in order to discover the rules which would generate all those sentences which could be recognised as standard English or Swahili or Chinese sentences by an ordinary speaker of English or Swahili or Chinese, and would exclude all those sentences which could not be so recognised.

Chomsky regards the grammar of a language not only as something which will enable us to specify those rules a grasp of which constitutes competence in a native speaker. He also believes that a linguistic theory which can specify an adequate grammar will furnish us with an explanation of how the child acquires its large ability to use language from the materials with which it is presented. An adequate linguistic theory will tell us what those principles are—native to the human being and presumably embodied in the structure of the brain—which make language-acquisition possible and give to language the character it has. Descartes's innate ideas have once more come into their own; and Chomsky does see his own linguistic theory as the heir to the linguistic theories of the rationalist philosophers of the 17th century.

In describing Chomsky's work I have mostly written of "language" rather than of "languages." This was not a slip. Chomsky believes— as other linguists such as Roman Jakobson have done, but on other grounds—that there are certain formal structures which underlie any language and which therefore constitute a universal grammar. He arrives at this conclusion from considering further the complex relationship between structure and sense in languages, on the one hand, and languages as merely physical systems on the other. Any adequate grammar correlates sense and sound or shape; it explains why such and such a sequence of noises or shapes constitutes a meaningful sentence in a particular language and such and such other sequence of noises or shapes does not. Now suppose that we ask, for example, as Chomsky did in the discussion with Stuart Hampshire which appears in this issue, why we can, from the sentence "John kept the car in the garage," form a question by bringing the expression "the garage" to the beginning of the sentence and replacing it by "What" (so that we get "What did John keep the car in?"); but we cannot apply the same process to the sentence: "John kept the car that was in the garage." We discover that not only in English, but, so Chomsky seems to claim, in all languages, there are some complex noun phrases which do not allow for this process of question-formation. We cannot say intelligibly: "What did John keep the car that was in?" It does just seem to be the case that such forms and such transformations are ruled out, that the rules which govern our acquisition and use of language restrict us from forming such sentences and performing such transformations. Such observations are presumably important clues as to the character of the internalised rules.

There are finally three points one ought to make about Chomsky's achievement. The first is that it lies not merely in pointing out that there must be deep grammatical structures and rules of the type I have indicated, but in actually mapping them. In trying to map them a large number of individual problems are thrown up. One central problem, the interest and importance of which is easily grasped, concerns ambiguity. Take such sentences as "I had a car stolen" or that used by G. B. Shaw in replying to young writers who had sent him their work, "I shall lose no time in reading your book," or John Berryman's line: "My psychiatrist can lick your psychiatrist." When such sentences are set in a context we normally assign them their intended sense without having to give any thought to the matter. But just how does context enable us to use and to understand unambiguously such ambiguous sentences? We could only answer this question if we had successfully clarified the relation between deep and surface grammatical structures.

Secondly, Chomsky's work has not only had important effects within linguistics. It also raises questions about the structure of the brain, about the analogies between the output of certain types of computer and language, about the nature of the algebra which we need to map deep grammatical structures and about the relationship of linguistics to philosophy. It is in fact a paradigmatic example of the type of work which breaks down conventional boundaries between disciplines. To be properly understood, Chomsky's work would have also to be placed in the context of all the other discussions that have been going on in linguistics, if only to understand that such an approach necessarily has limitations as well as achievements. Chomsky urges us to study, not linguistic performance, but linguistic competence, not the character of the strings of sounds and meanings that are produced, but the character of the rules which determine which strings are produced and which are not. But fairly obviously, linguistic performance must be studied and is determined by other factors as well as by the type of rule which Chomsky is interested in.

Let me give a simple example. We can form more complex sentences from simpler sentences by repeating certain operations over and over again. This is the cat that killed the rat that ate the malt that . . ." We can apparently go on, so far as the rules which govern what is a well-formed English sentence are concerned, indefinitely. But of course in fact we cannot. The length of sentences is affected by limitations upon our powers of comprehension which seem to have nothing to do with the rules which govern what is a well-formed English sentence.

Consider another crucial point. Chomsky's work is concerned with *sentences*. Now the same sentence may be used to say quite different things, and this is not at all a matter of ambiguity. The sentence "All men are mortal" is quite unambiguous; but it may be used not only to assert that all men are mortal but also among other things to answer the request: "Give me an example of a major premise in a syllogism." We shall not understand language-using until we understand how this can be the case, and for this we require more than a theory of syntax: we require an adequate semantic theory. We do not at the moment possess one. Nonetheless we can be sure that in this, as in several other fields, it is not only the case that Chomsky has helped to provide some new answers to some very old questions: he has also made it possible to ask questions which no one has ever asked before.

STUART HAMPSHIRE: Am I right in thinking that your studies of language have led you to the conclusion that there are certain underlying structures common to all languages, which constitute something like a universal grammar?

NOAM CHOMSKY: It seems to me that the evidence available to us suggests that there must be some very deep inborn principles, probably of a highly restrictive nature, that determine how knowledge of language emerges in the individual, given the scattered and degenerate data available to him.

HAMPSHIRE: Your evidence is derived from a study of the learning of language?

CHOMSKY: If one wants to study learning in a serious way, what one really has to do is to study a kind of an input/output situation. We have an organism of which we know nothing. We know, or can discover, what kind of data is available to it, and the first question we must try to answer is: what kind of a mental structure does the organism develop when that evidence is presented to it? And after we have answered that question—that is, when we have some conception of what is the knowledge that results—we can ask the question about the processes that intervened, that led from the data available to the knowledge that resulted. We study the input data available to the child, or in principle we might study that, but the more intensive study is directed to the "output" knowledge that is possessed by the person who has mastered a language. The input/output situation is this: a child who initially does not have knowledge of a language constructs for himself knowledge of a language on the basis of a certain amount of data; the input is the data, the output—which of course is internally represented—is the knowledge of a language. It's this relationship between the data available, and the knowledge of the language which results from the child's mental activities, which constitutes the data for the study of learning—of how the transition takes place from the input data to the resulting knowledge.

HAMPSHIRE: I understand that your evidence is sufficient to establish that this learning isn't the kind that can be explained on the stimulus-response model.

CHOMSKY: When we analyse carefully the nature of the knowledge of language that a person has, once he has mastered his language, we discover that it simply does not have the properties which are implied by the stimulus-response concept of how learning takes place. The stimulus-response theory can only lead to a system of habits—a network of associations, or some structure of that sort. And it is quite impossible to formulate as a system of habits or as a network of associations the processes which will account for the sound-meaning relation that all of us know intuitively when we've mastered English. To take a sentence such as "John kept the car in the garage," if one thinks for a minute it becomes clear that the sentence is ambiguous: it can mean either that John kept the car that happened to be in the garage and sold the other one, or that the place where John kept the car was in the garage. On the other hand, if I form a question from that sentence, if I say, "What garage did John keep the car in?" it's unambiguous. It can't be referring any more to the car that was in the garage, and in fact from the sentence "John kept the car that was in the garage" I can't form that sort of question at all. You can't say in English: "What garage did John keep the car that was in?" This kind of evidence relates to well-formedness of sentences, to the association of sound and meaning. Some sentences are ambiguous, some are unambiguous. Some are connected with one another as paraphrases or by implicational relations and so on. When one organises all of this information and tries to formulate the principles that underlie it, what I would call a grammar—a theory of the sound-meaning relations in

language—then this grammar has properties that are quite inconsistent with the notion of associative net or of habit structure.

The striking properties of the grammars that we are led to by this
study are two in this connection. The first is that they have what one
might call a creative aspect to them, that is that they, in the technical
sense, generate—they specify or characterise—an indefinitely large
number of sentences, each with its associated interpretation. And of
course it's a crucial fact about language that a person is quite capable
of using and understanding sentences that have no physical similarity
—no point-by-point relationship—to any that he's come across in his
linguistic experience or has produced earlier. This creative aspect of
language is quite incompatible with the idea that language is a habit-
structure. Whatever a habit-structure is, it's clear that you can't inno-
vate by habit, and the characteristic use of language, both by a
speaker and by a hearer, is innovation. You're constantly producing
new sentences in your lifetime—that's the normal use of language.
When you read the newspapers or walk down the street you are constantly coming across new linguistic structures which you immediately
understand, which have no feeling of lack of familiarity, but which are
nevertheless not in any definable way similar to others that you've
experienced before. So much for the notion of habit-structure. Of
course there are elements of skill involved.

HAMPSHIRE: But doesn't this only show so far that we are predisposed to make some associations of meaning and sound? Would this
give us any grounds for saying that the predisposition was in its content something general?

CHOMSKY: No, it doesn't as yet. I think in order to reach that further
conclusion, one would want to turn to another very characteristic
aspect of the grammars that we are led to when we study such sound-
meaning connections as I illustrated in the example I gave. In order
to account for such facts, we are led to postulate highly abstract
structures—structures which have no direct connection with the
physical facts, which are related to the physical facts only by a long
chain of operations of a very specific and unique and highly abstract
character. This is the second aspect of grammar I mentioned, in addition to what I called "the creative aspect": the abstract character of
the structures that we must postulate in order to account for such
phenomena as the ones I mentioned. This abstractness is of a sort
which cannot be represented as an associative net. It's a technical
matter to show that, but I don't think it's very difficult. Furthermore,
when we look at these abstract structures, and the intricate set of
processes that relate them to the physical event, we discover that the

structures and the processes meet highly restrictive conditions. One can think of many possible formal operations which are not permitted in a natural language, even though they're very simple, and one has to ask the question why this is so. I mentioned a moment ago the process of forming a question. We have a sentence such as "John kept the car in the garage," and we can form a question by transposing "the garage" to the front of the sentence and replacing it by "what," so we get: "What did John keep the car in?" On the other hand, we can't apply that process to the sentence: "John kept the car that was in the garage." Now it's a very general property of English—and of all language, I suppose—that there are certain complex noun phrases, such as "the car that was in the garage," from which a noun phrase cannot be extracted by an operation of question-formation or anything else. That is apparently a linguistic universal. And it's not only universal but also unlearnable. As language-learners, we had very little evidence, in fact I think no evidence, to show us that you cannot form the question: "What did John keep the car that was in?" Of course we've never heard such a sentence, but for that matter we've never heard most sentences that we come across, so the fact that we know you can't do that must be because of some intrinsic limitation on the operations that we are permitted to construct.

HAMPSHIRE: So the evidence both comes from observation of the actual learning process and also has a comparative linguistic side. It's important to you to find that there are in fact no languages which don't exhibit exactly these transformations?

CHOMSKY: There is a comparative linguistic side to it very definitely, but I really think that at the present stage of the subject, though this may seem paradoxical, the best evidence as to what is a universal property of language comes from study of a single language. The reason is this: that if one thinks again of the process—suppose you think of yourself as a scientist who's trying to study a black box which has certain data as input and a grammar as output—well, any property of the output which goes beyond the organisation in the input must, vaguely speaking, be attributed to the character of the device. We have to ask what in the device led the output to have this specific property. Anything that must be attributed to the device, by virtue of the study of this input/output relation, must be a universal of language— that is, if we assume that people are not genetically endowed in such a way that they can learn one rather than another language. And by posing the problem in that manner we can really get a great deal of very strong evidence about what must be a linguistic universal from the deep study of a single language. Of course we have to test that against comparative evidence. Such a hypothesis must stand the test that it is not refuted by some other language. In this sense comparative evidence is relevant but it is actually less illuminating, at the moment at least, than deep study of a single language.

HAMPSHIRE: I ask this question principally because I am thinking of the classical theories of philosophers who have believed in doctrines of innate ideas, of innate predispositions to form certain ideas, or who have held that there are certain categories of thought which will be reflected in any language which is successfully used in communication. They have wished to speak of the human species as a whole, with no suspicion that they're merely saying there must be *some* such predispositions in any successful language use. I just wondered whether, when you speak of linguistic universals, you are really saying what they said—namely, not only that there must be some predispositions, but that they must be universal ones?

CHOMSKY: Making the assumption—which is an empirical assumption, but I think no doubt it's correct—that there is no racial differentiation detectable as far as ability to acquire a language is concerned, if we assume that much uniformity in the human species, then we must assume that what we demonstrate about the person who has learned English, about the intrinsic capacities that made it possible to learn English, will also be true of the intrinsic capacities that made it possible to learn Japanese or Russian or some African language. Now I think that the logic of the argument that I was sketching a moment ago is rather similar to that of the people you mentioned—for example, Descartes—who did really try to discover the principles that determined how our knowledge is formed by looking at the disparity between data and knowledge. Descartes asks: how is it that when we see a sort of irregular figure drawn in front of us we see it as a triangle? He observes, quite correctly, that there's a disparity between the data presented to us and the percept that we construct, and the knowledge of the properties of triangles that we automatically use in dealing with this data. And he argues, I think quite plausibly, that we see the figure as a triangle because there's something about the nature of our minds which makes the image of a triangle easily constructible by the mind: it's a kind of schema that automatically one imposes on data instead of some irregular figure which logically speaking could have just as well been the basis for our interpretation of experience. Quite similarly, here we have a human being—a child, let's say—who has certain data before him. He constructs on the basis of this data a certain grammar the detailed characteristics of which must reflect properties of his mind, since on the basis of the data that was presented many alternative grammars could have been constructed. Yet he picks a particular one. And that must be because of certain mental properties that restrict his interpretation of this data. Other people pick the same one, which simply shows that they are like him in their innate mental properties.

HAMPSHIRE: I think a certain amount hinges, if one is to speak of innate ideas, on how abstract the transformations are. Are they so abstract that you couldn't properly speak of them as a specific grammar, in the sense in which one speaks of a grammar of a particular language? The notion of a universal grammar has always been open to the charge that, insofar as it's universal, it'll be so abstract as scarcely to amount to a grammar.

CHOMSKY: I think again this is an empirical issue, and my feeling is that universal grammar, that set of properties which is common to any natural language by biological necessity, is really a very rich and highly articulated structure, with very explicit restrictions on the kinds of operations that can occur, restrictions which we can easily imagine violating. If a mathematician were asked to design operations on sentences, he would think automatically of certain very elementary operations—such as reading the sentences back to front or permuting the third word with the tenth word—and he might study such simple operations. However, such operations simply do not exist in natural language: for example, there's no natural language which forms questions by reading declarative sentences backwards. It's not so obvious why that should be so, because that's a very simple operation. It's a much simpler operation to state than the operation by which we formulate questions in English, let's say. Nevertheless, the principles that determine what operations may apply in a natural language preclude such simple operations as reading the sentence backwards or permuting the third and tenth words. And all these operations meet very interesting formal properties which are by no means obvious: they are what you might call structure-dependent operations, operations which apply to a sequence of words, not by virtue of the internal content of that sequence, but by virtue of an abstract structure associated with them—its structure as a set of phrases and so on. And it's by no means a trivial property of natural language that all of the operations that apply to sentences are structure-dependent operations in this sense. That's an example of a simple linguistic universal that you can't explain on the grounds of communicative efficiency or simplicity or anything of that sort: it must simply be a biological property of the human mind.

HAMPSHIRE: I was just going to ask that. Do you begin to have the possibility of functional explanations of just these structures being chosen from the indefinite variety of structures that might have been? Because, after all, philosophers have continuously argued that there are certain necessities of human thought in communication—that, for example, noun phrases must function in a certain way, that statement-making itself requires this. This was all, in their case, *a priori* and uncontrolled by detailed observations, and the argument was essentially, so to speak, a functional one: what is required for human beings, who are medium-sized objects, to make references and statements.

CHOMSKY: What is interesting are the kinds of principles which meet two conditions: first, they are universal but not merely by accident, not merely because no language violates them, but rather because no language could violate them. Secondly, they do not have the property that you have just mentioned—namely, that they're somehow necessary for organisms of approximately our size and role in the world. I think the interesting universals are the ones which are not necessary in this sense and there are many such. I've just mentioned two actually. One, the principle that makes it impossible to form a question such as "What garage did John keep the car that was in?" That's an impossible question, on the basis of some universal principle. Second, the principle that makes it impossible to form a question, let's say, by reading a sentence back to front. Neither of these principles is at all necessary for communicative efficiency. Neither has any connection whatsoever with our function in a world of a certain sort. These are formal principles. One can easily imagine a language which violated these principles, a language which did not have only structure-dependent operations, and such a language would be just as usable as our own. You could say the same things in it that we can say. Instead of having our complicated rule for formation of questions, this language would have a very simple rule, so that the question associated with "John saw Bill yesterday" would be "Yesterday Bill saw John." From my position I would certainly have to predict that if an artificial language were constructed which violated some of these general principles, then it would not be learned at all, or at least not learned with the ease and efficiency with which a normal child will learn human language. For example, I would have to predict that if someone were to construct a language which was like English, except that it had structure-independent operations in it, a child presented with the data from this language would have a very hard time learning and using it.

HAMPSHIRE: And that's not only because it had two principles of organisation within it but because one of the principles of organisation was an unlearnable one?

CHOMSKY: One which is not adapted to his language faculty. He might be able to learn it in some other way, like solving a puzzle. For example, we could certainly, as intelligent human beings, break a code that used structure-independent operations. If I were presented with a kind of Martian system which formed questions by reading declaratives back to front, probably I'd be able to figure it out: but not by means of those properties of mind which the child applies to the data presented to him to discover a grammar.

I think that we could show this empirically: we should be able to show that there would be a qualitative difference in the way I would interpret and master this material as compared with the way I would master and interpret the material from a normal human language. Preliminary experiments of this sort have been carried out by a group around George Miller, the Harvard psychologist. He has a project in which he's tried to construct what are from a mathematical point of view extremely simple languages: these are languages described by finite-state automata. And what he's trying to discover is whether humans will find it harder to learn the organising principles for such languages than they would to discover the organising principles of natural languages. My guess is that he'll get a positive answer in this experiment. It's a very hard experiment to do, because he has to have a long exposure period and it's not of the order of the usual psychological experiment.

HAMPSHIRE: Could I ask a different question: does this hypothesis have definite implications for the teaching of language?

CHOMSKY: I think it has some implications, perhaps of a rather negative sort. A good deal of the foreign-language instruction that's going on now, particularly in the United States, is based on a concept of language diametrically opposed to this. It's based on the assumption that language really is a habit structure, that language is a system of skills and ought to be taught by a drill and by the formation of stimulus-response associations. I think the evidence is very convincing that that view of language structure is entirely erroneous, and that it's a very bad way—certainly an unprincipled way—to teach language. If it happens to work, it would be an accident for some other reason. Certainly it is not a method that is based on any understanding of the nature of language. As I mentioned earlier, our understanding of the nature of language seems to me to show quite convincingly that language is not a habit structure, but that it has a kind of a creative property and is based on abstract formal principles and operations of a complex kind. My own feeling is that from our knowledge of the organisation of language and of the principles that determine language structure one cannot immediately construct a teaching programme. All we can suggest is that a teaching programme be designed in such a way as to give free play to those creative principles that humans bring to the process of language-learning, and I presume to the learning of anything else. I think we should probably try to create a rich linguistic environment for the intuitive heuristics that the normal human automatically possesses.

HAMPSHIRE: As in classical literary education?

CHOMSKY: As in the classical literary education, which I think was on the right track. It certainly fits much more closely to my feeling about the knowledge of language than does the modern linguistic approach, with its emphasis on habit and skill and pronunciation ability.

HAMPSHIRE: What is peculiar about this is that here we have a traditional philosophical claim—the claim of empiricist philosophy at all periods, or at any rate from the 18th century onwards—that language is learnt by association of ideas and by reinforcing responses, that concepts are formed in this way by abstraction, and that our grammar is a cultural phenomenon which varies with different cultures, with no common underlying structure and no necessity to prefer one structure to another; and then one has a contrary philosophical tradition, that there are predispositions to form certain ideas and to organise concepts in a certain order, and even more strongly, that these ideas can be stated in a propositional form. The suggestion now is that a set of experiments, together with adequate statistical theory, show that one of these philosophical traditions was misguided and that the other—although we don't yet know how specific these abstract transformational principles are and whether they be anything like the traditional innate ideas—was correct. Is the conclusion you have reached one which is subject to controversy among others working in this field?

CHOMSKY: It's highly controversial, though much of the controversy is somewhat beside the point and I'm sure things will become sorted out over the years. A good deal of the controversy does not have to do with the conclusions but with the nature of the goals. This approach to the study of language and the study of mental processes in general does, as you say, run counter to a long-standing tradition, and I think one of the major problems that make it difficult for people even to investigate the correctness of what is being proposed here is that they first have to see that there is nothing necessary in the tradition that it opposes. The empiricist view is so deep-seated in our way of looking at the human mind that it almost has the character of a superstition.

HAMPSHIRE: But supposing we take other features of human behaviour which have nothing like the same function or the same complexity, but which bear a certain analogy to what might metaphorically be called the language of gesture. One might find that there was a predisposition in children to acquire gestures, expressions, which they couldn't have seen or learnt in the classical empirical way, that the output bore very little relation to the input. This would lead one to say that somehow in the physiological structure there was a predisposition to behave in this sort of area in a certain way.

CHOMSKY: For example, smiling rather than crying when you're happy.

HAMPSHIRE: One would accept in general about human behaviour that it must be a genetic inheritance with a cultural layer on top, and similarly for ritual behaviours of various kinds. No doubt if one carried out the same analysis of the games that children play and saw the alternatives and the speed with which they learnt them, one would be deeply impressed by this.

CHOMSKY: I'm sure they would not be able to learn other sorts of games, which are from an abstract point of view equally simple, because they are not well adapted to their particular mental structures.

HAMPSHIRE: So one ought not to be surprised by this in respect of language. On the other hand, there is a peculiar factor that enters with language, which relates it to the philosophical tradition we were speaking of, the empiricist tradition which has always denied that there was anything that could be called innate ideas, meaning by this substantial propositions, beliefs as opposed to predispositions to behave in certain ways. Supposing one found that there were preferences for certain sound orders or word orders that really were very general, this might seem a feature of human behaviour which in no way upsets the empiricist's picture—any more than it would if there was a predisposition to represent a scene on a piece of paper, given a pen, in a certain way.

CHOMSKY: Well, I don't quite agree with that, you see. It seems to me that empiricists have been a bit fuzzy on this. If you look at the actual mechanisms of learning proposed by classical empiricism—by Hume, for example—or at such modern variants of empiricism as so-called learning theory in psychology, then these mechanisms really do not leave any room for such things as the principles of the sort that you mentioned. Particular principles of representation have no place within Humian learning theory. Humian learning theory says, after all, that there are impressions presumably determined by the nature of the sense organs and that these impressions are associated by certain specified mechanisms—contiguity, similarity and so forth. Modern psychology adds very little, frankly, to this picture. One can add certain assumptions about stimulus sampling or about techniques of building up hierarchies, but the additions that have been made in modern learning theory don't seem to me to go beyond this sort of domain or process in any fundamental fashion; this domain simply does not incorporate general principles about how knowledge is organised of the sort I mentioned in connection with language, of the sort that you're describing in connection with techniques of representation or of the organisation of games.

HAMPSHIRE: I suppose that the contrast here, which empiricists would insist on, would be between knowledge in the sense of propositional knowledge, which is said to be innate, and features of behaviour, such as the tendency to represent on paper a solid body in a certain way, which may greatly vary culturally. Nonetheless, given all the possibilities there are of representation as something built-in, I don't see why empiricists should be upset by this feature of behaviour, though they should be distressed if these predispositions amounted to something that could be called propositional knowledge or even to restricted categories of thought.

CHOMSKY: At this point we are running into a difficulty with the concept of knowledge as it is customarily used in the modern philosophical tradition, which is very different from the way in which it was used in classical rationalist philosophy. And this makes it very hard to come to grips with the issue that divides the classical rationalists and the empiricists. I would want to use "knowledge" in the sense in which Leibnitz uses it: as referring to unconscious knowledge, principles which form the sinews and connections of thought but which may not be conscious principles, which we know must be functioning although we may not be able to introspect into them. The classical rationalist's view is that there are many principles which determine the organisation of knowledge which we may not be conscious of. You can think of these principles as propositional in form, but in any event they're not expressible. You can't get a person to tell you what these principles are. Incidentally, I think that the rationalists didn't go at all far enough: in fact the one fundamental mistake that I think is made by the Leibnitzian theory of mind is its assumption that one could dredge out these principles, that if you really worked hard at it and introspected, you could bring to consciousness the contents of the mind. I don't see any reason to believe that the sinews and connections of thought, in Leibnitz's sense, are even in principle available to introspection. They may interrelate in some complicated way with certain principles that are available to introspection, but there's no more reason to suppose these principles to be available to introspection than there is to suppose that the principles that determine visual perception should be accessible to introspection—the principles, as in the case of Descartes' example, that make us see a certain irregular figure as a distorted triangle.

Ultimately I think that there will definitely some day be a physiological explanation for the mental processes that we are now discovering, but I think this will be proved true for a not very interesting reason. It seems to me that the whole issue of whether there's a physical basis for mental structures is a rather empty issue, for the simple reason that if you look over the course of the history of modern science, what you discover is that the concept "physical" has been extended step by step to cover anything that we understand. For a Cartesian physicist, the idea of attraction at a distance was not a physical process, and in fact for Newton himself it was an occult quality of objects. Well, when this became absorbed into understanding, then of course it became a physical process, because the notion "physical" was extended. Similarly electro-magnetic phenomena that would not be physical processes in the sense of Descartes, which didn't involve pushing and pulling, became physical processes when we began to understand them. When we ultimately begin to understand the properties of mind, we shall simply, I'm sure, extend the notion "physical" to cover these processes as well. What is at issue is only whether the physiological processes and physical processes that we now understand are already rich enough in principle—and maybe in fact—to cover the mental phenomena which are beginning to emerge. That's an empirical question. I don't know what the answer to it is, but I have no doubt that if they are not rich enough, we shall add new principles and call them physical principles.

HAMPSHIRE: Yes. But one is thinking now of those principles which you have to acknowledge in trying to write an accurate grammar— which is what it amounts to—these in-built predispositions. One thinks of facing a certain restriction on human thought as if we were wearing spectacles—if we took them off, we couldn't see at all. Does the discovery of these predispositions and principles—in their most specific form, assuming that they can be discovered—offer the possibility of bursting out of the restriction?

CHOMSKY: It seems to me that the right approach to this problem is to go back to another long-discarded idea which I think is nevertheless quite appropriate: the idea that there are faculties of the mind. If we want to develop an understanding of the structure of something as complex as the human mind, we shall be forced to recognise many sorts of logical components which could be called faculties, and which differ from one another in their properties and interrelate in complex ways. One of the faculties of the mind, I suppose, is the language faculty, which has certain restrictive principles such as those that I've mentioned. But there are many other components to the mind aside from the language faculty. That's why I said earlier that we might very well be able to break a code that violates some of the principles of language that are incorporated in the language faculty.

HAMPSHIRE: You think of logical and mathematical powers as really distinct?

CHOMSKY: They might be quite distinct from our particular language faculty. I think that the language faculty is that property of the mind which, when applied to the normal linguistic data of everyday life, develops this very highly articulated, very abstract structure of human grammar which determines knowledge of language. However, we have many other mental faculties apart from this. Ability to acquire a language is not our only mental faculty and I have no doubt that these other mental faculties also have their limitations. That there are such limitations would seem to me to follow from the fact that we are a biological organism. We can tell what a frog's limitations are, and some more complicated organism than us might be able to tell what our limitations are. I don't see that there's any contradiction in the idea that we could discover what our own limitations are in some fashion, but at the moment of course we can't get anywhere near that, except possibly in the case of certain artificially isolated components of the mind like the language faculty.

HAMPSHIRE: Yes, but you're therefore making rather strong contrasts between the faculty that is exercised, say, in pure mathematics and the faculty that's exercised in recognising and constructing new sentences. From the historical point of view, there's a certain paradox here if these two are separated too absolutely, because one would suppose that the logical structure and the linguistic argumentative structure have to be kept somehow under a single faculty.

CHOMSKY: I think it would be dogmatic at the moment to take any position on this issue. All we can say is that we have evidence that the language faculty has such-and-such properties. We know for a fact that those properties are not a general limitation of human intelligence. We know perfectly well that we would be able to figure out a language that had structure—independent operations of certain sorts. All right, so that just tells us that there are faculties beyond the language faculty. What the nature of those faculties are, how they are interrelated to the language faculty—these are questions that have yet to be discovered by the study of other cognitive systems, by a study which may be analogous to the study of language. One of the reasons why I think the present-day study of language is most interesting is that it suggests a way in which other cognitive systems could be studied. There are many other things that we know besides language, and I think it would be very reasonable to look into some other system of knowledge that we have, rather as the rationalist philosopher suggested that we look into our belief system about the external world to see if we can construct something analogous to a grammar of this belief system, and then ask how that "grammar" was developed on the basis of the data available to us and what this input/output relation shows us about the intrinsic nature of the mind that mediated this connection.

HAMPSHIRE: Do you think that when one thinks of these principles of order and transformation and preferred structures in language as restrictions, they set a restriction on scientific thought?

CHOMSKY: I suspect that the properties of the language faculty are probably closely associated to the faculties that lead us to what we call common sense—our common-sense knowledge of the world, that is. At the level of maturity at which a child is acquiring competence in language, he's also acquiring a vast amount of highly structured knowledge of the physical world and of human action and motivation. We don't know too much about the nature of that knowledge but there's no question that it's intricate, complex, highly organised and so on. This whole mass of knowledge falls into what we roughly call common sense and we know from the history of science that common-sense knowledge has had its limitations, that it's necessary to try to make this incredibly difficult leap beyond common sense to some sort of abstract picture of the nature of experience, of the nature of the physical world. Making this leap is a uniquely human ability, and it involves properties of the mind that we do not yet even begin to understand. I would suppose that there are restrictions on these further faculties. And a very fascinating question would be to try to think of a way of discovering these restrictions. If we could discover some of them, we could begin to say something about the possible bounds of human knowledge.

PART II

*The Application of
Transformational Grammar
to English Teaching*

RICHARD OHMANN

Generative Grammars and the Concept of Literary Style

INTRODUCTION

For Ohmann, an author's style is his characteristic way of writing. The task of the student of style is to identify in some precise way what it is that distinguishes one way of writing from another. Ohmann lists a dozen ways that this task has been approached, and concludes that, in spite of partial successes, these approaches have failed "to yield a full and convincing explication of the notion of style."

Ohmann argues that the study of style (stylistics) is dependent on a theory of linguistics and a theory of semantics because these two latter theories describe the system of language. A style is a characteristic *use* of the options within the system. As Ohmann puts it, "it is difficult to see how the *uses* of a system can be understood unless the system itself has been mapped out." The relative failure of the various approaches to stylistic analysis resulted from not having as a base an adequate theory of language.

Ohmann then makes two claims: (1) that transformational grammar provides such an adequate theory of language, and (2) that it is now possible to make significant advances "in the practice of stylistic analysis." He

Reprinted by permission of the author from *Word*, Vol. XX (December), 1964, pp. 423–439.

then adds, "I hope to state a case for the first of these claims, and to make a very modest initial thrust toward documenting the second." The argument for the first claim begins by clarifying what is meant by a *way* of doing something. In human actions, there are areas of restriction and areas of freedom. Ohmann illustrates this by considering the actions of a pianist and a tennis player; each has to follow certain conventions, but each has a number of options within the conventions. Style, in this sense, is the habitual or recurrent use of those options.

Ohmann then raises the question of whether such a distinction between restriction and freedom exists in literature. Some literary critics believe that form (the way in which it is written) is inseparable from the work's meaning. To change a word is to change the meaning, or to say it another way, to get exactly *this* meaning, exactly *these* words had to have been used. Thus, it follows that style does not exist since there are no options that the writer could have used in creating this particular work, that is, if a single word were changed, it would be a different work with a different meaning. Ohmann rejects this conclusion as being counterintuitive.

Ohmann argues that the very concept of style implies that the words on the page could be changed without changing the basic meaning. Thus, a writer's style is his characteristic way of exercising the options available within the system of the language. Another writer, with a different style, could convey the same meaning, but he would choose his own way of expressing it. Style, then, involves the notion that there are alternative ways of saying the same thing.

The transformational component of a generative grammar has three characteristics which afford promising insights into the notion of alternativeness: (1) optional transformational rules will produce alternative sets of sentences that mean the same thing. Ohmann illustrates this by the set, "Dickens wrote *Bleak House*; *Bleak House* was written by Dickens; and Dickens was the writer of *Bleak House*." The second and third sentences result from the applications of optional rules to the first sentence. (2) Transformational rules, even though they alter the form of the sentence to which they are applied, preserve some of the features of the original (kernel) sentence. Thus, "transformational alternatives seem to be different renderings of the same proposition." (3) Transformational rules also govern the way kernel sentences are combined to make complex sentences. This is important because the complexity of sentence structure seems to be closely related to what the reader perceives as the writer's style. Ohmann concludes the first part of his paper by saying, "there is at least some reason, then, to hold that a style is in part a characteristic way of deploying the transformational apparatus of a language, and to expect that transformational analysis will be a valuable aid to the description of actual styles."

The second of the two claims was to show that, with transformational grammar providing a theoretical base, a more refined stylistic analysis is now possible. Ohmann does this by contrasting four modern writers:

Faulkner, Hemingway, James, and D. H. Lawrence. He selects a brief passage from each author and reduces the passage to strings of kernel sentences. One of Ohmann's main points is that writers who have a distinctive style often have a characteristic way of combining kernel sentences, that is, they have a favorite group of transformational rules. Ohmann illustrates this by contrasting the transformational rules employed in the passages from Faulkner and Hemingway. Faulkner favors the relative clause transformation, the conjunction transformation and the comparative transformation, all of which are *additive*, that is, they add "information about a 'thing' with a minimum of repetition." Hemingway, on the other hand, relies on the transformations that produce indirect discourse. Ohmann argues that the author's habitual use of certain types of transformations implies that these writers have "a certain conceptual orientation, a preferred way of organizing experience."

Ohmann discusses two other ways in which transformational grammar gives insight into style. Some writers have a characteristic way of *ordering* the elementary sentences. Sentences may be developed to the right or left of the main clause (termed right and left branching), or the main clause can be split by adding additional material in the middle (termed self-embedding). Self-embedding is usually avoided because it puts such a strain on the memory. One of the things that characterizes Henry James' idiosyncratic style is his fondness for self-embedded constructions at the expense of the more normal right- and left-branching ones.

Finally, a style may be characterized by a preference for a certain type of *operation* (as opposed to rule). There are many transformational rules, but all of them can be subsumed under one of four basic operations. Rules either add, delete, reorder, or combine. We have seen above that writers can favor individual rules. Ohmann points out that writers can favor certain operations as well. He shows that while D. H. Lawrence uses a variety of transformational rules, they tend to have the same effect—the operation of deletion, a fact which Ohmann connects with the "driving insistence" one feels in reading Lawrence's style.

A style is a way of writing—that is what the word means. And that is almost as much as one can say with assurance on the subject, which has been remarkably unencumbered by theoretical insights. Yet we know a good deal more than that, in a way: the same way, roughly in which a native speaker "knows" the grammar of English, although no existing grammatical analysis gives a full and adequate account of his linguistic intuition. Readers familiar with literature have what might sensibly be called a *stylistic* intuition, a rather loosely structured, but often reliable, feeling for the quiddity of a writer's linguistic method, a sense of differences between stretches of literary discourse which are not differences in content. In fact many readers can tell, by skimming a batch of unfamiliar passages, not only that the differences are there, but who the authors are. Read the first few paragraphs of a *New Yorker* story and you can often (without a surreptitious glance at the end) identify it as a Cheever, an O'Hara, an Updike, or a Salinger, even if the subject matter is uncharacteristic. Further evidence, if any is needed, of the reliability of stylistic intuitions is the ability of some to write convincing parodies, and of others to recognize them as such. Thus the theorist of style is confronted by a kind of task that is commonplace enough in most fields: the task of explicating and toughening up for rigorous use a notion already familiar to the layman.

But in stylistics the scholar has always had to make do with a theoretical apparatus not far removed from that of the layman. And although many practitioners have plied their craft with great subtlety, a survey of their work leaves one far from certain what that craft *is*. For the attempt to isolate the cues one attends to in identifying styles and in writing stylistic parody has sprawled out into an almost embarrassing profusion of critical methods. And most of these methods, I believe, are interesting in inverse proportion to their emphasis on what we sense as style. The following list will suggest, but not exhaust, the multiplicity of approaches:

1. What might be called "diachronic stylistics," the study of changes in national literary style from one period to the next. Clearly this approach presupposes a mastery of what might be called

2. "Synchronic stylistics," or the study of this or that period style. Since the style of a period can only be the sum of linguistic habits shared by most writers of that period, synchronic stylistics presupposes in turn the ability to describe the style of a single writer. But there is little agreement upon how such description is to be managed; many methods compete for critical attention.

3. Impressionism: the application of metaphorical labels to styles ("masculine," "limber," "staccato," "flowing," "involuted," etc.), and the attempt to evaluate (Swift's style is the best, or the most natural to English). This sort of criticism makes agreeable parlor conversation, records something of the critic's emotional response, and gives intuition its due, but little else can be said in its favor.

4. The study of sound, especially of rhythm. This approach is capable of some rigor, but the more rigor (that is, the more strictly the critic attends to physical or to phonemic features), the less relevance to what we sense as style. For—let me state this dogmatically—

in prose, at least, rhythm as perceived is largely dependent upon syntax, and even upon content, not upon stress, intonation, and juncture alone.

5. The study of tropes. Attention to metaphor, antithesis, synecdoche, zeugma, and the other figures of classical rhetoric often proceeds from a desire to see the writer's style in terms of what he thought he was doing, and to this extent points away from a descriptive analysis of style, and toward the history or philosophy of rhetorical theory. Even when the studies of figurative language maintain a descriptive focus, they embrace only a small, though important, part of style, and liberally mixed with content, at that.

6. The study of imagery. The fact that a writer favors images of disease, money, battle, or the like, is frequently of great interest, but imagery divorced from its syntactic embodiment is surely more a matter of content than of style.

7. The study of what is variously called "tone," "stance," "role," and so on: roughly, the writer's attitude toward what he is saying, toward his reader, and toward himself, as suggested by his language. The critic in this vein infers, from the locutions on the printed page, a hypothetical live situation in which such language would be appropriate, and discusses the social and emotional features of that situation. This approach has unquestionably been fruitful. Its success depends on a highly developed sense of connotative meaning, both of words and of constructions, and this sense is something that many critics possess in abundance. Tone, however, like figurative language, is only a part of style, and the question remains in what measure tone itself is a product of formal linguistic features.

8. The study of literary structure, which, like the study of tropes and tone, has flourished among the new critics. And to be sure, patterns of organization in a literary work are *related* to style (the way a novel is put together may have an analogue in the way a sentence is put together), but to consider structure a *component* of style, except perhaps in a short poem, stretches the meaning of the term "style" to its limits.

9. The analysis of particular and local effects—a change of verb tense, or the placement of an interrogative, for instance, in a certain passage. Clearly, individual strategies of this sort fit more comfortably under the heading of *technique* than of style, for style has to do primarily with the habitual, the recurrent.

10. The study of special idiosyncrasies, such as the omission of causal connectives from contexts where they usually appear. Such quirks are doubtless stylistic elements, and they can richly reward analysis, as a number of studies by Leo Spitzer have shown. But a few

idiosyncrasies do not add up to a style, by any method of calculation.

11. The study of a writer's lexicon, as pursued, for example, by Josephine Miles. Lexical preferences, unless seen in the context of a ramified system of word classes, are like imagery patterns, in that they reveal more about content than about style.

12. The statistical study of grammatical features—abstract nouns, adjectives, subordinate clauses, questions, and the like. This method is without doubt pertinent, but significant results have been highly elusive. One reason is the crudeness of the categories which traditional grammar has made available to critics, whose knowledge of linguistics generally seems to lag by a few decades. (Linguists, by and large, have not busied themselves with stylistics.) Another reason, equally important, is the overwhelming inefficiency of the procedure, given the very large number of grammatical categories, and the lack of any grammatical system that relates them in meaningful, formally motivated ways. Without such a theory, a collection of counts is simply a collection of counts.

And indeed, the inability of these and other methods, in spite of many partial successes, to yield a full and convincing explication of the notion of style seems in general to follow from the absence of an appropriate underlying linguistic and semantic theory. A style is a characteristic use of language, and it is difficult to see how the *uses* of a system can be understood unless the system itself has been mapped out. It is no surprise, in other words, to find stylistics in a state of disorganization when syntax and semantics, upon which stylistics clearly depends, have themselves been hampered by the lack of a theory that is inclusive, unified, and plausible.

The situation in stylistics is understandably analogous to that in the philosophy of language,* though more muddled still. Just as philosophers have tended to concentrate on this or that discrete feature of language—words, or groups of words, or grammatical predication, or the relation of reference, or logical structure—in isolation from the rest, so analysts of style have talked about sound, tropes, images, diction, devices of conjunction, parallel structure, and so on, without any apparent sense of priority or centrality among these concerns. Thus, in a time when linguistic theory and practice have passed through at least one renaissance, the most serviceable studies of style† continue to pro-

---

* See Jerrold Katz and Jerry Fodor, "What's Wrong with the Philosophy of Language?," *Inquiry* V (1962), pp. 197–237.

† William K. Wimsatt, *The Prose Style of Samuel Johnson* (New Haven, 1941), and Jonas Barish, *Ben Johnson and the Language of Prose Comedy* (Cambridge, Mass., 1960), to name just two of the best.

ceed from the critic's naked intuition, fortified against the winds of ignorance only by literary sophistication and the tattered garments of traditional grammar. Especially damaging is the critic's inability, for lack of a theory, to take into account the deeper structural features of language, precisely those which should enter most revealingly into a stylistic description.

It is my contention that recent developments in generative grammar, particularly on the transformational model, promise, first, to clear away a good deal of the mist from stylistic theory, and, second, to make possible a corresponding refinement in the practice of stylistic analysis. In the remainder of this paper I hope to state a case for the first of these claims, and to make a very modest initial thrust toward documenting the second.

That Chomsky's formulation of grammatical theory is potentially useful should become apparent from an examination of the common sense notion of style. In general that notion applies to human action that is partly invariant and partly variable. A style is a *way* of doing *it*. Now this picture leads to few complications if the action is playing the piano or playing tennis. The pianist performing a Mozart concerto must strike certain notes in a certain order, under certain restrictions of tempo, in a certain relation to the orchestra, and so on. These limitations define the part of his behavior that is fixed. Likewise, the tennis player must hit the ball over the net with the racket in a way partly determined by the rules of the game (errors and cheating are not style). But each has a significant amount of freedom, beyond these established regularities: the tennis player, for instance, chooses from a repertory of strokes, shots, and possible placements (analogous, perhaps, to the linguistic resources of the writer or speaker), and he also has freedom of intensity, smoothness, flamboyance, etc. (as the writer or speaker has freedom in the use of paralinguistic resources like loudness and emphatic punctuation). The tennis player's use of these options, in so far as it is habitual or recurrent, constitutes his style. But the relevant division between fixed and variable components in literature is by no means so obvious. What *is* content, and what is form, or style? The attack on a dichotomy of form and content has been persistent in modern criticism; to change so much as a word, the argument runs, is to change the meaning as well. This austere doctrine has a certain theoretical appeal, given the supposed impossibility of finding exact synonyms, and the ontological queerness of disembodied content—propositions, for instance—divorced from any verbal expression. Yet at the same time this doctrine leads to the altogether counterintuitive conclusion that there can be no such thing as style, or that style is simply a part of content.‡

To put the problem more concretely, the idea of style implies that words on a page might have been different, or differently arranged, without a corresponding difference in substance. Another writer would have said *it* another *way*. For the idea of style to apply, in short, writing must involve choices of verbal formulation. Yet suppose we try to list the alternatives to a given segment of prose: "After dinner, the senator made a speech." A dozen close approximations may suggest themselves ("When dinner was over, the senator made a speech," "The senator made a speech after dinner," "A speech was made by the senator after dinner," etc.), as well as a very large number of more distant renderings ("The senator made a post-prandial oration," "The termination of dinner brought a speech from the senator," etc.). Which ones represent stylistic variations on the original, and which ones say different things? We may have intuitions, but to support them is no trivial undertaking. Clearly it would help to have a grammar that provided certain relationships, formally statable, of alternativeness among constructions. One such relationship, for example, might be that which holds between two different constructions that are derived from the same starting point. And, of course, a generative grammar allows the formulation of precisely this sort of relationship.

In the phrase structure component, to begin with, there are alternate ways of proceeding from identically labeled nodes, alternate ways of expanding (or rewriting) a symbol. A verb phrase may be expanded§ into a transitive verb plus a noun phrase, a copula plus an adjective, a copula plus a noun phrase, or any one of several other combinations.‖ The various possibilities for rewriting at this stage of the grammar account for some of the major sentence types in English, and since the structural meaning of, say, $V_t + NP$ differs considerably from that of $Be + Adj$, a writer's preference for one or another of these forms may be a stylistic choice of some interest.

‡ For an earlier attempt by the present author to deal with this problem, see "Prolegomena to the Analysis of Prose Style," in *Style in Prose Fiction; English Institute Essays*, 1958, Harold C. Martin, Ed. (New York, 1959), pp. 1–24.

§ I do not mean to suggest that a speaker or writer actually performs these operations. But the different possibilities of expansion in the grammar do offer an analogue to the choices open to the writer.

‖ Possibly some other order of expansion is preferable, such as the one Lees uses: VP→ (Prev) Aux+MV. See Robert B. Lees, *The Grammar of English Nominalizations*, Part II, *International Journal of American Linguistics* XXVI 3 (1960), 5. If the grammar takes this form, then the choice I am speaking of enters only with the expansion of the main verb. Such questions are immaterial, however, to my point.

But notice that the possibility of alternative routings in the phrase structure component does not really solve the problem of style in a satisfactory way. I have been looking for linguistically constant features that may be expressed in different ways. The difficulty with taking a unit like the verb phrase for such a constant is its abstractness, its lack of structure. The symbol VP merely stands for a *position* in a string at one level of description. Two different expansions of VP will both occupy the same position, but will not necessarily retain any structural feature in common. Nor will the sentences that ultimately result from the two derivations necessarily share any morphemes or even morphemes from the same classes. Thus, the rewriting of VP as $V_t + NP$ is part of a derivation that leads eventually to the sentence "Columbus discovered America," among others. But there is no kernel sentence corresponding (semantically) to this one which results from a derivation in which NP is rewritten Be + Adj. Sentences like "Columbus was brave," or possibly "Columbus was nautical" are about as close as one can come. And certainly they are not stylistically different expressions of the same thing, in the sense required for stylistics—not in the way that "America was discovered by Columbus" is. The phrase structure part of the grammar does not account for intuitively felt relationships of sameness and difference between sentences, for the possibility of saying one "thing" in two different ways. Perhaps this is one reason why almost no important work in stylistic criticism has evolved from the grammatical analyses of American linguists.

To be of genuine interest for stylistics, a grammar must do more than simply provide for alternate derivations from the same point of origin. There are at least three important characteristics of transformational rules which make them more promising as a source of insight into style than phrase structure rules. In the first place, a large number of transformations are optional, and in quite a different sense from the sense in which it is optional how VP is expanded. VP must *be* expanded by one of the various rules, or of course no sentence will result from the derivation. But an optional transformation need not be applied at all. Given a string or pair of strings so structured that a certain optional transformation can apply, failure to apply it will not keep the derivation from terminating in a sentence.[#] Thus "Dickens wrote *Bleak House*" is a sentence, as well as "*Bleak House* was written by Dickens," which has undergone the passive transformation. Likewise, "Dickens was the writer of *Bleak House*" is a sentence, one that comes from the same kernel string as the other two, via a different optional transforma-

---

[#] This is simply to rephrase the definition of an optional transformation; see Noam Chomsky, *Syntactic Structures* ('s-Gravenhage, 1957), p. 45.

tion: agentive nominalization.** Technically, transformations apply to underlying strings with certain structures, but for the purposes of this paper they may be thought of as manipulations—reordering, combination, addition, deletion—performed on fully formed sentences, rather than as ways of *getting* to parts of fully formed sentences from incomplete, abstract symbols such as NP. Each application of a different optional transformation to a sentence results in a new sentence, similar in some ways to the original one. Thus a grammar with transformational rules will generate many pairs and limited sets of sentences, like the set of three sentences about Dickens, which belong together in an intimate structural way—not simply by virtue of being sentences. Many such sets of sentences will strike a speaker as saying "the same thing"—as being alternatives, that is, in precisely the sense required for stylistics.

A second and related reason why transformational happenings are relevant to style is the very fact that a transformation applies to one or more *strings,* or elements with structure, not to single symbols like VP, and that it applies to those strings by virtue of their structure. A transformation works changes on structure, but normally leaves *part* of the structure unchanged. And in any case, the new structure bears a precisely specifiable relationship to the old one, a relationship, incidentally, that speakers of the language will intuitively feel. Moreover, the transform retains at least some morphemes from the original string; that is, transformations are specified in such a way that "Columbus discovered America" cannot become, under the passive transformation, "*Bleak House* was written by Dickens," although this sentence has the same structure as the proper transform "America was discovered by Columbus." This property of transformations—their preserving some features from the original string—accounts for the fact that sets of sentences which are transformational alternatives seem to be different renderings of the same proposition.†† Again, this is the sort of relationship which seems intuitively to underlie the notion of style, and for which only a transformational grammar offers a formal analogue.

The third value of a transformational grammar to the analyst of style is its power to explain how complex sentences are generated, and how they are related to simple sentences. Writers differ noticeably in the amounts and kinds of syntactic complexity they habitually allow themselves, but these matters have been hard to approach through conventional methods of analysis. Since the complexity of a sentence is the

---

** Lees, *op. cit.,* p. 70 (transformation T47).

†† Notice that many such sets, including the three sentences about Dickens, will share the same *truth conditions,* to use the philosopher's term. This fact gives further encouragement to anyone who would treat transformational alernatives as different expressions of the same proposition.

product of the generalized transformations it has gone through, a breakdown of the sentence into its component simple sentences and the generalized transformations applied (in the order of application) will be an account of its complexity.‡‡ And since the same set of simple sentences may usually be combined in different ways, a set of complex sentences may be generated from them, each of which differs from the others only in transformational history, while embodying the same simple "propositions." Such differences should be interestingly approachable through transformational analysis. So should major variations in type of compounding: self-embedding as against left- and right-branching, for example, or the formation of endocentric as against the formation of exocentric constructions. These deep grammatical possibilities in a language may well be exploited differently from writer to writer, and if so, the differences will certainly be of stylistic interest.

Let me summarize. A generative grammar with a transformational component provides apparatus for breaking down a sentence in a stretch of discourse into underlying kernel sentences (or strings, strictly speaking) and for specifying the grammatical operations that have been performed upon them. It also permits the analyst to construct, from the same set of kernel sentences, other non-kernel sentences. These may reasonably be thought of as *alternatives* to the original sentence, in that they are simply different constructs out of the identical elementary grammatical units.§§ Thus the idea of alternative phrasings, which is crucial to the notion of style, has a clear analogue within the framework of a transformational grammar.

But is it the *right* analogue? What I have called "transformational alternatives" are different derivatives from the same kernel sentences. The notion of style calls for different ways of expressing the same content. Kernel sentences are not "content," to be sure. Yet they *have* content, and much of that content is preserved through transformational operations. "Dickens was the writer of *Bleak House* and America was discovered by Columbus" says much the same thing, if not exactly the same thing, as "Dickens wrote *Bleak House*; Columbus discovered

‡‡ Since deletions and additions will probably have taken place in the course of the derivation, the complex sentence will naturally not contain all and only all of the linguistic elements contained in the component sentences. These must be reconstructed and supplied with appropriate hypothetical elements, but there is generally a strong formal motivation for reconstructing the component sentences in one way rather than another.

§§ Of course the alternative forms need not be complete sentences, or single sentences. That is, the alternatives to sentence A may include (1) sentence B, (2) part of sentence C, and (3) the group of sentences, D, E, and F. The most interesting alternatives to a given sentence often arrange the kernel material in units of different lengths.

America." Of course some transformations import new content, others eliminate features of content, and no transformation leaves content absolutely unaltered. The analogue is not perfect. But it is worth remembering that other kinds of tampering with sentences (e.g., substitution of synonyms) also change content. And, to look at it another way, the most useful sense of "content"—*cognitive* content—may be such that transformations do generally leave it unaltered (and such that synonyms do exist).‖ ‖ In any case, transformational alternatives come as close to "different expressions of the same content" as other sorts of alternatives; moreover, they have the practical advantage of being accessible to formal, rather than to impressionistic, analysis. There is at least some reason, then, to hold that a style is in part a characteristic way of deploying the transformational apparatus of a language, and to expect that transformational analysis will be a valuable aid to the description of actual styles.

So much for theory and prophecy. The final proof must come, if it comes at all, from a fairly extensive attempt to study literary styles in the way I am suggesting. For a transformational analysis, however appealing theoretically, will not be worth much unless it can implement better stylistic descriptions than have been achieved by other methods—"better" in that they isolate more fully, economically, and demonstrably the linguistic features to which a perceptive reader responds in sensing one style to be different from another. The space available here will not suffice for a full scale demonstration, nor do I now have at my disposal nearly enough stylistic description to prove my case. Besides, the necessary grammatical machinery is by no means available yet (in fact, it is too early to say with certainty that Chomsky's plan for grammars is the right one—there are many dissenters). I shall use the rest of this paper merely to outline, by example, a simple analytic procedure that draws on the concept of grammatical transformations, and to suggest some virtues of this procedure.

My first specimen passage comes from Faulkner's story, "The Bear." It is part of a sentence nearly two pages long, and its style is complex, highly individual, and difficult—if it is read aloud, most hearers will not grasp it on first hearing. It is also, I believe, quite typically Faulknerian:

> the desk and the shelf above it on which rested the letters in which
> McCaslin recorded the slow outward trickle of food and supplies and
> equipment which returned each fall as cotton made and ginned and

‖ ‖ I owe this point and several others to correspondence and conversation with Noam Chomsky.

sold (two threads frail as truth and impalpable as equators yet cable-strong to bind for life them who made the cotton to the land their sweat fell on), and the older ledgers clumsy and archaic in size and shape, on the yellowed pages of which were recorded in the faded hand of his father Theophilus and his uncle Amodeus during the two decades before the Civil War, the manumission in title at least of Carothers McCaslin's slaves: . . .##

I propose to reduce the complexity of the passage by reversing the effects of three generalized transformations, plus a few related singulary transformations:

1. The relative clause transformation (GT 19 in Lees' *The Grammar of English Nominalizations*, p. 89), along with the WH-transformations (Lees, T5 and T6, p. 39), the transformation which later deletes "which" and "be" to leave post-nominal modifiers (Lees, T58, p. 94), and the transformation which shifts these modifiers to prenominal position (Lees, T64, p. 98).***

2. The conjunction transformation (Chomsky, *Syntactic Structures*, p. 36).

3. The comparative transformation, which, along with several reduction transformations and one order change,††† is responsible for sentences like "George is as tall as John."‡‡‡

Without this grammatical apparatus, the passage reads as follows:

the desk. The shelf was above it. The ledgers₁ rested on the shelf. The ledgers₁ were old. McCaslin recorded the trickle of food in the ledgers₁. McCaslin recorded the trickle of supplies in the ledgers₁. McCaslin recorded the trickle of equipment in the ledgers₁. The trickle was slow. The trickle was outward. The trickle returned each fall as cotton. The cotton was made. The cotton was ginned. The cotton was sold. The trickle was a thread. The cotton was a thread. The threads were frail. Truth is frail. The threads were impalpable. Equators are impalpable. The threads were strong to bind them for life to the land. They made the cotton. Their sweat fell on the land. Cables are strong. The ledgers₂ were old. The ledgers₂ rested on the shelf. The ledgers₂

William Faulkner, "The Bear," in *Go Down Moses* (New York: Modern Library, 1942), pp. 255–256.

*** For another version of these transformations, see Carlota S. Smith, "A Class of Complex Modifiers in English," *Language* XXXVII (1961), pp. 347–348, 361–362.

††† Strong as cables→cable-strong.

‡‡‡ Lees, "Grammatical Analysis of the English Comparative Construction," *Word* XVII (1961), pp. 182–183. Carlota S. Smith, in "A Class of Complex Modifiers in English," offers a fuller treatment of such constructions, but Lees' simpler analysis is adequate for my present purposes.

were clumsy in size. The ledgers$_2$ were clumsy in shape. The ledgers$_2$ were archaic in size. The ledgers$_2$ were archaic in shape. On the pages of the ledgers$_2$ were recorded in the hand of his father during the two decades the manumission in title at least of Carothers McCaslin's slaves. On the pages of the ledgers$_2$ were recorded in the hand of his uncle during the two decades the manumission in title at least of Carothers McCaslin slaves. The pages were yellowed. The hand was faded. The decades were before the Civil War. His father was Theophilus. His uncle was Amodeus.§§§

There is some artificiality in this process, of course. The order of the reduced sentences is in part arbitrary. More important, the transformations I have reversed are not the last ones applied in the generation of the original construction; hence precisely the set of sentences (strings) above would not have occurred at any point in the derivation. Nonetheless, this drastic reduction of the original passage reveals several important things:

1. The content of the passage remains roughly the same: aside from the loss of distinctions between "and" and "yet," "as ——— as" and "more _____ than," relative clauses and conjoined sentences, and the like, changes in content are minor. But the style, obviously, has undergone a revolution. In the reduced form of the passage there are virtually no traces of what we recognize as Faulkner's style.

2. This denaturing has been accomplished by reversing the effects of only three generalized transformations, as well as a few related singulary transformations. The total number of optional transformations involved is negligible as against the total number that apparently exist in the grammar as a whole. In other words, the style of the original passage leans heavily upon a very small amount of grammatical apparatus.

3. Most of the sentences in the reduced version of the passage are kernel sentences. Most of the rest are only one transformation away from kernel sentences. Further reduction, by undoing any number of other transformations, would not change the passage or its style nearly so much as has already been done.‖ ‖ ‖

4. The three major transformations I have deleted have an important feature in common. Each of them combines two sentences that share at least one morpheme.### and in such a way that the transform

---

§§§ Subscripts mark differences in referent.

‖ ‖ ‖ Passives and pronouns are also fairly prominent here, but not enough to make them striking as stylistic features.

Except that conjunction may also operate on two sentences with no common morphemes.

may contain only one occurrence of that morpheme (or those morphemes), while preserving the unshared parts of the original sentences.
That is to say, these transformations are all what might be called
"additive." To put the matter semantically, they offer methods of
adding information about a single "thing" with a minimum of repetition. Thus the two sentences "The threads were impalpable" and
"The threads were frail" might be combined through any one of the
three generalized transformations at issue here: "The threads which
were impalpable were frail" (relative); "The threads were frail and
impalpable" (conjunction); and "The threads were more frail than
impalpable" (comparison). The three transforms are somewhat similar,
both formally and semantically; and it seems reasonable to suppose
that a writer whose style is so largely based on just these three
semantically related transformations demonstrates in that style a certain conceptual orientation, a preferred way of organizing experience.**** If that orientation could be specified, it would almost certainly
provide insight into other, non-stylistic features of Faulkner's thought
and artistry. The possibility of such insight is one of the main justifi-
cations for studying style.

The move from formal description of styles to critical and semantic
interpretation should be the ultimate goal of stylistics, but in this
article I am concerned only with the first step: description. My first
example shows that the style of at least one short passage can be
rather efficiently and informatively described in terms of a few grammatical operations. It might be objected, however, that the transformations I have concentrated on in destroying the style of the Faulkner
passage are of such prominence in the grammar, and in the use of
English, that *any* writer must depend heavily upon them. To show
that this is not universally the case, it is sufficient to perform the same
reductions on a characteristic passage from the work of another writer
with a quite different style. Consider, therefore, the conclusion of
Hemingway's story, "Soldier's Home":

> So his mother prayed for him and then they stood up and Krebs
> kissed his mother and went out of the house. He had tried so to keep
> his life from being complicated. Still, none of it had touched him. He
> had felt sorry for his mother and she had made him lie. He would go
> to Kansas City and get a job and she would feel all right about it.
> There would be one more scene maybe before he got away. He would

---

**** It is apparently common for stylistic features to cluster like this in the
work of an author. See my study, *Shaw; The Style and the Man* (Middletown,
Conn., 1962), for numerous examples, and for an attempt to link style with
cognitive orientation.

not go down to his father's office. He would miss that one. He wanted
his life to go smoothly. It had just gotten going that way. Well, that
was all over now, anyway. He would go over to the schoolyard and
watch Helen play indoor baseball.††††

Reversing the effects of the relative and comparative transformations barely alters the passage: only the prenominal modifier "indoor"
is affected. Removing the conjunctions does result in some changes:

> So his mother prayed for him. Then they stood up. Krebs kissed his
> mother. Krebs went out of the house. He had tried so to keep his life
> from being complicated. Still, none of it had touched him. He had felt
> sorry for his mother. She had made him lie. He would go to Kansas
> City. He would get a job. She would feel all right about it. There
> would be one more scene maybe before he got away. He would not
> go down to his father's office. He would miss that one. He wanted his
> life to go smoothly. It had just gotten going that way. Well, that was
> all over now, anyway. He would go over to the schoolyard. He would
> watch Helen play indoor baseball.

Notice that the reduced passage still sounds very much like Hemingway. Nothing has been changed that seems crucial to his style. Note
too that although the revised passage is quite simple, none of the
sentences is from the kernel. Hemingway is not innocent of transformations: he is relying on pronominalization, on a group of nominalizations, and, most notably, on a sequence of transformations responsible
for what critics call the *"style indirect libre."* These transformations
work this way:

1. GT; quotation, or reported thought:

$$\text{He} \left. \begin{cases} \begin{Bmatrix} \text{thought} \\ \text{said} \\ \text{felt} \\ \text{etc.} \end{Bmatrix} \text{NPabst} \\ \text{She has made me lie} \end{cases} \right\} \rightarrow \text{He thought, "She has made me lie"}$$

2. Indirect discourse (change of pronouns and of verb tense):

    He thought, "She has made me lie" → He thought that she had made
    him lie

††††*The Short Stories of Ernest Hemingway* (New York, 1953), pp. 152–153.

3. Deletion:

He thought that she had made him lie → She had made him lie‡‡‡‡

The original passage, stripped of the effects of these transformations, reads as follows:

> So his mother prayed for him and they stood up and Krebs kissed his mother and went out of the house. He thought this: I have tried so to keep my life from being complicated. Still, none of it has touched me. I have felt sorry for my mother and she has made me lie. I will go to Kansas City and get a job and she will feel all right about it. There will be one more scene maybe before I get away. I will not go down to my father's office. I will miss that one. I want my life to go smoothly. It has just gotten going that way. Well, that is all over now, anyway. I will go over to the schoolyard and watch Helen play indoor baseball.

The peculiar double vision of the style, the sense of the narrator peering into the character's mind and scrupulously reporting its contents, the possibility of distance and gentle irony—all these are gone with the transformational wind.

To be sure, these transformations do not in themselves distinguish Hemingway's style from the styles of many other writers (Virginia Woolf, Ford Madox Ford, James Joyce, etc.). But it is interesting, and promising, that a stylistic difference so huge as that between the Faulkner and Hemingway passages can be largely explained on the basis of so little grammatical apparatus.

Up to this point, I have been exploring some effects on style of particular transformations and groups of transformations, and arguing that this method of description has, potentially, considerable value for literary critics. But there are at least two other ways in which transformational machinery will aid the analyst of style.

First, it has often been pointed out that constructions may be left-branching ("Once George had left, the host and hostess gossiped briskly"), right-branching ("The host and hostess gossiped briskly, once George had left"), or self-embedding ("The host and hostess, once George had left, gossiped briskly"). Neither left- nor right-

‡‡‡‡ Morris Halle (Massachusetts Institute of Technology) explained these transformations to me. He is treating them in a forthcoming article on Virginia Woolf's style, and I make no attempt here to put the rules in proper and complete form. It should be noted though, that there is at present no justification for the grammar to contain rule number three as a transformation, since the transform is already generated by other rules.

branching constructions tax the hearer's understanding, even when compounded at some length ("a very few not at all well liked union officials"; "the dog that worried the cat that chased the rat that ate the cheese that lay in the house that Jack built"). But layers of self-embedding quickly put too great a strain on the unaided memory ("the house in which the cheese that the rat that the cat that the dog worried chased ate lay was built by Jack"). Even a relatively small amount of self-embedding in a written passage can slow a reader down considerably.

With these preliminaries, consider the following sentence, which begins a short story:

> She had practically, he believed, conveyed the intimation, the horrid, brutal, vulgar menace, in the course of their last dreadful conversation, when, for whatever was left him of pluck or confidence—confidence in what he would fain have called a little more aggressively the strength of his position—he had judged best not to take it up.§§§§

The style is idiosyncratic in the highest degree, and the writer is, of course, Henry James. His special brand of complexity is impossible to unravel through the method I pursued with Faulkner. A number of *different* transformations are involved. But notice that most of this complexity results from self-embedding. With the embedded elements removed the sentence is still far from simple, but the Jamesian intricacy is gone:

> She had practically conveyed the intimation in the course of their last dreadful conversation, when he had judged best not to take it up.

The following are the deleted sentences, with their full structure restored:

> He believed [it].
> [The intimation was a] horrid, brutal, vulgar menace.
> [Something] was left him of pluck or confidence.
> [It was] confidence in the strength of his position.
> He would fain have called [it that], a little more aggressively.

The embedded elements, in short, significantly outweigh the main sentence itself, and needless to say, the strain on attention and memory required to follow the progress of the main sentence over and

§§§§ "The Bench of Desolation," *Ten Short Stories of Henry James,* Michael Swan, Ed. (London, 1948), p. 284.

around so many obstacles is considerable. The difficulty, as well as the Jamesian flavor, is considerably lessened merely by substituting left- and right-branching constructions for self-embedding, even though all the kernel sentences are retained:

> He believed that in the course of their last dreadful conversation she had practically conveyed the intimation, a horrid, brutal, vulgar menace, which he had then judged best not to take up, for whatever was left him of pluck or confidence—confidence in the strength of his position, as he would fain have called it, a little more aggressively.

It seems likely that much of James's later style can be laid to this syntactic device—a matter of *positioning* various constructions, rather than of favoring a few particular constructions. The relevance of positioning to style is, to be sure, no news. But again, transformational analysis should clarify the subject, both by providing descriptive rigor and by making available a set of alternatives to each complex sentence.

Finally, styles may also contrast in the kinds of transformational operations on which they are built. There are four possibilities: addition, deletion, reordering, and combination. Of these, my final sample depends heavily on deletion. The passage is from D. H. Lawrence's *Studies in Classic American Literature*, a book with an especially brusque, emphatic style, which results partly from Lawrence's affection for kernel sentences. But his main idiosyncrasy is the use of truncated sentences, which have gone through a variety of deletion transformations. Here is the excerpt:

> The renegade hates life itself. He wants the death of life. So these many "reformers" and "idealists" who glorify the savages in America. They are death-birds, life-haters. Renegades.
> We can't go back. And Melville couldn't. Much as he hated the civilized humanity he knew. He couldn't go back to the savages. He wanted to. He tried to. And he couldn't.
> Because in the first place, it made him sick.‖ ‖ ‖ ‖

With the deleted segments replaced, the passage reads, somewhat absurdly, like this:

> The renegade hates life itself. He wants the death of life. So these many "reformers" and "idealists" who glorify the savages in America [want the death of life]. They are death-birds. [They are] life-haters. [They are] renegades.
> We can't go back. And Melville couldn't [go back]. [Melville

‖ ‖ ‖ ‖ D. H. Lawrence, *Studies in Classic American Literature* (New York: Anchor Books, 1955), p. 149.

couldn't go back, as] much as he hated the civilized humanity he knew. He couldn't go back to the savages. He wanted to [go back to the savages]. He tried to [go back to the savages]. And he couldn't [go back to the savages].

[He couldn't go back to the savages] because, in the first place, it made him sick [to go back to the savages].

One does not need grammatical theory to see that Lawrence is deleting. But the restoration of the full form which is allowed by the grammar does reveal two interesting things. First, there is a large amount of repetition in the original passage, much more than actually shows. Perhaps this fact accounts for the driving insistence one feels in reading it. Second, Lawrentian deletion is a stylistic alternative to *conjunction*, which can also take place whenever there are two sentences partly alike in their constituents. The reasons for Lawrence's preferring deletion to conjunction might well be worth some study.

And in general, study of that sort should be the goal of stylistic analysis. All I have done here is outline, briefly and in part informally, a fruitful method of stylistic *description*. But no *analysis* of a style, in the fuller sense, can get off the ground until there are adequate methods for the humble task of description. Such methods, I think, are provided by transformational grammar. Furthermore, I have argued, such a grammar is especially useful for this purpose in that it alone is powerful enough to set forth, formally and accurately, stylistic *alternatives* to a given passage or a given set of linguistic habits.

Now there is no reason to generalize from four passages to infinity, and in fact full stylistic descriptions of the work of even the four writers I have discussed would need to be far more elaborate than the sketches I have offered here. Moreover, many styles that readers perceive as distinctive are more complex in their syntactic patterns than these four. Finally, though syntax seems to be a central determinant of style, it is admittedly not the whole of style. Imagery, figures of speech, and the rest are often quite important. But to perform on various styles the kind of analysis I have attempted in this paper is to be convinced that transformational patterns constitute a significant part of what the sensitive reader perceives as style. Transformational analysis of literary discourse promises to the critic stylistic descriptions which are at once simpler and deeper than any hitherto available, and therefore more adequate foundations for critical interpretation. Not only that: if, as seems likely to happen, generative grammars with transformational rules help the linguist or critic to explicate convincingly the elusive but persistent notion of style, that achievement will stand as one more piece of evidence in favor of such grammars.

RICHARD OHMANN

Literature as Sentences

INTRODUCTION

The essay begins with a distinction between surface structure and deep structure, "typically, a surface structure overlays a deep structure which it may resemble but little, and which determines the 'content' of the sentence." Notice that Ohmann has connected "content" with the deep structure. Throughout the essay Ohmann draws a distinction between "form" and the surface structure on the one hand and "content" and the deep structure on the other. At the close of the essay Ohmann makes the distinction explicit:

> I have indicated some areas where a rich exchange between linguistics and critical theory might eventually take place. To wit, the elusive intuition we have of *form* and *content* may turn out to be anchored in a distinction between the surface structures and the deep structures of sentences.

To illustrate how the theory of transformational grammar can assist the literary critic in his task of relating form and meaning, Ohmann gives two

Reprinted by permission of the author, the National Council of Teachers of English, from *College English*, Vol. 27, No. 4 (January), 1966 pp. 261–267.

samples, the final sentence of Joseph Conrad's "The Secret Sharer" and the first sentence of Dylan Thomas' "A Winter's Tale."

In his comments on "The Secret Sharer" Ohmann makes these points:

1. The surface structure feeds information to the reader at a certain rate and in a certain way. The surface structure gives the writer control over the way the reader comes to understand the meaning of the passage. Stated in slightly different terms, the author's control of the surface structure determines the progression of the reader's understanding of the deep structure. In the passage he cites from Conrad, Ohmann says,

> This progression in the deep structure rather precisely mirrors both the rhetorical movement of the sentence from the narrator to Leggatt via the hat that links them, and the thematic effect of the sentence, which is to transfer Leggatt's experience to the narrator via the narrator's vicarious and actual participation in it.

2. A word can be heavily emphasized in the deep structure without being repeated in the surface structure. In this case, the word *share* is of key thematic importance in understanding the whole work, yet it appears in the surface structure of the last sentence only once. However, in the deep structure, Ohmann points out that thirteen sentences "go to the semantic development of 'sharer.'" *Share* thus plays a complex syntactic role in the deep structure. Ohmann argues that the very act of understanding the sentence concentrates the reader's attention on the word *share*. Words that have many separate functions in the deep structure are said to have a high degree of "syntactic density."

3. By a greater conscious understanding of the deep structure, the reader may better understand the structuring ("the build") of the thematic meaning of the whole work.

4. Finally, a point which Ohmann develops at length in his article "Generative Grammars and the Concept of Literary Style." Each writer tends to exercise the options in the grammar in a characteristic way:

> his style, in other words, rests on syntactic options within sentences . . . these syntactic preferences correlate with habits of meaning that tell us something about his mode of conceiving experience.

In the case of Conrad, Ohmann claims that "Conrad draws heavily on operations that link one thing with another associatively."

Dylan Thomas' "A Winter's Tale" raises a different kind of critical question: the ungrammatical or deviant use of language which is common in modern poetry. Ohmann begins by rejecting the notion that such deviance is simply a reflection of the irrational nature of the world. Quite the opposite:

> And if he (the poet) strays from grammatical patterns he does not thereby leave language or reason behind: if anything, he draws the

more deeply on linguistic structure and on the processes of human understanding that are implicit in our use of well-formed sentences.

Ohmann's main point is that the reader interprets the surface deviance in terms of "the base sentences that lie beneath ungrammatical constructions." The surface deviance is corrected by analogy to similar grammatical constructions. For instance, when the word *twilight* is used as the subject of *ferry* we can resolve the surface ungrammaticality by interpreting *twilight* as an animate noun. Another example is the interpretation of the phrase *river wended vales*. Ohmann's own interpretation is that the normally intransitive verb *wend* is interpreted as being analogous to the class of verbs that can be either transitive or intransitive, such as *paint* or *rub*. *Wend* is then interpreted by Ohmann to mean "make a mark on the surface of, by traversing." The key point here is that *wend* is doing double duty. In addition to its own ordinary intransitive meaning, it has picked up additional meanings from the class that it is analogized with. As Ohmann explains it:

> I have been leading up to the point that every syntactically deviant construction has more than one possible interpretation, and that readers resolve the conflict by a process that involves deep and intricately motivated decisions and thus puts to work considerable linguistic knowledge, syntactic as well as semantic.

Ohmann's final major point is that a poet's use of deviance is not random: the deviancy has a kind of consistency in it which springs from "particular semantic impulses, particular ways of looking at experience." Ohmann shows that Thomas' deviancy

> converts juxtaposition into action, inanimate into human, abstract into physical, static into active. Now, much of Thomas' poetry displays the world as process, as interacting forces and repeating cycles, in which human beings and human thought are indifferently caught up. I suggest that Thomas' syntactical irregularities often serve this vision of things.

Critics permit themselves, for this or that purpose, to identify literature with great books, with imaginative writing, with expressiveness in writing, with the non-referential and non-pragmatic, with beauty in language, with order, with myth, with structured and formed discourse—the list of definitions is nearly endless—with verbal play, with uses of language that stress the medium itself, with the expression of an age, with dogma, with the *cri de coeur*, with neurosis. Now of course literature is itself and not another thing, to paraphrase Bishop Butler; yet analogies and classifications have merit. For a short space let us think of literature as sentences.

To do so will not tax the imagination, because the work of literature indubitably *is* composed of sentences, most of them well-ordered, many of them deviant (no pejorative meant), some of them incomplete. But since much the same holds for dust-jacket copy, the Congressional Record, and transcripts of board meetings, the small effort required to think of literature as sentences may be repaid by a correspondingly small insight into literature as such. Although I do not believe this to be so, for the moment I shall hold the question in abeyance, and stay mainly within the territory held in common by all forms of discourse. In other words, I am not asking what is special about the sentences *of literature*, but what is special about *sentences* that they should interest the student of literature. Although I employ the framework of generative grammar and scraps of its terminology,* what I have to say should not ring in the traditionally educated grammatical ear with outlandish discord.

First, then, the sentence is the primary unit of understanding. Linguists have so trenchantly discredited the old definition—"a sentence is a complete thought"—that the truth therein has fallen into neglect. To be sure, we delimit the class of sentences by formal criteria, but each of the structures that qualifies will express a semantic unity not characteristic of greater or lesser structures. The meanings borne by morphemes, phrases, and clauses hook together to express a meaning that can stand more or less by itself. This point, far from denying the structuralist's definition of a sentence as a single free utterance, or *form*, seems the inevitable corollary of such definitions: forms carry meanings, and it is natural that an independent form should carry an independent meaning. Or, to come at the thing another way, consider that one task of a grammar is to supply structural descriptions, and that the sentence is the unit so described. A structural description specifies the way each part of a sentence is tied to each other part, and the semantic rules of a grammar use the structural description as starting point in interpreting the whole. A reader or hearer does something analogous when he resolves the structures and meanings of sentences, and thereby understands them. Still another way to approach the primacy of the sentence is to notice that the initial symbol for all

---

* I draw especially on Noam Chomsky, *Aspects of the Theory of Syntax* (Cambridge, Mass., 1965) and Jerrold J. Katz and Paul Postal, *An Integrated Theory of Linguistic Descriptions* (Cambridge, Mass., 1964).

derivations in a generative grammar is "S" for sentence: the sentence is the domain of grammatical structure—rather like the equation in algebra—and hence the domain of meaning.

These remarks, which will seem truisms to some and heresy to others, cannot be elaborated here. Instead, I want to register an obvious comment on their relevance to literary theory and literary criticism. Criticism, whatever else it does, must interpret works of literature. Theory concerns itself in part with the question, "what things legitimately bear on critical interpretation?" But beyond a doubt, interpretation begins with sentences. Whatever complex apprehension the critic develops of the whole work, that understanding arrives mundanely, sentence by sentence. For this reason, and because the form of a sentence dictates a rudimentary mode of understanding, sentences have a good deal to do with the subliminal meaning (and form) of a literary work. They prepare and direct the reader's attention in particular ways.

My second point about sentences should dispel some of the abstractness of the first. Most sentences directly and obliquely put more linguistic apparatus into operation than is readily apparent, and call on more of the reader's linguistic competence. Typically, a surface structure overlays a deep structure which it may resemble but little, and which determines the "content" of the sentence. For concreteness, take this rather ordinary example, an independent clause from Joyce's "Araby": "Gazing up into the darkness I saw myself as a creature driven and derided by vanity." The surface structure may be represented as follows, using the convention of labeled brackets:[†]

$^S[^{Adv}[V + Part \, ^{PP}[P \, ^{NP}[D + N]]] \, ^{Nuc}[N \, ^{VP}[V + N \, ^{PP}[P \, ^{NP}[D + N \, ^{Adj}[V + and + V \, ^{PP}[P + N]]]]]]]$

The nucleus has a transitive verb with a direct object. In the deep structure, by contrast, the matrix sentence is of the form $^S[NP \, ^{VP}[V + Complement + NP]]$: "I + saw + as a creature + me." It has embedded in it one sentence with an intransitive verb and an adverb of location—"I gazed up into the darkness"—and two additional sentences with transitive verbs and direct objects—"Vanity drove the creature," and "Vanity derided the creature." Since "darkness" and "vanity" are derived nouns, the embedded sentences must in turn contain embeddings, of, say "(Something) is dark" and "(Someone) is vain." Thus the word "vanity," object of a preposition in the surface

---

[†] Each set of brackets encloses the constituent indicated by its superscript label. The notation is equivalent to a tree diagram. Symbols: S = Sentence, Adv = Adverbial, V = Verb, Part = Particle, PP = Prepositional Phrase, P = Preposition, NP = Noun Phrase, D = Determiner, N = Noun, Nuc = Nucleus, VP = Verb Phrase, Adj = Adjectival.

structure, is subject of two verbs in the deep, and its root is a predicate adjective. The word "creature," object of a preposition in the surface structure, also has a triple function in the deep structure: verbal complement, direct object of "drive," and direct object of "deride." Several transformations (including the passive) deform the six basic sentences, and several others relate them to each other. The complexity goes much farther, but this is enough to suggest that a number of grammatical processes are required to generate the initial sentence and that its structure is moderately involved. Moreover, a reader will not understand the sentence unless he grasps the relations marked in the deep structure. As it draws on a variety of syntactic resources, the sentence also activates a variety of semantic processes and modes of comprehension, yet in brief compass and in a surface *form* that radically permutes *content.*

I choose these terms wilfully: that there are interesting grounds here for a form-content division seems to me quite certain. Joyce might have written, "I gazed up into the darkness. I saw myself as a creature. The creature was driven by vanity. The creature was derided by vanity." Or, "Vanity drove and derided the creature I saw myself as, gazer up, gazer into the darkness." Content remains roughly the same, for the basic sentences are unchanged. But the style is different. And each revision structures and screens the content differently. The original sentence acquires part of its meaning and part of its unique character by resonating against these unwritten alternatives. It is at the level of sentences, I would argue, that the distinction between form and content comes clear, and that the intuition of style has its formal equivalent.‡

Sentences play on structure in still another way, more shadowy, but of considerable interest for criticism. It is a commonplace that not every noun can serve as object of every verb, that a given noun can be modified only by adjectives of certain classes, and so on. For instance, a well-defined group of verbs, including "exasperate," "delight," "please," and "astound," require animate objects; another group, including "exert," "behave," and "pride," need reflexive objects. Such interdependencies abound in a grammar, which must account for them by subcategorizing nouns, adjectives, and the other major classes.§ The importance of categorical restrictions is clearest in sentences that disregard them—deviant sentences. It happens that the example from

‡ I have argued the point at length in "Generative Grammars and the Concept of Literary Style," *Word,* 20 (Dec. 1964), 423–439.

§ Chomsky discusses ways of doing this in *Aspects of the Theory of Syntax,* Chapter 2.

Joyce is slightly deviant in this way: in one of the underlying sentences —"Vanity derided the creature"—a verb that requires a human subject in fact has as its subject the abstract noun "vanity." The dislocation forces the reader to use a supplementary method of interpretation: here, presumably he aligns "vanity" (the word) with the class of human nouns and sees vanity (the thing) as a distinct, active power in the narrator's psyche. Such deviance is so common in metaphor and elsewhere that one scarcely notices it, yet it helps to specify the way things happen in the writer's special world, and the modes of thought appropriate to that world.

I have meant to suggest that sentences normally comprise intricacies of form and meaning whose effects are not the less substantial for their subtlety. From this point, what sorts of critical description follow? Perhaps I can direct attention toward a few tentative answers, out of the many that warrant study, and come finally to a word on critical theory. Two samples must carry the discussion; one is the final sentence of "The Secret Sharer":

> Walking to the taffrail, I was in time to make out, on the very edge of a darkness thrown by a towering black mass like the very gateway of Erebus—yes, I was in time to catch an evanescent glimpse of my white hat left behind to mark the spot where the secret sharer of my cabin and of my thoughts, as though he were my second self, had lowered himself into the water to take his punishment: a free man, a proud swimmer striking out for a new destiny.

I hope others will agree that the sentence justly represents its author: that it portrays a mind energetically stretching to subdue a dazzling experience *outside* the self, in a way that has innumerable counterparts elsewhere in Conrad. How does scrutiny of the deep structure support this intuition? First, notice a matter of emphasis, of rhetoric. The matrix sentence, which lends a surface form to the whole, is "# S # I was in time # S #" (repeated twice). The embedded sentences that complete it are "I walked to the taffrail," "I made out + NP," and "I caught + NP." The point of departure, then, is the narrator himself: where he was, what he did, what he saw. But a glance at the deep structure will explain why one feels a quite different emphasis in the sentence as a whole: seven of the embedded sentences have "sharer" as grammatical subject; in another three the subject is a noun linked to "sharer" by the copula; in two "sharer" is direct object; and in two more "share" is the verb. Thus thirteen sentences go to the semantic development of "sharer," as follows:

1. The secret sharer had lowered the secret sharer into the water.
2. The secret sharer took his punishment.
3. The secret sharer swam.
4. The secret sharer was a swimmer.
5. The swimmer was proud.
6. The swimmer struck out for a new destiny.
7. The secret sharer was a man.
8. The man was free.
9. The secret sharer was my second self.
10. The secret sharer had (it).
11. (Someone) punished the secret sharer.
12. (Someone) shared my cabin.
13. (Someone) shared my thoughts.

In a fundamental way, the sentence is mainly *about* Leggatt, although the surface structure indicates otherwise.

Yet the surface structure does not simply throw a false scent, and the way the sentence comes to focus on the secret sharer is also instructive. It begins with the narrator, as we have seen, and "I" is the subject of five basic sentences early on. Then "hat" takes over as the syntactic focus, receiving development in seven base sentences. Finally, the sentence arrives at "sharer." This progression in the deep structure rather precisely mirrors both the rhetorical movement of the sentence from the narrator to Leggatt via the hat that links them, and the thematic effect of the sentence, which is to transfer Leggatt's experience to the narrator via the narrator's vicarious and actual participation in it. Here I shall leave this abbreviated rhetorical analysis, with a cautionary word: I do not mean to suggest that only an examination of deep structure reveals Conrad's skillful emphasis—on the contrary, such an examination supports and in a sense explains what any careful reader of the story notices.

A second critical point adjoins the first. The morpheme "share" appears once in the sentence, but it performs at least twelve separate functions, as the deep structure shows. "I," "hat," and "mass" also play complex roles. Thus at certain points the sentence has extraordinary "density," as I shall call it. Since a reader must register these multiple functions in order to understand the sentence, it is reasonable to suppose that the very process of understanding concentrates his attention on centers of density. Syntactic density, I am suggesting, exercises an important influence on literary comprehension.

Third, by tuning in on deep structures, the critic may often apprehend more fully the build of a literary work. I have already mentioned how the syntax of Conrad's final sentence develops his theme. Consider two related points. First, "The Secret Sharer" is an initiation story in which the hero, through moral and mental effort, locates himself vis à vis society and the natural world, and thus passes into full manhood. The syntax of the last sentence schematizes the relationships he has achieved, in identifying with Leggatt's heroic defection, and in fixing on a point of reference—the hat—that connects him to the darker powers of nature. Second, the syntax and meaning of the last sentence bring to completion the pattern initiated by the syntax and meaning of the first few sentences, which present human beings and natural objects in thought-bewildering disarray. I can do no more than mention these structural connections here, but I am convinced that they supplement and help explain an ordinary critical reading of the story.

Another kind of critical point concerns habits of meaning revealed by sentence structure. One example must suffice. We have already marked how the sentence shifts its focus from "I" to "hat" to "sharer." A similar process goes on in the first part of the sentence: "I" is the initial subject, with "hat" as object. "Hat" is subject of another base sentence that ends with "edge," the object of a preposition in a locative phrase. "Edge" in turn becomes object of a sentence that has "darkness" as subject. "Darkness" is object in one with "mass" as subject, and in much the same way the emphasis passes to "gateway" and "Erebus." The syntax executes a chaining effect here which cuts across various kinds of construction. Chaining is far from the only type of syntactic expansion, but it is one Conrad favors. I would suggest this hypothesis: that syntactically and in other ways Conrad draws heavily on operations that link one thing with another associatively. This may be untrue, or if true it may be unrevealing; certainly it needs clearer expression. But I think it comes close to something that we all notice in Conrad, and in any case the general critical point exemplified here deserves exploration: that each writer tends to exploit deep linguistic resources in characteristic ways—that his style, in other words, rests on syntactic options within sentences (see fn. ‡)—and that these syntactic preferences correlate with habits of meaning that tell us something about his mode of conceiving experience.

My other sample passage is the first sentence of Dylan Thomas' "A Winter's Tale":‖

> It is a winter's tale
> That the snow blind twilight ferries over the lakes
> And floating fields from the farm in the cup of the vales,
> Gliding windless through the hand folded flakes,
> The pale breath of cattle at the stealthy sail,
>
> And the stars falling cold,
> And the smell of hay in the snow, and the far owl
> Warning among the folds, and the frozen hold
> Flocked with the sheep white smoke of the farm house cowl
> In the river wended vales where the tale was told.

Some of the language here raises a large and familiar critical question, that of unorthodox grammar in modern poetry, which has traditionally received a somewhat facile answer. We say that loss of confidence in order and reason leads to dislocation of syntax, as if errant grammar were an appeal to the irrational. A cursory examination of deep structure in verse like Thomas', or even in wildly deviant verse like some of Cummings', will show the matter to be more complex than that.

How can deviance be most penetratingly analyzed? Normally, I think, in terms of the base sentences that lie beneath ungrammatical constructions. Surface structure alone does not show "the river wended vales" (line 10) to be deviant, since we have many well-formed constructions of the same word-class sequence: "machine made toys," "sun dried earth," and so on. The particular deviance of "the river wended vales" becomes apparent when we try to refer it to an appropriate underlying structure. A natural one to consider is "the river wends the vales" (cf. "the sun dries the earth"), but of course this makes "wend" a transitive verb, which it is not, except in the idiomatic "wend its way." So does another possibility, "NP + wends the vales with rivers" (cf. "NP + makes the toys by machine"). This reading adds still other kinds of deviance, in that the Noun Phrase will have to be animate, and in that rivers are too cumbersome to be used instrumentally in the way implied. Let us assume that the reader rejects the more flagrant deviance in favor of the less, and we are back to "the river wends the vales." Suppose now that "the vales" is not after all a direct object, but a locative construction, as in "the wolf prowls the forest"; this preserves the intransitivity of "wend," and thereby avoids a serious form of deviance. But notice that there is *no* transformation in English that converts "the wolf prowls the forest" into "the wolf prowled forest," and so this path is blocked as well. Assume, finally, that given a choice between shifting a word like "wend" from one subclass to another and adding a transformational rule to the grammar, a reader will choose the former course; hence he selects the first interpretation mentioned: "the river wends the vales."

If so, how does he understand the anomalous transitive use of "wend"? Perhaps by assimilating the verb to a certain class that may be either transitive or intransitive: "paint," "rub," and the like. Then he will take "wend" to mean something like "make a mark on the surface of, by traversing"; in fact, this is roughly how I read Thomas' phrase. But I may be wrong, and in any case my goal is not to solve the riddle. Rather, I have been leading up to the point that every syntactically deviant construction has more than one possible interpretation, and that readers resolve the conflict by a process that involves deep and intricately motivated decisions and thus puts to work considerable linguistic knowledge, syntactic as well as semantic.# The decisions nearly always go on implicitly, but aside from that I see no reason to think that deviance of this sort is an appeal to, or an expression of, irrationality.

Moreover, when a poet deviates from normal syntax he is not doing what comes most habitually, but is making a special sort of choice. And since there are innumerable kinds of deviance, we should expect that the ones elected by a poem or poet spring from particular semantic impulses, particular ways of looking at experience. For instance, I think such a tendency displays itself in Thomas' lines. The construction just noted conceives the passing of rivers through vales as an agent acting upon an object. Likewise, "flocked" in line 9 becomes a transitive verb, and the spatial connection Thomas refers to—flocks in a hold—is reshaped into an action—flocking—performed by an unnamed agent upon the hold. There are many other examples in the poem of deviance that projects unaccustomed activity and process upon nature. Next, notice that beneath line 2 is the sentence "the twilight is blind," in which an inanimate noun takes an animate adjective, and that in line 5 "sail" takes the animate adjective "stealthy." This type of deviance also runs throughout the poem: Thomas sees nature as personal. Again, "twilight" is subject of "ferries," and should thus be a concrete noun, as should the object, "tale." Here and elsewhere in the poem the division between substance and abstraction tends to disappear. Again and again syntactic deviance breaks down

---

See Jerrold J. Katz, "Semi-sentences," in Jerry A. Fodor and Jerrold J. Katz, Eds., *The Structure of Language* (1964), pp. 400–416. The same volume includes two other relevant papers, Chomsky, "Degrees of Grammaticalness," pp. 384–389, and Paul Ziff, "On Understanding 'Understanding Utterances,'" pp. 390–399. Samuel R. Levin has briefly discussed ungrammatical poetry within a similar framework in *Linguistic Structures in Poetry* (The Hague, 1962), Chapters 2 and 3.

categorical boundaries and converts juxtaposition into action, inanimate into human, abstract into physical, static into active. Now, much
of Thomas' poetry displays the world as process, as interacting forces
and repeating cycles, in which human beings and human thought are
indifferently caught up.** I suggest that Thomas' syntactical irregularities often serve this vision of things. To say so, of course, is only
to extend the natural critical premise that a good poet sets linguistic
forms to work for him in the cause of artistic and thematic form. And
if he strays from grammatical patterns he does not thereby leave language or reason behind: if anything, he draws the more deeply on
linguistic structure and on the processes of human understanding that
are implicit in our use of well-formed sentences.

Most of what I have said falls short of adequate precision, and much
of the detail rests on conjecture about English grammar, which at this
point is by no means fully understood. But I hope that in loosely
stringing together several hypotheses about the fundamental role of
the sentence I have indicated some areas where a rich exchange
between linguistics and critical theory might eventually take place.
To wit, the elusive intuition we have of *form* and *content* may turn
out to be anchored in a distinction between the surface structures and
the deep structures of sentences. If so, syntactic theory will also feed
into the theory of *style*. Still more evidently, the proper *analysis* of
styles waits on a satisfactory analysis of sentences. Matters of *rhetoric*,
such as emphasis and order, also promise to come clearer as we better
understand internal relations in sentences. More generally, we may
be able to enlarge and deepen our concept of literary *structure* as we
are increasingly able to make it subsume linguistic structure—including especially the structure of deviant sentences. And most important,
since critical understanding follows and builds on understanding of
sentences, generative grammar should eventually be a reliable assistant
in the effort of seeing just how a given literary work sifts through a
reader's mind, what cognitive and emotional processes it sets in
motion, and what organization of experience it encourages. In so far
as critical theory concerns itself with meaning, it cannot afford to
bypass the complex and elegant structures that lie at the inception of
all verbal meaning.

** Ralph Maud's fine study, *Entrances to Dylan Thomas' Poetry* (Pittsburgh,
1963), describes the phenomenon well in a chapter called "Process Poems."

JOSEPH C. BEAVER

A Grammar of Prosody

INTRODUCTION

The starting point for Beaver's article is a paraphrase of the main thesis
of Morris Halle and Samuel J. Keyser's article "Chaucer and the Study of
Prosody" in the December 1966 issue of *College English*. In their article,
Halle and Keyser develop a set of rules which, according to Beaver, provides "a grammar of meter, comparable to the generative grammarian's
'rules of competence,' which will determine (that is, provide a metrical
description of) what are metrical and what are unmetrical lines."

Beaver reprints the set of three rules (called "principles" by Halle and
Keyser) and extends them to cover different kinds of meter other than iambic
pentameter. The first principle is that a line of verse consists of a fixed
number of positions. The second principle states that a position is normally
occupied by a single syllable, but gives certain conditions under which the
position may be occupied by two syllables or by none. The third principle
(as extended by Beaver) states that in order for a line to be metrical, a
stress maximum may occupy only even positions in iambic verse and odd
positions in trochaic verse. Halle and Keyser explicitly define a stress maximum as "a syllable bearing linguistically determined stress that is greater

Reprinted by permission of the author and the National Council of Teachers of
English, from *College English*, Vol. 29, No. 4 (January), 1968, pp. 310–321.

than that of the two syllables adjacent to it in the same verse." A stress maximum is thus a valley-peak-valley stress pattern.

It is important to realize that a stress maximum does not correspond to a "foot" in traditional metrics. In a line of iambic pentameter, for instance, there are by definition, five feet, each foot with two syllables, the first syllable bearing a lighter stress than the second. From the view-point of the Halle-Keyser metrics, however, a line of iambic pentameter is regular if the stress maximums in the line (if there are any) fall on the even syllables. The line would be unmetrical only if a stress maximum fell on an odd-numbered syllable. Beaver points out that,

> These metrical rules, or principles, may be regarded as claims about the metrical competence of the poet. It could be said that it is claimed the poet internalizes, not a poetic foot (some recurring pattern of stress and unstress), but a sequence of positions to be occupied by syllables; it is claimed that he is aware somehow of whether a given syllable Y occurs in an arithmetically even or arithmetically odd position; it is claimed further that the poet is metrically conscious only of stress maxima (linguistically determined lexical stress sandwiched by unstressed syllables, without intervening major syntactic boundary); it is claimed that he allows these to occur, or accepts their occurrence, only in even positions for iambic meter and only in odd positions for trochaic meter.

The advantage of the Halle-Keyser metrics over the traditional foot metrics is the explanatory power of the former. For example, Beaver points out that in Shakespeare's pentameter sonnets, more lines actually begin with trochaic feet than with iambic. Beaver comments on such a line from Sonnet II:

> "Proving his beauty by succession thine."

> Traditional prosody finds itself in the uncomfortable position, here, of saying that the most common occurrence is the allowable exception. In our view, an initial "trochee" is entirely regular—all that matters is that stress maxima occur, when they occur at all, in even positions.

The remainder of the article is devoted to further illustrating the explanatory power of the Halle-Keyser metrical theory. Beaver here summarizes his main points:

> The principles, together with the stress rules here suggested, offer a unified explanation for the fact that the majority of iambic lines begin with trochaic feet; for the absence of regular feet at various other positions in the line; for our acceptance of strong stress before or after juncture, even in odd-numbered positions; for the fact that special intonation features do not appear to violate the acceptability of metrical lines; for the rejection of iambs in trochaic verse; for the fact

that poetry in duple meter in verse lines shorter than decasyllabic appears to be more irresistably metrical. Finally, they offer a well-defined procedure for basic metrical-stylistic analysis.

In their recent study of Chaucerian meter, Morris Halle and Samuel Jay Keyser propose a theory of prosody which they hope may serve as a framework for the study of "a major portion of English poets."[*] The rules of stress assignment and meter they have discovered for Chaucer's iambic pentameter appear to me quite convincing (with some minor reservations to be discussed later), and metrical rules of this sort should be of considerable help in stylistic analysis, whether for individual poets or for different periods of poetry. But I think the major role of the Halle-Keyser rules (or, ultimately, more refined rules of this kind) will be to constitute essentially a grammar of meter, comparable to the generative grammarian's "rules of competence," which will determine (i.e., provide a metrical description of) what are metrical and what are unmetrical lines. And in this role, in addition to providing a basic framework for stylistic analysis, which may have to be supplemented with something comparable to "rules of performance,"[†] such rules should be useful in providing explanations for metrical phenomena, and in determining various prosodic questions, some of major importance. For example, why has the decasyllabic line (iambic pentameter) been the overwhelmingly predominant vehicle for English verse? Or, alternatively, in what way does it provide the freedom and flexibility the poet obviously finds there? Why do shorter line lengths (tetrameter, trimeter) in duple meter appear to be so much more "rhythmic" than pentameter, exhibiting always a more insistent beat or accent? Why does trochaic meter appear more inflexible than iambic (i.e., why does it seem peculiarly beat-insistent, or, why does it show such a low tolerance for "irregular feet")? The purpose of the present article is to explore, in a preliminary way, some of these questions, to examine possible extensions of the rules Halle and Keyser have proposed, to suggest a different set of stress rules to use in con-

---

[*] Morris Halle and Samuel J. Keyser, "Chaucer and the Study of Prosody," *College English*, Vol. 28 (Dec. 1966), pp. 187–219.

[†] For those unfamiliar with generative terminology, Chomsky has distinguished between rules of competence (in effect, these are the grammar of the language; they are the rules which will generate grammatical sentences), and rules of performance (stylistic rules, which will allow grammatically deviant sentences, or place certain restrictions upon the use of what would be, technically, grammatical sentences). See Noam Chomsky, *Aspects of the Theory of Syntax* (Cambridge, Mass., 1965), pp. 8–15, and *passim*.

junction with the Halle-Keyser principles of meter (for purposes of analysis of English poetry of the past three centuries), and to provide a critical commentary on the new prosodic system.

Two sets of rules are essential to the system: rules of stress, and rules (Halle and Keyser use the word "principles") of meter. It is the rules of meter Halle and Keyser think may have provided the system of prosody for a major portion of English poets, and I reproduce them here.

Principle 1

The iambic pentameter verse consists of ten positions to which may be appended one or two extra-metrical syllables.

Principle 2

A position is normally occupied by a single syllable, but under certain conditions it may be occupied by more than one syllable, or by none.

Condition 1

Two vowels may constitute a single position provided that they adjoin, or are separated by a liquid or nasal or by a word boundary which may be followed by *h*-, and provided that one of them is a weakly stressed or unstressed vowel.

Condition 2

An unstressed or weakly stressed mono-syllabic word may constitute a single metrical position with a preceding stressed or unstressed syllable.

Principle 3

A stress maximum may only occupy even positions within a verse, but not every even position need be so occupied.

Definition

A stress maximum is constituted by a syllable bearing linguistically determined stress that is greater than that of the two syllables adjacent to it in the same verse.‡

‡ Halle and Keyser, p. 197. The *stress maximum* is reminiscent of Jespersen, who, in "Notes on Meter," points out that the initial syllable of a verse can not be judged to bear ictus until the second syllable occurs—because there is nothing

For purposes of this article, I assume that these three principles are in fact the principles of all English regular-metered verse, and extend them, as Halle and Keyser suggest, to embrace different kinds of meter in obvious ways:

> 1A. a tetrameter iambic or trochaic line consists of 8 positions, a trimeter line of 6, etc.
>
> 3A. for trochaic verse, stress maxima may occupy only odd positions, though not every odd position need be occupied.

Turning now to rules of stress (which are needed to determine stress maxima—see "Definition" under 3), it could be argued that a different set would be needed for every period of verse (and every dialect). But I think that a set can be constructed—perhaps somewhat primitive, but adequate to our purpose—sufficient to provide a working tool for most English verse of the last three centuries. We adopt Seymour Chatman's distinction of five types of syllables for purposes of arriving at linguistically determined "lexical stress," and we identify stress maxima from certain configurations of these syllable types.§ The five kinds of syllables are:

---

preceding the first syllable for purposes of comparison. For this reason, an initial trochee in iambic verse disappoints only in the second syllable, not in the first. If this is the only disappointment in a decasyllabic line, and if the third syllable carries even less stress than the second (Jespersen uses four degrees of stress), the line will show only 10% disappointment, as compared to a 20% occasioned by an initial iamb in a trochaic line. The recognition of stress relationship to adjacent syllables and the concomitant notion that stress next to nothing can not be optimum stress are key elements of the Halle-Keyser rules. See Otto Jespersen, "Notes on Metre," in *Essays in the Language of Literature,* ed. Seymour Chatman and Samuel R. Levin (New York 1967), pp. 71–90.

§ Seymour Chatman, *A Theory of Meter,* (The Hague. 1965), pp. 123 ff. Note that one could also evolve a theory of phrase and clause accent to supplement lexical stress. One could for example postulate that in prepositional phrases the head word bears phrase accent, that in determiner-adjective-noun phrases the noun bears phrase accent (in American English, if not in British English), that in NV-terminal juncture clauses, the V bears clausal accent, that in NV-adverb clauses, the adverb bears clausal accent, and so forth.

The supplementing of rules of lexical stress with accent rules of this kind would yield some additional stress maxima, specifically where two back to back lexically stressed syllables would otherwise cancel each other out. Halle and Keyser do propose to include rules of this kind in their theory on the grounds that one should make as strong a hypothesis as the facts will support (personal communication). I do not employ such rules in the present exploratory article. Like lexical secondary stress (which I also do not use in the present article), it is not at present clear to me that such rules need be a part of the metrical rules determining stress maxima, even though they are clearly a part of the phonological rules of the language.

a. full-voweled monosyllabic words with non-reducible vowels (*e.g.,* "straight," "bright," etc.)

b. reducible full-voweled monosyllabic words ("a," "to," "shall," "you," "it," "can," etc. In general, most non-lexical monosyllabic words can reduce the vowel coloring to /i/

c. stressed syllables of polysyllabic words

d. full-vowelled unstressed syllables in polysyllabic words

e. unstressed syllables in polysyllabic words with reduced vowels

We now assume that a syllable of type a or c, preceded and followed by syllables of types b, d, or e will constitute a *stress maximum,* unless a syntactic juncture intervenes—for, following Halle-Keyser, we will maintain that if a major syntactic boundary intervenes between two metrical positions, neutralization occurs, which is to say, the adjacent positions cannot carry stress maxima.‖

The center syllable, then, of any sequence of three syllables which meets this description is a stress maximum:

$$\text{Syll.} \qquad \text{Syll.} \qquad \text{Syll.}$$

$$\begin{bmatrix} \begin{Bmatrix} b \\ d \\ e \end{Bmatrix} \end{bmatrix} \qquad \begin{bmatrix} \begin{Bmatrix} a \\ c \end{Bmatrix} \end{bmatrix} \qquad \begin{bmatrix} \begin{Bmatrix} b \\ d \\ e \end{Bmatrix} \end{bmatrix}$$

In essence, what is proposed for the determination of stress maxima is a rule which is *lexically* based, but which operates as a determinant of *underlying* stress in any phrase segment of three sequential syllables.

Since it is *capacity* for reduction that determines the membership of "b," rather than whether the monosyllable is in fact reduced in a given instance, and since the rule deals with only two stresses (stress and unstress), the system proposed here will find a somewhat different set of stress maxima than any alternative system that assigns four (or even three) degrees of stress, or that assigns phrasal and clausal stress on a basis of syntactic order.

To briefly illustrate the use of the Halle-Keyser rules of prosody in combination with the rules of stress I propose consider the familiar lines from Hamlet:

    1   2   3   4   5   6   7   8   9   10
    Oh that this too too solid flesh would melt,

    1   2   3   4   5 6   7 8 9 10
    Thaw, and resolve itself into a dew.

‖ Halle and Keyser, pp. 203, 204. Notice that for the same reason (incapacity for stress subordination) a syllable at the beginning of a line cannot bear stress maximum, no matter what the meter; nor can the syllable at the end of a line, unless there is appended an extra-metrical syllable.

Both lines have ten positions occupied with syllables, and there are no problems of extra-metrical syllables. The lines are iambic pentameter, and our rules call for stress maxima, if there are any, to fall only on even-numbered positions.

The syllables that could, by virtue of their linguistically determined stress, conceivably carry stress maxima are: "Oh," the first syllable of "solid," "flesh," "melt," "thaw," the second syllables of "resolve" and "itself," and "dew." These are either the accented syllables of poly-syllabic words (*solid*), or else they are non-reducible full-vowelled monosyllables (*melt*):

  1   2   3   4   5 6 7 8   9   10
Oh that this too too *solid flesh* would *melt*,

  1   2   3   4   5 6 7 8 9 10
Thaw, and re*solve* it*self* *into* a *dew*.

The unitalicized syllables are of types b, d, or e. Most of them are type b, reducible full-voweled monosyllables. For example, "too" is a full voweled syllable (/tuw/) but it frequently reduces to a neutralized vowel (/tɨ/), as in "too much" said rapidly, with stress on "much." It is important to note that it is this capacity for reduction, rather than how the word may actually be said in a particular instance, which determines its classification.

Let us now examine the italicized syllables, those with linguistically determined stress. The first syllables in both lines carry linguistic stress (they are type a: non-reducible full-vowelled monosyllables). However, neither "Oh" nor "Thaw" is a stress maximum, and for two reasons. First, no syllable precedes them in their respective lines, and they thus cannot be thrown into relief by unaccented syllables on each side. For this reason, neither the first, nor the last syllable of a line (unless an extra-metrical syllable follows) may be a stress maximum. So "melt" and "dew," though both are linguistically stressed (they are non-reducible full-vowelled monosyllables), also do not constitute stress maxima.

But there is a second reason why neither "Oh" nor "thaw" can be a stress maximum, namely, that these syllables are followed by major syntactic junctures, which have the effect of neutralization: neither the syllable before, nor the syllable after major syntactic juncture, may carry stress maxima.

This leaves five candidates for stress maxima, positions 6 and 8 in line one (*solid flesh*) and positions 4, 6, and 7 in line two (re*solve* it*self into*). The second syllable of "itself" and the first of "into" have linguistically determined stress (they are type c—accented syllables of polysyllabic words), but they are back to back. Thus each keeps the other from being a stress maximum: neither can be bordered on both sides by non-stressed syllables.

This leaves then only three linguistically stressed syllables to consider: "flesh," the first of "solid," and the second of "resolve." In each of these cases, unstressed syllables are to be found on both sides, without intervening juncture. These three syllables, then, do constitute stress maxima. Further, they fall on even positions, so the two lines are metrical by our rules, the first showing positions 6 and 8 occupied, and the second showing only position 4 occupied (not every even position need be occupied):

$$\overset{1}{\text{Oh}} \quad \overset{2}{\text{that}} \quad \overset{3}{\text{this}} \quad \overset{4}{\text{too}} \quad \overset{5}{\text{too}} \quad \overset{6}{\textit{solid}} \quad \overset{8}{\textit{flesh}} \quad \overset{9}{\text{would}} \quad \overset{10}{\text{melt,}}$$

$$\overset{1}{\text{Thaw}} \quad \overset{2}{\text{and}} \quad \overset{3}{\text{re}}\overset{4}{\textit{solve}} \quad \overset{5}{\text{itself}} \quad \overset{7\,8\,9}{\text{into}} \quad \overset{10}{\text{a}} \quad \text{dew.}$$

❊   ❊   ❊   ❊   ❊   ❊

These metrical rules, or principles, may be regarded as claims about the metrical competence of the poet.[#] It could be said that it is claimed the poet internalizes, not a poetic foot (some recurring pattern of stress and unstress), but a sequence of positions to be occupied by syllables; it is claimed that he is aware somehow of whether a given syllable Y occurs in an arithmetically even or arithmetically odd position; it is claimed further that the poet is metrically conscious only of stress maxima (linguistically determined lexical stress sandwiched by unstressed syllables, without intervening major syntactic boundary); it is claimed that he allows these to occur, or accepts their occurrence, only in even positions for iambic meter and only in odd positions for trochaic meter.[**] His grammar, *per se,* is not concerned with mere "accent" (though possibly his rules of performance might register cognition of these and other refinements).

❊   ❊   ❊   ❊   ❊   ❊

[#] It would be useful to have a word comparable, in this metrical context, to "native speaker" in the more general linguistic situation. The claims in any event are of the competence of the poet and of those attuned to poetry in some metrical sense, but I shall use the word "poet," in this situation, to refer to both. By "competence" is meant what the poet and the attuned reader know (though not necessarily what they can articulate) about the rules of meter.

[**] Or, obviously, some other pattern of position occupancy in the cases of dactyllic or anapestic verse.

By way of comparison, it could be said that traditional "school-room" prosody also may be reduced to a set of claims: namely that the poet internalizes a recurring group of stressed and unstressed syllables in a certain sequence—this is essentially the claim of the "foot" concept.

Let us turn now to such matters as the greater rhythmic regularity of short-line verse (tetrameter and trimeter), and the long noted and frequently debated difference in character between iambic and trochaic verse. Otto Jespersen, for example, contends that trochaic meter is characterized by a "falling" rhythm, and iambic meter by a "rising" rhythm; in the former, there is a tendency to "linger" on the stressed syllable.†† This suggests that the trochaic "foot" might be quantitatively longer than the iambic. No measurements of performance that I know of have established this,‡‡ but even those who do not accept the foot (Chatman, and Jespersen himself, in part—p. 74) unite in finding a more regular and insistent beat to trochaic verse.

If we assume, however, that the difference attributed to trochaic verse is in fact a difference to be found generally in *all* short-lined verse whether trochaic *or* iambic, there can be found an explanation for the assumed difference. Since most trochaic verse in English is in short-lines, and since our impressions of iambic verse are derived almost entirely from pentameter, it would seem entirely possible that the issue has been falsely formulated—that the differences of rhythm encountered are attributed not to the type of foot, but to the length of line in which the foot characteristically appears. And it will be argued below that the more regular beat of short-lined verse is accounted for by the fact that a much higher percentage of positions available for stress maxima are occupied than is the case in decasyllabic verse.

In English, most trochaic poems are in tetrameter, or trimeter.§§

†† Otto Jespersen, "Notes on Metre," in *Essays in the Language of Literature,* ed. Seymour Chatman and Samuel R. Levin (New York, 1967), pp. 86–88.

‡‡ One, in fact, shows the iambic foot as longer: Ada Snell, "An Objective Study of Syllabic Quantity in English Verse," *PMLA* XXXIII (1918), 396–408; XXXIV (1919), 416–435. Though this was not her principle objective, her measurements did show the average iambic foot to be of .69 seconds duration, and the average trochaic foot to be .55 (XXXIV, p. 433).

However, her tabulations on p. 432 show the average short syllable (unstressed) of the trochaic foot to be .35 seconds, and the average long syllable (stressed) as .20! Obviously, from an examination of the other figures, the two columns were accidentally reversed in the printing, a fact which may possibly have contributed to what seems to me Chatman's misleading conclusion that her figures "demonstrated clearly that syllable length was not necessarily an indication of metrical ictus, that indeed unstressed syllables could last longer than adjacent stressed syllables" (Chatman, p. 80). On the contrary, Snell's figures, to me, suggest that there is a clear general correspondence between the classical prosodist's length and ictus, so far as performance is concerned.

§§ Poe claimed that he wrote "The Raven" in trochaic "octameter acatalectic" alternating with "heptametre catalectic" but the heavy internal junctures after the fourth foot in most lines, and the internal rhyme, clearly suggest that the poem is in fact tetrameter.

Once up*on* a *mi*dnight *dreary*
While **I** *ponde*red *weak* and *weary*

Here, for example are two 10 line passages from Longfellow's "The Song of Hiawatha," the syllables carrying stress maxima, in accordance with rules here adopted, printed in italics.

> Till at *length* a small green *feather*
> From the earth shot slowly *up*ward,
> Then *an*other and *an*other,
> And be*fore* the *Sum*mer *end*ed
> Stood the *maize* in *all* its *beauty*,
> With its *shin*ing *robes* a*bout* it,
> And its long, soft, yellow *tres*ses:
> And in *rap*ture Hia*wa*tha
> Cried aloud, "It is Mon*dam*in!
> Yes, the *friend* of man, Mon*dam*in!"

> "The Song of Hiawatha,"
> Section V.

> Straight be*tween* them *ran* the *path*way.
> Never *grew* the *grass* up*on* it;
> Singing birds, that *ut*ter *false*hoods,
> Story-*tell*ers, mischief-*mak*ers,
> Found no *eag*er *ear* to *lis*ten,
> Could not breed ill-will be*tween* them,
> For they *kept* each *oth*er's *coun*sel,
> Spake with *nak*ed *hearts* to*geth*er,
> Pondering *much* and *much* con*triv*ing
> How the *tribes* of *men* might *pros*per.

> "The Song of Hiawatha,"
> Section VI.

A tetrameter line has available only three positions (2, 4, and 6 for iambic, 3, 5, and 7 for trochaic) for occupancy by stress maxima—a trimeter line only two. Pentameter has four. In the lines quoted from "The Song of Hiawatha," 46 of 60 available positions are occupied by stress maxima, for a 77% occupancy. Various randomly selected pas-

---

> Over *many* a *quaint* and *cur*ious
> Volume (of) for*got*ten lore

Note in the four lines (as I have rearranged them) that ten of the eleven available positions carry stress maxima, which are indicated by italics. The position not occupied is enclosed in parentheses.

sages in "Hiawatha" show an average 75% occupancy.‖ ‖ By contrast, an analysis of 10 of Shakespeare's sonnets (where there are four available positions per line, or 56 per sonnet) show an average of only 27.7 stress maxima per sonnet, or 49% occupancy.##

But the high occupancy ratio in Longfellow's trochaic verse is matched by that in various randomly sampled short-lined *iambic* poems. A. E. Housman's ballad stanzas show about 75% occupancy; even so varied a poem, metrically, as "Loveliest of trees, the *cherry* now" (the first line with only one stress maximum) shows 27 out of 35 positions occupied, or 77%.

Nor does the type of poet, or the type of verse (e.g., sonnet, or blank verse) seem ordinarily to affect the density of stress maxima. Edwin Arlington Robinson's blank verse dramatic monologues show about the same occupancy as Shakespeare's sonnets, and so do Robert Frost's blank verse and e. e. cummings' sonnets and other pentameter poems.*** (The condition indeed appears so general that when we find poetry departing significantly from the pattern, the occupancy ratio and distribution provide a basic tool for initial stylistic analysis, as we shall see a little later.)

It appears then that the often noticed difference between trochaic and iambic verse, if understood as actually a perceived difference between poems of different line length, may be correlated with the much greater density of stress maxima in short-lined verse: about 75% occupancy for short-lined verse, contrasted to 50% occupancy for decasyllabic verse. Put another way, there is 50% greater density of occupancy in short line verse.

Such an explanation follows naturally upon the concepts of positions and stress maxima. But the concept of feet does not explain it, for in fact just as high a percentage of iambs is found in pentameter as in shorter lines (or troches in trochaic lines). Shakespeare's sonnet LXXXIX, for example, which shows only 27 stress maxima in 56 available positions, shows 66 iambic feet out of a possible 70 (defining an iambic foot for this purpose as one which can be read, by any reasonable stretch of performance rules, as a lesser stressed syllable followed by a more greatly stressed syllable). For purposes of direct compari-

---

‖ ‖ The lowest percentage of occupancy I found in Hiawatha was 64%, in a thirteen line passage, also from section V. Four of the thirteen lines contain only one stress maximum each: "Sorrowing for her Hia*wa*tha," "He meanwhile sat weary *wai*ting," "Till the sun dropped from the *hea*ven," and "As a red leaf in the *au*tumn."

The following sonnets were analyzed; I, II, XXIX, LV, LVIII, LXXIII, LXXXIX, XC, XCI, CVII.

*** I am indebted to Helen Tulsky for work with e. e. cummings' poetry.

son, here is Sonnet LXXXIX, with stress maxima italicized, and with only those "feet" which do *not* seem, to me, susceptible to an iambic reading printed in capital letters:

> SAY THAT thou didst for*sake* me for some fault,
> And I will com*MENT* UP*on* that offense.
> SPEAK OF my *lame*ness, and I *straight* will halt,
> Ag*ainst* thy *reasons making* no defence.
> Thou canst not, love, dis*grace* me *half* so ill,
> To *set* a *form* up*on* de*sired* change,
> As I'll my*self* disgrace, KNOWING thy will.
> I will ac*quaint*ance *strang*le, and look strange,
> Be *ab*sent from thy walks, and in thy tongue
> Thy *sweet* be*loved name* no more shall dwell,
> Lest I, too much profane, should *do* it wrong
> And *hap*ly of our *old* ac*quaint*ance tell.
>   For thee, *against* my*self* I'll *vow* debate,
>   For I must ne'er love him whom thou dost hate.

I have designated 28 stress maxima here, but count only 27 that fall in an even position, since the stress on the second syllable of "upon" in line 2 falls on position 7, thus making that line unmetrical. The point is that there are 66 syllables in even position capable of some kind of stress, but only 27 of these are stress maxima.

✲   ✲   ✲   ✲   ✲   ✲

Glancing now at English triple meters, anapestic and dactyllic, it might at first appear that the insistent beat in these meters is at odds with our assumption that the phenomenon is associated with "short line verse," for most triple meters are in lines longer than decasyllabic. Indeed, the percentage of occupancy of available positions by stress maxima in anapestic verse appears to run higher than for the short line verse examined earlier. Byron's "Destruction of Sennacherib" and "On the Day of the Destruction of Jerusalem by Titus" show 96 stress maxima out of a possible 117 positions, for somewhat over 80% occupancy.

But in this case I think we must look for a different explanation of the rhythmic insistency. If the phenomenon in short line duple meters is to be accounted for—as I think it must—by a relative numerical scarcity of available positions as these relate to the syntactic units that normally comprise a line, in triple meter verse I think it is to be explained by the fact that the poet has to rely excessively on preposition-determiner-noun sequences, and other set syntactic patterns of English, to throw the stress always on the third syllable. It is worth noting, however, that complete lines without any stress maxima are possible in triple meter, as witness Byron's "When the blue wave rolls nightly on deep Galilee," where each potential stress maximum is cancelled by an adjacent non-reducible full-vowelled monosyllabic or accented syllable of a polysyllabic.†††

❁   ❁   ❁   ❁   ❁   ❁

Certain aspects of the Halle-Keyser principles of meter may provoke attack, and there remain some formal problems to be solved. For one thing, there is the claim—if I am right in postulating that their first principle in effect makes a claim—having to do with internalizing in some manner a sequence of positions (up to 10, in the case of decasyllabic verse) and identifying within this chain those positions which may be legitimately occupied with stress maxima. At first consideration, this might appear counter-intuitive. The claim asks nothing of rhythmic or temporal considerations. It is quasi-arithmetic, and on the face of it seems harder to believe than what amounts to the traditional claim that what is internalized is a recurring rhythmic pattern consisting of stronger and weaker pulses (which claim, of course, has support from psychological research).

To this objection, it might be answered that counting is the basis of all rhythm, musical as well as poetic. But how much counting (up to what number, without assistance of metrical grouping) is another question. In music, for example, one does not "count" higher than four in most cases—indeed, it can be argued that one does not have to internalize a count higher than three, since the various quadruple meters lend themselves to subdivision so easily. Herein lies the strength of the foot concept, since it hypothesizes only a recurring pattern of stress and unstress that never exceeds three (in English). The stress maximum concept on the other hand (at least in its unsupported version) implies that we can internalize 10 positions and be satisfied— to use Jespersen's word—by an event in the 8th position (which may

††† These comments on triple meter are based on the assumption of a set of rules that would provide, in anapestic tetrameter, for a 12 position verse, with stress maxima allowed to occupy only positions 3, 6, or 9, and with provisions for empty initial positions, and for extra-metrical syllables. In actuality, I think the framing of rules for triple meters in English poses difficulties not encountered in duple meters. Conditions for empty medial positions where there are terminal junctures would have to be set, for most poets who employ the medium.

not have occurred in 2, 4, or 6); or dissatisfied by an event in the 7th, even though we have no other occurrences anywhere in the line to use as an interval or distance estimate. Such observations suggest that rules for stress maxima should be supplemented by rules perhaps of another sort.

A quite minor detail is the fact that the rules of meter indicate that a position may under certain conditions be unoccupied, though the conditions are not specified in the rules. In fact, the only position which may be unoccupied appears to be the first position in iambic pentameter, though as I have suggested (footnote †††) provision for other empty positions would probably have to be made in other meters.

On this point, note that if we postulate a set of rules governing trochaic verse exactly parallel to those generating iambic verse (including the conditions of position occupancy by more than one syllable, and the possibility of zero occupancy), we have no way to distinguish consistently beheaded iambic verse (zero initial position) from consistently catalectic trochaic verse (zero final position). Thus, Tennyson's "Locksley Hall" and many others of this form:

> Cómrădes, léave mĕ hére ă líttlĕ, whĭle ăs yét 'tĭs éarlў́ mórn;
>
> Léave mĕ hére, ănd whén yŏu wánt mĕ, sóund ŭpón thĕ búglĕ hórn.

Tennyson's poem continues in a precisely similar metrical manner for 194 lines, with stress on the first and last syllables of each line. An obvious solution to this problem is to view such poems or portions of poems as metrically ambiguous in their surface structure, and postulate that they are, in their deep structure, either iambic with initial position always unoccupied, or trochaic, with final position always unoccupied.††† As a matter of fact, many poets have capitalized on this ambiguity. In "To a Skylark," Shelley chooses a stanza form which maintains the ambiguity through the first four lines of each stanza, resolving it in the iambic hexameter fifth line. And much of the charm of John Donne's "Go and catch a falling star," consists in precisely this ambiguity, which he maintains unresolved throughout the three stanzas.

Finally, it might be argued that the principles appear to offer no way of dealing with the reality of run-on lines—that is, if a line is in fact run on (proceeds without major juncture into the next), why then

††† "Locksley Hall," like "The Raven," seems to me misleadingly arranged with respect to line length. A major syntactic break occurs in the middle of each line; instead of rhyming octameter couplets (as Tennyson arranged it), these seem to me to be tetrameter quatrains, with lines 2 and 4 rhyming, and—as Poe would have put it—tetrameter trochaic acatalectic alternating with tetrameter trochaic catalectic.

can not the tenth syllable of the first line (or the first syllable of the second line, in trochaic verse) be considered occupied by stress maximum? The major difficulty is that if this be admitted, we will be forced in some cases to find stress maxima in initial position in iambic verse, thus losing the strength of our position (see next paragraph) that an initial stress does not make an irregular or unmetrical line. However, it must be remembered that our principles postulate a verse line as *a sequence of positions only*: the verse line is taken as a primitive, so to speak, and in this light, the foregoing objection loses some of its force.

Far more than offsetting these present possible inadequacies is the explanatory power of the principles. Initial "trochees" in iambic verse pose no problem at all: to say a line begins with a trochee is to say that the first position contains a stress greater than the second position, but no more: in our view, the first position cannot contain a stress maximum. And in fact, more of the lines in Shakespeare's sonnets begin on accented than on unaccented syllables: in the ten sonnets studied, only 52 of 140 lines had stress maxima in position 2. More common are lines like this one from Sonnet II:

"Proving his beauty by succession thine."

Traditional prosody finds itself in the uncomfortable position, here, of saying that the most common occurrence is the allowable exception. In our view, an initial "trochee" is entirely regular—all that matters is that stress maxima occur, when they occur at all, in even positions.

In a similar vein, the absence of bona fide iambs in various feet other than the first poses no problem. The fact that "by" in "Proving his beauty by succession thine" is unstressed does not embarrass the metrical theory. Traditional prosody, on the other hand, must say

that in some sense "*bý sŭccéssiŏn thíne*" occurs.

Our acceptance of strong accent after internal juncture also demonstrates the explanatory power of the rules. The following line shows an accented syllable in the wrong position, but it is not a stress maximum (because it is neutralized by juncture), and we intuitively feel that its occurrence does no violence to the meter.

"As I'll myself disgrace, *know*ing thy will"—Sonnet LXXXIX

We readily accept also special intonations which might appear to violate the meter, if meter is taken to be based on performance. But our principles and our stress rules say nothing at all about how lines may happen to be read. Stress maxima are defined in terms of linguistically determined stress (*i.e.*, not performance determined). In the present study, a syllable is one of the five kinds[§§§] distinguished by Chatman, and it belongs in that class *regardless of how it is performed.* The following lines may be performed with unusual stress on the italicized syllables in odd positions, but it does not make the lines unmetrical:

1. Say that thou didst forsake *me* for some fault—Sonnet LXXXIX

2. As he would add a shilling to *more* shillings—Robinson, "Ben Jonson Entertains a Visitor from Stratford."

3. Oh, that this too *too* solid flesh would melt—Hamlet

In 1, "sake" is the stressed syllable of a polysyllabic word, and "me" is a reducible full-vowelled monosyllabic (as are most pronouns). The fact that "me" may be said louder (perhaps to indicate that in the past the reverse had been true) or higher than "-sake" does not alter the linguistic fact. In 2, which has an extra-metrical syllable after the 10th position, "more" is a prenominal adjective and subject to reduction (even though it may not be so performed in this instance), and therefore is not a stress maximum. In each case, the performance can not alter what as native speakers we know, and our knowledge of inherent linguistic stress overrides performance. Ictus in our sense is not synonymous with what is phonetically higher or louder or with what is more carefully enunciated. Therefore we need no performance records to determine the meter of the poem—though we need a knowledge of "performance" i.e., a corpus) from which to derive our rules of stress in the first place.

And, as Halle and Keyser have demonstrated, our principles explain the otherwise unexplainable phenomenon that while iambic lines can accept initial trochees, trochaic lines frequently cannot accept initial iambs. In "Proving his beauty by succession thine," the initial accent on *"Proving"* cannot be a stress maximum, and thus its occurrence on an odd position in iambic verse does not alter the meter. But if, to parallel Jesperson's illustration, we change Longfellow's trochaic line

---

§§§ In fact four kinds, for in this analysis I do not distinguish between his types d and e: between full-vowelled unstressed syllables in polysyllabic words and unstressed syllables in polysyllabic words with neutralized vowels.

"Straight between them ran the pathway"

to read

"Be*tween* them straight ran the pathway"

we have created a stress maximum in an even position, thus violating the rule of trochaic meter.

So the Halle-Keyser prosodic system is first of all a grammar of verse: it is a set of rules which enables us to say that certain lines are metrical, and certain lines are not metrical. Beyond this lies the question of whether the rules can be used significantly for stylistic analysis. This article has not for the most part concerned itself with this question. The distinction drawn between short-line and long-line verse (75% density of stress maxima in the former, 50% in the latter) is not fundamentally a stylistic distinction. Rather, it would appear that the language mechanics of verse lines shorter than decasyllabic linguistically requires the higher percentage of occupancy because of the relatively fewer available positions for stress maxima in each line to correlate with normal syntactic units.

Perhaps we should look for stylistic devices to emanate from something corresponding to rules of performance, rather than to metrical competence. In effect performance—but in an oral production sense—is what earlier structuralist analyses of metrical stress dealt with.‖ ‖ ‖ If efforts are made to supplement rules for determination of stress maxima with rules showing how phrase accent and clause accent, etc., may be appended, these might have more to do with metrical performance (not oral-production) than with metrical competence.###

‖ ‖ ‖ Though Seymour Chatman has now shifted his position substantially, *A Theory of Meter* is still performance-oriented in this sense.

See footnote §. For a full "grammar of prosody," further refinement might be needed, but I think their necessity would have to be demonstrated. For example, I have not used secondary stress in polysyllabic words as stress maxima. Thus, Poe's line

1 2   3 4 5 67 8   9 10 11 12 13 14   15

To the tintinnabulation that so *mu*sically wells would show stress maxima in positions 7 and 11, but not in 3 or 5 or 13, all of which are occupied by syllables that possibly have secondary stress of some kind. A glance at several dictionaries will show how divided opinion is on the question of secondary stress. And the fact that secondary stress can be subordinated to primary stress seems to me to eliminate it from stress maximum status. Observe the behavior of the third syllable of "refuge" in the following triple meter:

The rĕfūgĕe cáme tŏ thĕ villăge hĕ knéw.

Additional conditions for occupancy of a position by more than one syllable might be needed, though I have so far encountered few situations that are not encompassed by those in the Halle-Keyser principles.

However, certain basic stylistic determinations may be derived from the rules. Relative density of stress maxima occupancy comes first to mind as a stylistic determinant. I have said that most of the deca-syllabic verse examined shows about 50% occupancy, and have sug-gested that this ordinarily obtains, irrespective of poet or period. But individual poems may show significant variance; and individual efforts in different verse forms may exhibit differences. An analysis of the first ten of John Donne's "Holy Sonnets" shows 236 of 560 positions occu-pied, for 42% density of occupancy, as compared to the 49% found for ten of Shakespeare's sonnets.

Predilection for placing stress maxima in certain positions would appear to be, potentially, a more telling stylistic determinant. My study of the sonnets of Shakespeare and Donne shows distribution of stress maxima in the four available positions (140 possibilities for each position) as follows:

POSITION	Number Stress Maxima		Percentage Stress Maxima	
	S.	D.	S.	D.
2	52	65	37%	46%
4	76	50	54%	36%
6	65	47	46%	33%
8	83	74	59%	53%

Shakespeare uses position 8 most, followed by 4, then 6, then 2. Donne also uses 8 most, but favors next position 2 (last with Shakespeare), then 4, then 6. This suggests, in Donne, a metrical structure tending to support stability at the extremities of the lines, somewhat like a suspension bridge, perhaps at the expense of medial stability. Shake-speare, on the other hand, tends to provide anchors at half way points. This possibly subjective interpretation might be represented in this manner:

John Donne

William Shakespeare

Distribution of the stress maxima does appear to provide the richest source for stylistic analysis. Many more possibilities suggest them-selves. For example, if a poet has employed positions 6 and 8 in one or two lines, how long will it be till he balances by placing maxima in 2 and 4? What overall distributional patterns of occupancy present themselves, and what is their significance? What lines show total occupancy? What show none? In the ten sonnets of Shakespeare, there were 10 lines with no stress maxima; in the sonnets of Donne, there were 11. The following are typical:

"Some glory in their birth, some in their skill"

Shakespeare, Sonnet XCI.

"My worlds both parts, and (oh) both parts must die"

Donne, Holy Sonnet 5.

The particular uses—and the frequency—of *un*metrical lines is another potential stylistic consideration. There is always the possibility of a lapse on the part of the poet, and occasionally a poet may be a poor metrist (see footnote †††), but some lines unmetrical by the rules seem calculated for effect. In the ten sonnets of Shakespeare I found only one clearly unmetrical line (which, incidentally, is about ⅔ of 1%, as compared to the 1% of unmetrical lines Halle and Keyser found in Chaucer), but four in Donne. The unmetrical line of Shakespeare's occurs in Sonnet LXXXIX:

"And I will comment up*on* that offense."

As pointed out earlier, a stress maximum falls on position 7, rendering the line unmetrical. This would seem to be merely a lapse.

John Donne's unmetrical lines, however, occur with sufficient frequency to suggest deliberation. He appears to seek the device which will capture attention, by departing from the usual (note that he does not attempt to achieve novelty—which would not have been novelty— by low frequency use of position 2, and the attendant stress in initial position). One of the ways of doing this is by deliberately placing stress maxima in off positions. In Sonnet I, we find:

"Thou hast *made* me, and shall thy *worke* decay?"

where the very first stress maximum occurs in position 3, perhaps underscoring the conflict, the contradiction in the two thoughts Donne contemplates. An unmetrical line in a passage that interests because of its use of double position occupancy occurs in Sonnet IV:

line 5 Or like a thiefe, which till deaths doome be read,

6 Wisheth him*selfe* deliverĕd from prison;

7 But *damn'd* and *hal'd* to execŭtion,

8 Wisheth that *still* he might be imprisonĕd.

Here "wisheth" is used in positions 1 and 2 of line 6, and the line is metrical (but the extra-metrical syllable at the end, the second of "prison," is made to carry the rhyme). Then in line 8, the two syllables of "wisheth" both occupy position one, which places the stress maximum in position 3 for an unmetrical line. Alternatively, if "wisheth" occupies two positions, "still" carries stress maximum in position 4, but now the stress maximum in "imprisoned" falls in position 9, for an unmetrical line. One could assign "be" and "im-" to the same position by condition one of the rules, and, with other adjustments, argue that the line is metrical. The other two unmetrical lines are printed without comment:

7

To where they're bred, and would *presse* me, to hell—

Sonnet VI.

9

Make sinnes, else equall, in mee more *heino*us?

Sonnet IX.

It may be noted in passing that Donne's experiments in position occupancy by more than one syllable are most interesting, and is another aspect which lends his verse its rough-hewn effect.

✻   ✻   ✻   ✻   ✻   ✻

In summary, the Halle-Keyser principles of prosody appear to bear a relationship to traditional prosody somewhat akin to that which transformational grammar bears to traditional grammar. Their approach represents an attempt to make explicit what had been only implicit. Pursuing the analogy, the principles appear also to represent certain claims about the nature of metrical competence, and though the claims may at first pose something of a credibility gap, in fact they stretch the credulity no more than the failure of implicit claims in traditional prosody to account for what would otherwise be an intolerable percentage of unmetrical lines. The principles, together with the stress rules here suggested, offer a unified explanation for the fact that the majority of iambic lines begin with trochaic feet; for the absence of regular feet at various other positions in the line; for our acceptance of strong stress before or after juncture, even in odd-numbered positions; for the fact that special intonation features do not appear to violate the acceptability of metrical lines, for the rejection of iambs in trochaic verse; for the fact that poetry in duple meter in verse lines shorter than decasyllabic appears to be more irresistably metrical. Finally, they offer a well-defined procedure for basic metrical-stylistic analysis.****

**** I would like to acknowledge the valuable assistance of Don Seigel, who read two versions of this paper and whose criticism has been most helpful.

I am indebted also to Morris Halle and Samuel Keyser for a detailed commentary. I have adopted some of their suggestions, but responsibility for the entire paper is my own.

George Hansen, Elsa Atkins, and Leonard Stenson have helped in various ways.

COMPOSITION

KELLOGG W. HUNT

How Little Sentences
Grow into Big Ones

INTRODUCTION

The article begins with a sketch of the main syntactic components of a
transformational grammar: the phrase structure rules, the simple transformational rules, and the sentence combining rules. The part of the grammar
that is of particular interest to Hunt is the last mentioned set of rules: the
sentence combining transformations. These rules are cyclical, that is, they
can be applied over and over, each time producing a longer and more
complex sentence. Hunt's main point is that

> the ability to combine more and more kernel sentences is a mark of
> maturity. The older a child becomes, the more he can combine. Appar-
> ently, too, the higher the IQ, the faster children learn to do this.

Hunt breaks the sentence combining transformations into two large families: (1) noun modification and (2) nominalization, that is, the reduction
of a whole sentence into a clause or phrase that functions like a unitary
noun. The strength of this article is that Hunt takes the reader through the
operation of the sentence combining transformations in "slow-motion."

Reprinted by permission of the author and the National Council of Teachers of
English, from *New Directions in Elementary English*, ed. by Alexander Frazier.

*

We are all aware of the planned obsolescence in automobiles. When I was a boy, cars were streamlined to reduce wind resistance. The ideal shape was the teardrop. Now instead, the outlines of cars are sharp and crisp, and no one talks of wind resistance, only of sales resistance. One year the ads proclaim the transcendent beauty of tail fins that shoot straight up like the tails on airplanes. But at the same moment, on the drawing boards of the car designers is the plan for the next year's model. Next year tail fins will shoot straight out like horizontal stabilizers instead.

In language arts teaching we have our obsolescence too, but it is never planned. No one advocates functional grammar or structural grammar because he knows it will not wear well. He advocates it instead because he thinks it is better than last year's model. It isn't always. Sometimes it wears badly.

The newest model in grammar is called generative-transformational.* It is called generative because it aims to be as explicit as the mathematical formulae that generate a circle or a straight line on a sheet of graph paper. An explicit formula is capable of being proved true or false. A vague statement is not capable of being proved either true or false. So generative grammar aims to say explicitly many of the things that traditional grammars have said only vaguely. It tries to generate the same sentences that people generate, and it tries to generate none of the nonsentences. This grammar is by no means complete, but no other grammar is complete either, as any experienced grammarian knows. (The second half of the generative-transformational label will be touched on later in this paper.)

NATURE OF GENERATIVE-TRANSFORMATIONAL GRAMMAR

So far, generative-transformational grammar appears only in the learned journals which most English teachers never read. There are only about three books on the subject which most English teachers can hope to wade through if they are diligent: Robert's *English Syntax*,† Rogovin's *Modern English Sentence Structure*,‡ and Thomas's

---

* For further information on the subject see Kellogg W. Hunt, "Recent Measures in Syntactic Development," *Elementary English,* 43 (November 1966), 732–739.
† Paul Roberts, *English Syntax* (New York: Harcourt, Brace, and World, Inc., 1964).
‡ Syrell Rogovin, *Modern English Sentence Structure* (New York: Random House, Inc., 1965).

Transformational Grammar and the Teacher of English.[§] So when I try to survey the subject from beginning to end so quickly, you can expect that I will sweep past many points where you would like to challenge me, if you do not first lose interest.

I will call the grammar by its initials, g-t. Ordinarily, g-t grammar is presented as a series of formulae that to many people look horribly scientific. Sample formulae look like this:

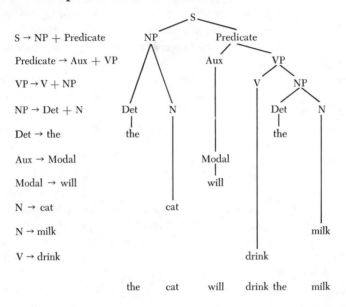

S → NP + Predicate

Predicate → Aux + VP

VP → V + NP

NP → Det + N

Det → the

Aux → Modal

Modal → will

N → cat

N → milk

V → drink

But what these formulae mean is not at all strange and forbidding. In fact it is so familiar to language arts teachers that I am afraid I will be dull and commonplace for the next several pages. I am going to talk about some things you know so well that you may never have noticed them. First, I will talk about little sentences. These formulae would produce or generate the one little sentence *The cat will drink the milk.* They also ascribe a structural description to that sentence. A structural description is somewhat like a sentence diagram, though it is also different in some respects. The structural description says that the sentence can be broken first of all into two parts: *The cat* is one part and *will drink the milk* is the second. It also says that the second part is composed of two subparts, *will* and *drink the milk*. It

§ Owen Thomas, *Transformational Grammar and the Teacher of English* (New York: Holt, Rinehart, and Winston, Inc., 1965).

breaks the second subpart into two sub-subparts *drink* and *the milk.*
It breaks *the milk* down into its two parts, *the* and *milk.*

Who cares what the structural description of a sentence is? Why
have we been analyzing sentences all these years? Have we known
why? Actually there are several reasons. First, the meaning of the
whole sentence is made from the meaning of exactly those components,
not other components. That is, one *the* forms a meaningful unit with
milk, but not with any other one word in the sentence: *drink the* is not
a meaningful unit, nor is *will drink the.* Furthermore, *the milk* next
forms a meaningful unit with drink: *drink the milk.* But *the cat the milk*
is not a meaningful unit. This larger unit *drink the milk* forms a meaningful unit with *will* to produce the next unit, and finally *will drink the
milk* joins with *the cat* to give the meaning of the whole sentence. Here
we happen to have worked from the small units to the large unit, but
we could have worked from large to small as we did in the formula.
When you listen you work from large to small, but when you speak or
write you work from small to large.

REASONS FOR STRUCTURAL DESCRIPTION OF SENTENCES

One reason to give the structural description of the sentence, then,
is to show which are the meaningful parts and what is the order in
which those parts are joined together one after another to give the
whole meaning of the sentence.

When I used to assemble model airplanes with my son, we had to
learn about subassemblies and sub-subassemblies. We had to glue the
parts together in the proper order or some part would be left over and
we would have to tear the whole thing apart to get it in. Sentences
too have their subassemblies, and the order of assembly is no chance
matter.

There are two other reasons to show the structural description of a
sentence. Some words are called nouns in this description and some
are called verbs and some are called modals. Which names we use
for these sets of words would not matter, except that these names have
been used for two thousand years. We could call them class 1, class 2,
class 3 words instead if we gained anything by the change. One reason
we group words into those various classes or sets is to show that
thousands of English sentences can be made simply by substituting
one noun in the same place as another noun and some new modal in
place of another modal. But we never can substitute a noun for a
modal or a modal for a noun. For instance if it is English to say

The cat will drink the milk.

we know it will also be English to say

John will drink the milk.
The dog will drink the milk.
Mary will drink the milk.

One animate noun substitutes here for another animate noun. Similarly one modal substitutes for another.

The cat   can   drink the milk.
The cat should drink the milk.
The cat   may   drink the milk.
The cat might drink the milk.

But we know too that a modal cannot be substituted for a noun. It is not English to say

Could will drink the milk.
The cat John the milk.

Regularities such as these make a language easy enough that people can learn it. When we learn a new word we unconsciously learn whether it is a noun or a verb, and so we unconsciously learn countless thousands of new sentences in which it can be used. So this is a second reason why the structural description of a sentence helps to show what we know when we know our language.

A third reason to show the structural description is to show what can be conjoined. For instance we said earlier that *the cat* is a grammatical unit, but that *drink the* is not. That tells us that it will not be English to conjoin *drink the* and *taste a* as in the sentence.

The cat will drink the and taste a milk.

However, it will be English to say

The cat will taste and drink the milk.

for *taste* and *drink* are both V's. But words are not all that can be conjoined. Larger structures can be too.

Here two VP's are conjoined though there is only one NP and one modal:

The cat will drink the milk and go to sleep.

But only the components generated by the rules can be conjoined. Words cannot be conjoined at random.

Just as one noun phrase can be substituted for another noun phrase but for nothing else, so one noun phrase can be conjoined with another noun phrase, but not with anything else. Just as a VP can be replaced by another VP but not by a modal or an NP, so one can be conjoined to another bearing the same label in the formulae.

So when we give the structural description of a sentence, we are simply pointing out explicitly some of the things we know unconsciously when we know our language.

That is not all that a g-t grammar shows about little sentences. It also assigns certain functional relations to certain components. What are here called functional relations are not the same as the grammatical categories. For instance, *the cat* is an NP and *the milk* is another NP. But one is subject and the other is object. And the subject NP does not mean the same as an object NP. In the following sentences both *John* and *Mary* are NP's, but in one sentence *John* is the subject, and in the other *Mary* is the subject. Any youngster knows the difference between the two.

John hit Mary first.
Mary hit John first.

One NP is often substitutable grammatically for another NP, whether subject or object, but an NP which is subject does not mean the same as it does when it is object.

Take another simple example.

The boy is easy to please.
The boy is eager to please.

In one sentence, the boy pleases other people and is eager to do so. In the other sentence, other people please the boy and to do so is easy. In one sentence, *the boy* has the subject meaning relationship to *please*. In the other sentence, *the boy* has the object meaning relationship to *please*. But in both sentences, *boy* is the formal subject of the verb *is*.

The g-t grammarian makes further distinctions between the formal subject and the formal object and the semantic subject and the semantic object. For instance, the two following sentences mean the same thing (that is, if one is true the other is true, and if one is false the other is false).

The boy pleases other people.
Other people are pleased by the boy.

The semantic subject in both sentences is *the boy*: the boy does the pleasing. But one verb agrees with the formal subject *the boy* which is singular, *the boy pleases*. The other verb agrees with the formal subject *other people* which is plural: *other people are pleased*. So in this sentence the semantic subject is not the same as the formal subject. The verb agrees with the formal subject and that may not be the semantic subject.

FORMULAE FOR MAKING BIGGER SENTENCES

The sentence we started out with was extremely simple. A g-t grammar gives formulae to produce all these different simplest sentences: sentences with direct objects, predicate nominals (John is a hero), predicate adjectives (John is heroic), indirect objects (John gave Mary a book), and many constituents which are not named in school book grammars. These simplest sentences used to be called kernel sentences by the g-t grammarian. That term is not being used in recent publications, but I shall continue to use it here.

A g-t grammar also gives you explicit directions on how to make big sentences out of little ones. Of course, being a native English speaker you know that, but you know it unconsciously without even knowing how you learned it. The grammar merely tries to describe what you know and what you do. But before I talk about how we make big sentences out of little sentences, I want to take a couple of minutes to give you a sample of how we make question sentences and imperative sentences and passive sentences out of statement or declarative sentences.

If you have a statement sentence with a modal, all you have to do to make it into a yes-no question sentence is to put the modal before the subject:

The cat will drink the milk.
Will the cat drink the milk?

The cat with the tiger markings and the ragged ears will drink the milk.
Will the cat with the tiger markings and the ragged ears drink the milk?

The formulae for other questions are almost as simple.

The inversion of modal and subject signals that a yes-no question is being asked. What is the meaning there signaled? It is simply "The speaker requests the listener to affirm or deny the following sentence." All yes-no questions bear that same relation to the statements from which they are formed. *Will the cat drink the milk?* means "The speaker requests the listener to affirm or deny the sentence, *The cat will drink the milk.*"

To produce an imperative sentence you must begin with a sentence that has *you*, meaning the listener, as the subject, and *will* (the volitional *will*, not the future tense *will*) as its modal: *You will be here on time tomorrow.* The verb following *will* is always in the uninflected form, and that is just the form we always want. We say *You are here*, *You will be here*, and consequently we say in the imperative *Be here*, not *Are here*. To form an imperative sentence from such a declarative sentence, all you have to do is delete the *you will*: *Be here on time tomorrow.* The absence of the subject and the uninflected form of the verb are the formal signals that an imperative has been uttered. We say that *you will* has been deleted, because if we add a tag question at the end of the imperative, we put the *you* and the *will* back in, though in negative form.

> Be here on time tomorrow, won't you?

The meaning signaled by the interrogative is "The speaker requests that you will: Be here on time tomorrow."

Passive sentences are formed from kernel sentences by as simple a formula. Take this example: *The cat will drink the milk: The milk will be drunk by the cat.* (1) Whatever expression functioned as semantic direct object now becomes formal subject. (2) Whatever expression functioned as semantic subject now follows *by* (or is deleted along with *by*) at the end of the sentence. (3) The proper form of *be* is inserted before the main verb and the main verb takes the past participle form. Thus:

> (1) The cat will (2) drink (3) the milk.
> (3) The milk will (2) be drunk by (1) the cat.

These are the formal signals of the passive. The meaning of the passive does not differ from that of the active, but in a passive sentence the semantic subject does not need to be mentioned. Instead of saying "Someone hurt him" we can say "He was hurt."

VARIETY OF TRANSFORMATIONS

These changes which we English speakers make on active declarative sentences to turn them into questions and imperatives and passives are called singulary transformations, because they change a single sentence of one sort into a single sentence of another sort. Children before they ever get to school can form questions and imperatives in an endless stream, though they have no conscious notion of the general rules which they have learned to follow.

Which comes first, the question or the statement? Which comes first, "He will come" or "Will he come?" It depends on what you mean by "comes first." If you mean, "Which does the child learn first?" then we have no certain answer. Having watched my own infants when they were angry and demanding, I feel certain that infants speak imperatives long before they speak any words at all. I remember too that four-year-olds generate questions much faster than their parents want to generate answers.

But the statement comes before the question in a thoroughly different sense. It is simpler to write a grammar which generates first the form and meaning of statements than to write one which generates questions first and then transforms them into statements.

In many elementary grammar books, I see questions and statements mixed together indiscriminately, though the relation of one to the other is never explained.

Far more useful for the language arts program, however, are the transformations which have been called sentence-combining. They take one sentence of a certain sort and another of a certain sort and combine them to produce one new sentence. The g-t grammar tries to tell exactly what changes are made in the process. The process of combining little sentences into bigger ones can be repeated an indefinite number of times so that two, three, four, five, and even ten or twenty can be combined into one complicated sentence. Below we will combine seventeen into one. Furthermore, the meaning of the complicated sentence is the meaning of all the simple sentences put together.

This process is particularly interesting because apparently the ability to combine more and more kernel sentences is a mark of maturity. The older a child becomes, the more he can combine. Apparently, too, the higher the IQ, the faster children learn to do this, so that by the time they are in the twelfth grade, the students with superior IQ's tend to be well ahead of students with average IQ's.

THE PROCESS OF COMBINING SENTENCES

I want to sketch for you that process of combining sentences.

Very young children combine two sentences into one by putting *and's* between. We can call this sentence coordination. Children in the earlier grades do this far more often than adults. In writing, fourth graders do so four or five times as often as twelfth graders in the same number of words. As they get older, they learn not to use sentence coordination so much. Also children use sentence coordination more often in speech than in writing. In fact, Dr. Griffin and his associates at Peabody have found that fifth graders use two or three times as much sentence coordination in their speech as they do in their writing for the same number of words.‖

So we may think of sentence coordination as a relatively immature device for joining little sentences into bigger ones. It is a device which they will outgrow, or, better yet, which they will replace with the other devices I will now describe. Sentence coordination is the only transformation that we know to be used *less* frequently by older students.

Often two adjoining sentences have a certain relation between them such that the event recorded in one sentence happened at the same time as that in the other. When such is the case, *when* can be put in front of one sentence, making it an adverbial clause with the other as the main or independent clause:

> My mother came home and I got spanked. (*When* my mother, etc.)
> We climbed out on the end of the limb and it broke. (*When* we climbed out, etc.)

There are many subordinators besides *when* which introduce movable adverbial clauses, and, in writing, students use a few more of them as they get older. Dr. Griffin finds that in the speech of students from kindergarten to seventh grade, there is a general increase in their number. I find that in writing there is also a slight increase from the fourth grade up to the twelfth.‖ ‖

So-called adjective relative clauses are also produced by sentence-combining transformations. They can be formed when one sentence contains the same noun or the same adverb of time or place as another

‖ Roy C. O'Donnell, William J. Griffin & R. C. Norris, *Syntax of Kindergarten and Elementary School Children: A Transformational Analysis* (Champaign, Illinois: National Council of Teachers of English, 1967).

‖ ‖ Kellogg W. Hunt, *Grammatical Structures Written at Three Grade Levels* (Champaign, Illinois: National Council of Teachers of English, 1965).

sentence contains. Let me take as my main clause *The man did something* and then combine with it a number of different sentences in the form of adjective clauses. At the same time, we will notice that in all the examples I happen to have chosen, the adjective clause can be reduced by deletion to a single word modifier of a noun or to a phrasal modifier of a noun.

> The man did something.
>
> The man was big.
> The man (who was big) did something.
> The (big) man did something.
>
> The man was at the door.
> The man (who was at the door) did something.
> The man (at the door) did something.
>
> The man had a derby.
> The man (who had a derby) did something.
> The man (with a derby) did something.
>
> The man was swinging a cane.
> The man (who was swinging a cane) did something.
> The man (swinging a cane) did something.

We find that as students mature they use more and more adjective clauses in their writing. Furthermore, as students mature they use more and more of these single-word or phrasal modifiers of nouns. So we see that the ability to combine sentences into adjective clauses and to delete parts of the clause to produce single word or single phrase modifiers is indeed a mark of maturity.

Now let us see how a twelfth grader can combine five sentences into one. You will see that the twelfth grader is telling about a sailor. In fact the word *sailor* is subject of each of the sentences which he has consolidated into one.

> The sailor was tall.
> The sailor was rather ugly.
> The sailor had a limp.
> The sailor had offered them the prize.
> The sailor finally came on deck.

There are lots of bad ways to combine these sentences. One is with sentence coordinators:

> The sailor was tall and he was rather ugly and he had a limp and he had offered them the prize and he finally came on deck.

I have seen fourth graders who wrote almost that way.

Another bad way to combine the sentences is to produce a great number of relative adjective clauses all modifying the word *sailor*. No one would ever write like this:

> The sailor who was tall and who was rather ugly and who had offered them the prize finally came on deck.

Rarely do we let more than one full adjective clause modify a single noun. Instead we reduce the potential clauses to single word modifiers or phrasal modifiers.

I fancy most of you are way ahead of me already. You have been so uncomfortable with these bad sentences that you have already rewritten them as the twelfth grader did. But even so I am going to ask you to combine these sentences with me, one by one, slow motion, so we can study the process.

Below, I have numbered the minimal sentences S1, S2, etc. The procedure will be as follows. First, I will state a general transformational rule for English sentences. Then we will apply that rule to two of the sentences and see what we come out with. Next I will state another transformational rule, or the same one again, and we will apply that rule in the third sentence plus what we produced the previous time. Or instead I may state a rule which changes what we produced though it does not incorporate a new sentence.

The rules read like this: If you have a sentence of one particular pattern and a second of another particular pattern, it will be good English if you rewrite them into one according to the formula. Instead of using abstract but more exact symbols like NP for noun phrase or VP for predicate, I have used the words *someone* or *something* for noun phrases, and the words *did something* for predicates in general. *A twelfth grader consolidates 5 sentences into 1, using noun modifiers.*

> S1 The sailor finally came on deck.
> S2 The sailor was tall.
> S3 The sailor was rather ugly.
> S4 The sailor had a limp.
> S5 The sailor had offered them a prize.

Transformation #1

> Someone did something + Someone did something else → The someone (who did something else) did something.

Application to S1 and S2:

> The sailor who was tall finally came on deck.

Transformation #2

> Someone (who was X) did something → Someone X did something
> (or some X person did something).

Application to what we produced last time:

> The tall sailor finally came on deck.

Transformation #1 again

> Someone did something + Someone did something else → The some-
> one (who did something else) did something.

Application to S3 plus what we produced last time:

> The tall sailor (who was rather ugly) finally came on deck.

Transformation #2 again

> Someone (who was X) did something → Someone X did something
> (or some X person did something).

Application to what we produced last time:

> The tall, rather ugly sailor finally came on deck.

Transformation #3

> Someone had something → someone with something.

Application to S4 plus what we produced before:

> The tall, rather ugly sailor with a limp finally came on deck.

Transformation #1 again

> Someone did something + Someone did something else → The some-
> one (who did something else) did something.

Application to S5 plus what we produced before:

> The tall, rather ugly sailor with a limp, who had offered them a prize, finally came on deck.

An average fourth grader does not write four modifiers to a single noun. He will write only two or at most three at a time. He would be likely to resort to *and's* and produce about three sentences.

> The sailor was tall and rather ugly and had a limp. He had offered them the prize. Finally he came on deck.

I have just finished talking about noun modifiers, attempting to show that syntactic maturity is the ability to consolidate several sentences by reducing some sentences to modifiers of a single noun.

THE NOMINALIZING TENDENCY IN CONSOLIDATION

The second tendency I will talk about today is called the nominalizing tendency. What the writer does is to take a whole sentence, or at least a whole predicate, and make it into a structure which can function like a noun. That is, the whole transformed sentence can now be subject in some other sentence, or object of a verb, or object of a preposition. This whole new sentence can then be nominalized in turn, and so on and so on. The best way to illustrate this process is to show you a number of kernel sentences and let you put them together.

A twelfth grader consolidates 6 sentences into 1, nominalizing some.

> S1 Macbeth breaks up the feast with something.
> S2 Macbeth remarks something.
> S3 Macbeth displays fear.
> S4 Macbeth fears a ghost.
> S5 Banquo is the ghost.
> S6 Only Macbeth sees the ghost.

Transformation #1

> Someone remarks about something → someone's remark about something.
> Someone displays something → someone's display of something.
> Someone fears something → someone's fear of something.

Application to S1 and S2:

Macbeth breaks up the feast with his remarks (about something).

Transformation #1 again, plus coordination plus deletion

(The coordination transformation is too complex to explain here.)

Application to S3 plus what we produced before:

Macbeth breaks up the feast with his remarks and his display of fear.

Transformation #1 again

Application to S4 plus what we produced before:

Macbeth breaks up the feast with his remarks and his display of fear of a ghost.

Transformation #2

Someone has something → the something of someone.

Application to S5 plus what we produced before:

Macbeth breaks up the feast with his remarks and his display of fear of a ghost of Banquo.

Transformation #3

Someone sees something → something is seeable (visible) to someone. (*Visible* replaces seeable somewhat as *edible* replaces *eatable*. *Understandable, divisible* are regular forms.)

Application to S6 plus what we produced before:

Macbeth breaks up the feast with his remarks and his display of fear of a ghost of Banquo visible only to him.

Here is still another sequence of transformations, this time showing the way in which a superior adult incorporates a great variety of kernel sentences as nominalizations, modifiers, etc., into a single sentence with highly complex relationships expressed between or among its constituent ideas.

A superior adult consolidates 17 sentences into 1, using modifiers, nominalizations, etc.

S1 He also noted S2.
S2 S3 would apply only to S4.
S3 Someone cuts back something.
    (Someone's cutback of something)
S4 Someone stockpiles weapons.
    (Someone's stockpiling of weapons)
    (He also noted that [someone's] cutback [of something] would apply only to [someone's stockpiling] of weapons.)
S5 The weapons are for an arsenal.
    (He also noted that the cutback would apply only to the stockpiling of weapons for an arsenal.)
S6 The arsenal is for atomic weapons (?)
    (. . . an atomic [weapon] arsenal)
S7 The arsenal already bulges.
    (. . . an already bulging atomic arsenal)
S8 S3 would not affect the strength.
    (He also noted that the cutback would apply only to the stockpiling of weapons for an already bulging atomic arsenal and would have no effect on the strength.)
S9 The strength overwhelms someone.
    (. . . the overwhelming strength)
S10 The strength retaliates.
    (. . . the overwhelming retaliatory strength)
S11 The SAC has the strength.
    (. . . the overwhelming retaliatory strength of the SAC)
S12 The force has the strength.
    (. . . strength of the SAC and of the force)
S13 The force carries missiles.
    (. . . the missile force)
S14 The missiles are intercontinental.
    (. . . the intercontinental missile force)
S15 The fleet has the strength.
    (. . . strength of the SAC, of the intercontinental missile force, or the fleet)
S16 The fleet carries missiles.
    (. . . the missile fleet)
S17 The missiles are Polaris.
    (. . . the Polaris missile fleet)
    He also noted that the cutback would apply only to the stockpiling of weapons for an already bulging atomic arsenal and would have no effect on the overwhelming retaliatory strength of the SAC, of the intercontinental missile force, or the Polaris missile fleet.

SUMMARY AND CONCLUSION

This has been an exceedingly rough sketch of g-t grammar. We started out with fairly explicit rules that generated an exceedingly simple sentence and also its structural description. Then we saw that questions, imperatives, and passives bear a certain explicit relationship to those simple active statement sentences, both in form and in meaning.

Then we saw that quite complicated sentences can be consolidated out of a number of exceedingly simple sentences. As children get older, they can consolidate larger and larger numbers of them. Average twelfth graders consolidate half a dozen with moderate frequency. But to find as many as seventeen consolidated into one, one must look to the highbrow magazines such as *Harper's* and *Atlantic*. Only superior adults can keep that many in mind at once and keep them all straight, too.

No one yet knows whether elementary school children can be hurried along this path.

KELLOGG W. HUNT

Recent Measures in
Syntactic Development

INTRODUCTION

According to Hunt, there are three well-established generalizations about the way in which the sentences of children change with the children's increasing maturity: (1) there are more of them, that is, children write more on a given topic as they get older; (2) the sentences become longer; and (3) the children use subordinate clauses more frequently. Hunt's investigation has led him to reformulate observations (2) and (3).

Hunt establishes a unit for measuring the frequencies of subordinate clauses and finds that, as expected, they increase as children mature. Next, he subclassifies the types of subordinate clauses to see if the various types all increase at the same rate. The result is that of the three main types— noun clauses, adverb clauses, and adjective clauses—the first two do not greatly increase with maturity. Consequently, point (3) above can be considerably refined: as children mature, they use more and more adjective clauses. As Hunt puts it, "we see, then, that the subordinate clause index is a team which moves ahead, but it moves ahead because one member does almost all the work."

Reprinted with permission of the author and the National Council of Teachers of English from *Elementary English,* Vol. XLIII (November), 1966, pp. 732–739.

Hunt points out that young children write strings of independent clauses whereas older children and adults reduce many of the independent clauses to subordinate clauses, particularly adjective clauses, which in turn are often reduced to adjectival phrases or even single words, for example, modifying adjectives and appositives. This process of reduction increases the total number of words per clause by decreasing the number of clauses. In effect, the older writers pack more information into fewer clauses by the grammatical processes known as embedding and deletion. As Hunt explains it,

> older students reduce more of their clauses to subordinate clause status, attaching them to other main clauses; and secondly . . . the clauses they do write, whether subordinate or main, happen to have more words in them.

In order to measure the amount of "packing" within the boundaries of the independent clause, Hunt proposes the "minimal terminable unit" or "T-unit" for short. Hunt defines the T-unit as "the shortest units into which a piece of discourse can be cut without leaving any sentence fragments as residue." Thus a T-unit always contains just one independent clause plus however many subordinate clauses there are attached to the independent clause. The T-unit can be used in several differer : ways. One way is to count the average *number* of T-units per sentence. Another way is to count the average *length* of T-units per sentence.

Hunt points out that fourth graders have more T-units on the average per sentence than superior adults do. This is a reflection of the comment made earlier that young children tend to make up sentences out of strings of independent clauses. The observation, incidentally, suggests that pure sentence length in itself is not a very revealing measure of syntactic sophistication.

On the other hand, the length of the average T-unit appears to be closely correlated with maturity of the writer. This, in turn, is a reflection of the earlier observation that older writers pack more into the T-unit by reducing independent clauses to subordinate clauses, and subordinate clauses to phrases and words. Hunt suggests that there are two possible ways to increasing the length of the T-unit: (1) add more dependent clauses and (2) lengthen the existing clauses by adding phrases and words (derived from reduced clauses). According to Hunt, both ways are important in increasing the size of the T-unit during the school years. In the writing of superior adults and superior twelfth graders, the length of the T-unit jumps significantly. Here the increased length seems to be solely the result of adding more words to the clauses without increasing their number. As Hunt puts it,

> to advance beyond the level of the average twelfth grader, the writer must learn to reduce and consolidate clauses much more often. Supe-

rior twelfth graders do not write more subordinate clauses than average twelfth graders. Instead they write much longer clauses, just as superior adults do.

Hunt closes the essay by turning the investigation to what makes a sentence hard to read. Longer sentences are harder to read than short ones. However, it is not sentence length that is the important factor, it is the fact that "the clauses are longer. And the clauses are longer, it can be inferred, only because more have been consolidated into a single one."

Any teacher of English can tell a fourth-grade theme from a twelfth-grade theme. Probably anyone in this room could make still finer distinctions: he could tell the average fourth-grade theme from the average eighth-grade theme. Just how would he detect the difference? For one thing he would rely on word choice. The vocabulary of the average eighth grader is measurably different from that of the average fourth grader. But also the teacher would feel that some of the sentence structures used by the eighth grader were too mature to be used by a fourth grader. Sentence structure, not vocabulary, is my subject for this paper.

The educational researcher respects the teacher's intuitive sense of maturity, but he wishes he knew how to measure it quantitatively, by counting something—if only he knew what to count. He knows of course that it takes centuries to build up a science. All during the Middle Ages the alchemists were poking away at the information which eventually led to modern scientific chemistry. It took centuries to establish the science. The science of measuring syntactic maturity is barely emerging from the stages of alchemy. It scarcely deserves to be called a science at all. But we do know a few things.

For the last thirty years we have known at least three things about the development of language structure. First, as children mature they tend to produce more words on any given subject. They have more to say. Second, as children mature, the sentences they use tend to be longer. Third, as children mature a larger proportion of their clauses are subordinate clauses.[*]

In the last two years it has been possible to add a few more measures, and I will come to them later. But first let me turn back to the statement about subordinate clauses and try to make clear its significance

[*] Dorothea McCarthy, "Language Development in Children." *Manual of Child Psychology*, ed. Leonard Carmichael. New York: John Wiley & Sons, Inc., 1954.

for the teaching program. It would be worse than useless for a fourth-grade teacher to say to her students, "Now if you will go back to your last paper and add more subordinate clauses to the main clauses, you will be writing like Miss Hill's wonderful sixth graders or Miss Summit's wonderful eighth graders instead of my own miserable fourth graders." Such an approach would be worse than useless. But the facts behind so useless a statement are not useless; they are useful if we know how to use them. Let us look at some fourth-grade writings. We find pairs of main clauses like this:

> There was a lady next door and the lady was a singer.

Now an older student would not be likely to repeat the noun *lady*. He might rewrite the two clauses in any of several ways: one way would be to reduce the second main clause to a relative adjective clause.

> There was a lady next door who was a singer.

Now instead of two main clauses and no subordinate clauses, we have one main clause and one subordinate clause.

Let me give you a few more examples of pairs of fourth-grade main clauses. In every instance one of the main clauses could have been reduced to a relative adjective clause.

> Moby Dick was a very big whale. He lived in the sea. (who lived in the sea.)
>
> His owner was a milkman. The milkman was very strict to the mother and babies. (who was very strict . . .)
>
> Once upon a time I had a cat. This cat was a beautiful cat. It was also mean. (who was a beautiful cat.)
>
> One day Nancy got a letter from her Uncle Joe. It was her great uncle. (who was her great uncle.)
>
> I have a new bicycle. I like to ride it. (which I like to ride.)
>
> We have a lot on Lake Talquin. This lot has a dock on it. (On Lake Talquin we have a lot which has a dock on it.)
>
> Today we went to see a film. The film was about a white-headed whale. (which was about a white-headed whale.)
>
> The jewel was in the drawer. It was red. (The jewel which was red . . .)
>
> Beautiful Joe was a dog, he was born on a farm. (that was born on a farm.)

> One colt was trembling. It was lying down on the hay. (One colt which was lying down . . .)

A convenient way to measure the frequency of subordinate clauses is to divide the total number of clauses, both subordinate and main, by the number of main clauses. I will call this the "subordinate clause index."[†] It is expressed as a decimal fraction. The index will always be 1 (for the main clause) plus whatever number of subordinate clauses are attached to it.

I find that average fourth-grade writers have a subordinate clause index of about 1.3; that is, they write a subordinate clause three-tenths as often as they write a main clause. Average eighth graders have an index of 1.4; they write a subordinate clause four-tenths as often as a main clause. Average twelfth graders have an index of 1.68. They write a subordinate clause about six-tenths as often as a main clause. If you jump now to the superior adult writers who produce articles for *Harper's* and *Atlantic* you find that they have an index of 1.78: they write about seven-tenths as many subordinate clauses as main clauses. However, some mature article writers have much higher indexes. One had a score of 2.36, indicating that his average main clause had one and a third subordinate clauses related to it.

The general trend of development is fairly clear: for fourth grade the score was 1.3, for eighth 1.4, for twelfth 1.6, and for superior adults 1.7.

It would be interesting to go back to the grades earlier than the fourth to see if the number of subordinate clauses is smaller back there. Fortunately Professors O'Donnell, Griffin, and Norris at Peabody have provided us with data within the last year.[‡] Reporting on their results for speech alone, they find a general increase in number of subordinate clauses from kindergarten to the seventh grade where the study ended. These kindergarten students have an index of 1.16. Putting their figures and mine together, we see that the trend is clear. From the first public school grade to the last the number of subordinate clauses increases steadily for every grade.

This tendency has implications for teaching language. Without ever using the words "main clause" and "subordinate clause," the language arts teacher who sees pairs of main clauses like those I have mentioned can show her students another way of saying the same thing.

[†] The "subordination ratio" which has been used for thirty years has usually been figured in another way.

[‡] Published as an NCTE research monograph entitled *A Transformational Analysis of the Language of Kindergarten and Elementary School Children*, NCTE Research Report #8. Champaign, Illinois, 1967.

One further refining statement can be made about subordinate clauses and the index of their frequency. There are three common kinds of such clauses: noun, movable adverb, and adjective. The other kinds, such as clauses of comparison, are uncommon. Though the total of all three increases with maturity, not all three increase equally. Noun clauses in general are no index of maturity: the number of them is determined instead by the mode of discourse, the subject matter, all the way from the early grades to maturity. Movable adverb clauses do seem to increase with maturity in the very early grades, but the ceiling is reached early, and after the middle grades the frequency of them tells more about mode of discourse and subject matter than about maturity. But adjective clauses are different. From the earliest grades to the latest the number of them increases steadily, and among skilled adults the adjective clause is still more frequent than it is with students finishing high school. We see, then, that the subordinate clause index is a team which moves ahead, but it moves ahead because one member does almost all the work. The other two sometimes pull ahead but sometimes pull back too, depending on factors other than mental maturity.

But of course subordinating clauses is not all there is to syntactic development. In every pair of examples I have given so far, it would have been possible to reduce one of the clauses still further so that it is no longer a clause at all, but merely a word or phrase consolidated inside the other clause. In this fashion two clauses will become one clause. The one clause will now be one word or one phrase longer than it was before, but it will be shorter than the two clauses were together. By throwing away some of one clause we will gain in succinctness. The final expression will be tighter, less diffuse, more mature.

Let me illustrate now with the same examples, and then back up the examples with figures to indicate that older students do indeed more often make one longer clause out of two shorter ones.

A clause with a predicate adjective can all be thrown away except for the adjective.

> Once upon a time I had a *beautiful, mean* cat.
> The *red* jewel was in the drawer.

Eighth graders write more than 150 percent as many single-word adjectives before nouns as fourth graders do.

If a clause contains a prepositional phrase after a form of *be* you can throw away all but that prepositional phrase.

The jewel *in the drawer* was red.
Today we saw a film *about Moby Dick.*

Eighth graders use such prepositional phrases to modify nouns 170 percent as often, and twelfth graders 240 percent as often, as fourth graders do.

If the clause contains a *have* you can often put what follows the *have* into a genitive form and throw away the rest.

I like to ride *my* new bicycle.
Our lot on Lake Talquin has a dock on it.

Twelfth graders used 130 percent as many genitives as fourth graders do.

If a clause contains a predicate nominal, it can become an appositive, and the rest can be thrown away.

There was a lady next door, *a singer.*
His owner, *a milkman,* was very strict to the mother and babies.
One day Nancy got a letter from her *great uncle* Joe.

Eighth graders wrote a third more appositives than fourth graders.

Often clauses with non-finite verbs can all be thrown away except for the verbs, which now become modifiers of nouns.

Beautiful Joe was a dog *born on a farm.*
One *trembling* colt was lying down on the hay.
One colt, *lying down on the hay,* was trembling.

Eighth graders wrote 160 percent and twelfth graders wrote 190 percent as many non-finite verb modifiers of nouns as fourth graders did.

I have used this set of examples twice now, to show two different things: first, how it is that older students reduce more of their clauses to subordinate clause status, attaching them to other main clauses; and secondly, how it is that the clauses they do write, whether subordinate or main, happen to have more words in them.§ Those extra added

§ A clause is here defined as one subject or one set of coordinate subjects with one finite verb or one finite set of coordinated verbs. Thus *I went home* is one clause, and so is *Jim and I went home and rode our bikes.*

The average clause length for any body of writing, however long or short, is simply the total number of words divided by the total number of clauses. For a sentence such as *She said he ought to try harder,* there are 7 words and 2 clauses, so the average clause length is 3.5 words for that body of writing.

words are not padding. They are all that is left out of useless whole clauses when the padding has been thrown away. From a six-word clause five words may be thrown away, with only one word salvaged. So adding that one more word to some other clause indicates a substantial gain. Though an increase of one word in clause length may not sound very impressive, a gain of five words or so in succinctness is indeed impressive. What was said in two clauses totalling twelve words is now said in one clause of seven words.

It is not as if some fourth-grade teacher had said "Add one word to each clause you have written." Instead it is as if she had said, "In this sentence you can throw away all but one word or one phrase. You can consolidate that word or phrase with this other expression into a larger, more comprehensively organized, unit of thought."

Substantial evidence is accumulating that as school children mature they do indeed learn to put their thoughts into longer and longer clauses. My own first research dealt with children of strictly average IQ, that is, with children having scores between 90 and 110. I worked first with three grades, fairly widely spaced: fourth grade, when students are just beginning to write with some degree of comfortableness; twelfth grade when the student of average IQ writes about as well as he ever will, perhaps; eighth grade, half way between the beginning and end of that public school period. The clauses written by these fourth graders were 6.6 words long. Clauses by eighth graders were 20 percent longer and clauses by twelfth graders were 30 percent longer. But development does not stop there. The writers of articles for *Harper's* and *Atlantic* write clauses about 175 percent as long as those written by fourth graders of average IQ. In fact, in clause length, the superior adult is farther ahead of the average twelfth grader than the average twelfth grader is ahead of his little brother back in the fourth grade.

If the evidence is as sound as it seems to be, then one ought to be able to predict on the basis of it. If this tendency to lengthen clauses is a general characteristic of linguistic development, then one might predict in several directions. He might predict that if growth is fairly steady after the fourth grade, then it probably is perceptible before the fourth grade too. And if growth occurs in writing, then it probably occurs in speech too. If one is going to measure the development which occurs earlier than the fourth grade, of course, it is speech, not writing, he must study.

Fortunately the Peabody study has provided us with some confirming evidence within the last few months. Notice the slight but steady

increase as I read these figures. The clauses spoken by the kindergarten children are 6.1 words long. For first graders, 6.7 words. For
second graders 7.1 words. Third graders 7.2. Fifth graders 7.5. Seventh
graders 7.8. At every grade level there is an increase in the clause
length of their speech. Clause length plots as a smooth rising curve, all
the way to the maturity of *Harper's* and *Atlantic* articles.

One might predict in yet another direction. He might predict that
children with superior IQ's will have matured more in language structure at even an early age. Since my results are not conclusive at this
time, I am not sure whether, as early as the fourth grade, children with
IQ scores above 130 write, on the average, slightly longer clauses and
write a larger proportion of subordinate clauses than fourth graders
with average IQ. By the time children of superior IQ reach the twelfth
grade, however, their superiority in clause-length is unmistakable.
They are almost as far ahead of average twelfth graders as average
twelfth graders are ahead of fourth graders. In fact, in clause length,
twelfth graders with IQ above 130 are closer to writers of *Harper's* and
Atlantic articles than they are to twelfth graders of average IQ.

These longer clauses written by older students are not produced by
combining just two clauses, but by combining four or six or eight.
Superior adults can combine a dozen clauses into one, by the process
already briefly suggested.

So, for a third time, I suggest that teachers who understand the findings of language development research may be able to apply those
findings in the classroom. For years teachers have occasionally combined pairs of clauses as we were doing here a few minutes ago. But
so far as I know it has never occurred to anyone to show that six or
eight or a dozen are often consolidated into one mature clause. It is
by this process that little sentences grow into big ones.‖

Here is a clause written by an average eighth grader. "He was a rare
white whale with a crooked jaw." That consolidates five clauses.
(1) He was a whale. (2) The whale was white. (3) The whale was
rare. (4) The whale had a jaw. (5) The jaw was crooked. Average
fourth graders do not ordinarily write like that. In fact, in five thousand
clauses written by fourth graders we found a single nominal that
resulted from as many as five of these consolidations only three times.
Five is simply too many for a fourth grader, but he often consolidates
three.

‖ See "How Little Sentences Grow into Big Ones," a paper by Kellogg W. Hunt
read at the NCTE's Spring Institute on New Directions in Elementary English,
Chicago, March 7, 1966, to be published with the proceedings of that institute.

Despite this eighth grader's relative maturity, even he failed to consolidate clauses where he might have. He missed opportunities. He wrote:

> Moby Dick was a dangerous whale. People had never been able to catch him. He was a rare white whale with a crooked jaw. He was a killer too. He was long and strong.

There are many ways to consolidate this further and I won't rewrite the whole passage. The first two clauses could well be consolidated and so could the last two:

> Moby Dick was a dangerous whale that people had never been able to catch. He was a killer too, long and strong.

I am recommending, then, that throughout the elementary and secondary grades the process of clause-consolidation is one of the things which the language arts program should study. Transformational grammarians speak of this process as the result of embedding and deletion transformations.

Finally I want to describe to you a new unit of measurement which is very convenient for syntactic development research. It is certainly more significant than sentence length which is still reported to be the most widely used measure of language maturity.[#] To introduce this unit let me read a theme as written by one of our fourth graders. The theme is one sentence long.

> I like the movie we saw about Moby Dick the white whale the captain said if you can kill the white whale Moby Dick I will give this gold to the one that can do it and it is worth sixteen dollars they tried and tried but while they were trying they killed a whale and used the oil for the lamps they almost caught the white whale.

In sentence length this fourth grader is superior to the average writer in *Harper's* and *Atlantic*. Now let me cut that sentence up into the new units. Each unit will consist of exactly one main clause plus whatever subordinate clauses happen to be attached to or embedded within it.

> 1. I like the movie we saw about Moby Dick, the white whale.
> 2. The captain said if you can kill the white whale, Moby Dick, I will give this gold to the one that can do it.

[#] For instance, see the article on "Language Development" in the 1960 edition of the *Encyclopaedia of Educational Research*.

3. And it is worth sixteen dollars.
4. They tried and tried.
5. But while they were trying they killed a whale and used the oil for the lamps.
6. They almost caught the white whale.

For lack of a better name I call these units "minimal terminable units." They are "terminable" in the sense that it is grammatically acceptable to terminate each one with a capital letter at the beginning and a period or question mark at the end. They are "minimal" in the sense that they are the shortest units into which a piece of discourse can be cut without leaving any sentence fragments as residue. They are thus "minimal terminable units." I wish I could call these units "the shortest allowable sentences" but instead I call them "T-units," for short. To repeat, each is exactly one main clause plus whatever subordinate clauses are attached to that main clause.

In ordinary prose about half the sentences consist of just one such T-unit. The other half of the sentences consist of two or more T-units, often joined with *and's*. Such sentences are "compound," or "compound-complex." Cutting a passage into T-units cuts each compound sentence or compound-complex sentence into two or more T-units. Now if it were true that as writers mature they put more and more T-units into their sentences, then sentence length would be a better measure of maturity than T-unit length. But such is not the case. Occasionally a very young student will string one T-unit after another after another, with *ands* between or nothing between. The passage I read a moment ago combined six T-units into one sentence. The result of this tendency is that my fourth graders average more T-units per sentence than superior adults do. That fact upsets sentence length as an index of maturity. That same fact explains why T-unit length is a better index of maturity than sentence length.

A useful name for the average number of T-units per sentence might be "main clause coordination index." It probably should not be called "sentence coordination index."

Now let us pull all these various indexes together into a single piece of arithmetic. "Average clause length" is the number of words per clause. "Subordinate clause index" is the number of clauses per T-unit. "Average T-unit length" is the number of words per T-unit. "Main clause coordination index" is the number of T-units per sentence. "Average sentence length" is the number of words per sentence.

These five measures are very useful analytically and are all related arithmetically. The number of words per clause times the number of

clauses per T-unit equals the number of words per T-unit. That times
the number of T-units per sentence gives the number of words per
sentence. The first index times the second equals the third. The third
times the fourth equals the fifth. Clause length times subordinate
clause index equals T-unit length. That figure times main clause coordination index equals sentence length.**

Finally, as a review, let me mention again the tendencies that have
been known for thirty years concerning the development of language
structure. First, as students mature they tend to have more to say
about any subject. Second, as students mature their sentences tend to
get longer. Third, as students mature they tend to write more subordinate clauses per main clause.

In the last few years a few more statements about syntactic development have been added. First, as students mature they tend to produce
longer clauses. From kindergarten to at least the seventh grade, and
probably beyond that time, this appears to be true of speech. And
from the beginning to at least the twelfth grade this appears to be true
of writing. Clause length is a better index of language maturity than
sentence length. You will recall that clauses can be lengthened by a
process that is here described as reduction and consolidation. That
same process is described by generative-transformational grammarians
as embedding transformations. Second, a convenient unit, intervening
in size between the clause and the compound sentence is the "minimal
terminable unit," defined as one main clause plus whatever subordinate
clauses are attached to it or embedded within. This too is a better
index of language maturity than sentence length. You will recall that
"T-units" can be lengthened either by lengthening clauses or by increasing the number of subordinate clauses per T-unit. In the writing
of average students throughout the public school grades, the one factor
is about as influential as the other in effecting longer T-units. But the
equality of influence stops there. The average twelfth grader has
approached the ceiling in number of subordinate clauses. To advance
beyond the level of the average twelfth grader, the writer must learn
to reduce and consolidate clauses much more often. Superior twelfth
graders do not write more subordinate clauses than average twelfth
graders. Instead they write much longer clauses, just as superior adults
do.

But making one clause out of two is child's play. Long before the

** Kellogg W. Hunt, "A Synopsis of Clause-to-Sentence Factors," *English
Journal*, 54 (April 1965) 300–309. Also Kellogg W. Hunt, *Grammatical Structures
Written at Three Grade Levels*, Research Report #3, NCTE, Champaign, Ill.,
1965.

average child gets to the fourth grade he can consolidate two, though he does not do so very often. Some average fourth graders consolidate three into one. Some average eight graders consolidate four into one. Some average twelfth graders consolidate five into one. Superior twelfth graders consolidate six and seven. Superior adults consolidate more than that.†† For a teacher to stretch a youngster, to push against the limits of his present accomplishment, two is nowhere near enough.

So far I have talked only about building up little sentences into bigger ones. Before I close I want to mention the other side of the coin, breaking big sentences down into little ones, as the mature reader or listener does with such lightning speed.

In recent months we have compared the syntactic traits that make a sentence hard to write and the syntactic traits that make it hard to read. We have compared the sentences written by children with those read by them but written by adults. For our reading samples we have used the *McCall-Crabbs Reading Lessons,* since the readability of each passage therein is supposedly already established. The passages cover roughly grades four to nine.

We find that sentences more difficult to read do not have more T-units per sentence. The number is about the same whether the sentences are easy or difficult. Listen to this sameness for grades 4 to 9: 1.13, 1.12, 1.13, 1.10, 1.13, 1.10.

You will remember that as children mature they tend to write subordinate clauses more often. But as sentences written by adults get easier or harder to read there seems to be no change. Listen to this sameness for passages that are 80 percent comprehensible to children in grades 4 through 9: 1.4, 1.4, 1.4, 1.4, 1.4, 1.4. (It sounds as if the record player were stuck in the same groove.)

But the clause length of passages, for 80 percent comprehension, increases steadily for grades 4 through 9 just as it increases as children write. Here are our figures so far: 8.45, 9.13, 9.59, 10.19, 11.01, 10.83.

In other words, the difficulty in reading sentences usually lies down inside the clause. Longer clauses tend to be more difficult. On the basis of previous research on what constitutes these clauses, it seems clear what it is that makes longer clauses harder to read and harder to write. On the whole, longer clauses have a larger number of sentences or clauses reduced and consolidated into one. It is by that process that little clauses grow into big ones.

†† Kellogg W. Hunt, *Sentence Structures Used by Superior Students in Grades Four and Twelve, and by Superior Adults.* USOE Research Project No. 5-0313. Available from ERIC Document Reproducing Service, Bell and Howell, 1700 Shaw Boulevard, Cleveland, Ohio 44112.

Little by little the evidence piles up that the reduction and consolidation of many clauses into one is intimately related to syntactic growth both in writing and reading. If writers must build up clauses, then readers must break them down. A whole new range of applications is opened up for approaching reading difficulty.

For many years we have known that longer sentences tend to be harder to read. But in the last few months we have learned more about why that is true. It is not because longer sentences have more T-units coordinated into them, for they do not. It is not because they have more subordinate clauses attached to main clauses, for they do not. Instead it is because the clauses are longer. And the clauses are longer, it can be inferred, only because more have been consolidated into a single one.

All this has implications for the teaching of reading in the early grades. Teachers need to be trained in clause-consolidation so that children can be taught what otherwise they must discover unaided. They will discover it. That we know. But at present they must do so unaided.

Here is another place where the results of research should crawl out of the learned journals and into the classroom.

MARK LESTER

The Value of Transformational
Grammar in Teaching Composition

INTRODUCTION

The essay begins with the assertion that "there simply appears to be no
correlation between a writer's conscious study of grammar and his ability
to write." If we accept this view, will the study of transformational grammar succeed in improving writing where earlier theories of grammar have
failed? Lester answers that it will not for several reasons: (1) the entry
price for transformational grammar is high. In order to apply transformational grammar to the problems of style, the student must first learn the
grammar. On the college level, at least, there is simply not enough time to
teach both the fundamental theory of transformational grammar and also its
application to writing within the compass of the usual freshman English
course. (2) The theory of transformational grammar itself suggests that the
conscious study of language may have only a remote connection with
language behavior.

Lester argues that a transformational grammar is a deductive approach
to language, as opposed to structural linguistics which used an inductive
approach. In crude terms, a deductive approach begins with abstract rules

Reprinted with permission of the author and the National Council of Teachers
of English from *College Composition and Communication*, Vol. XVIII, No. 5
(December), 1967, pp. 227–231.

and moves to tangible data to show the operation of these rules, whereas an inductive theory begins with data and works toward abstract generalizations about the data. In the transformational view, a child approaches the data of his language deductively, that is, he deduces a grammar for his own language from the innate general principles that must underlie all human languages. These abstract general principles are completely beyond his conscious awareness. The structural view is that the child discovers the patterns of his language in an inductive way. The transformational grammarians draw a distinction between competence and performance. Competence is the amazing linguistic capacity every speaker of a language possesses for his language. Performance is the tangible produce of competence. Lester claims that performance is the proper subject matter of the composition class because it can be discussed and compared with other performances. Competence is simply too abstract to grapple with. Lester's main point is that

> the complexity of human language competence is so vast that we can hardly expect our petty tinkering with the surface of performance to produce lasting results.

The balance of the essay is devoted to a slightly different topic. Lester notes that a student's level of verbal performance often seems to outstrip his level of written performance. If we assume that the same linguistic competence underlies both, the fact that the two levels of performance are not the same seems counter to the theory. Lester argues that the faults we find with student composition, "abrupt transitions, vague pronoun references, poor organization, unintended ambiguity" and the like, are characteristic of spoken communication, even by the most careful speakers. The point is that in conversation the speaker receives a feedback from the hearer which enables him to make the necessary corrections and explanations. Obviously, in written communication the writer seldom receives any immediate and continuous feedback from the reader. However, the writer does have the advantage of being able to rewrite at his leisure. Unless the writer is able to seize this advantage and comes to see his performance as the reader will see it, he will have great difficulty in communicating clearly. Lester claims that

> the writer's inability to project himself into the role of a reader is the single most important cause for the difference in levels of verbal and written performances.

Lester argues that there is a quite specific reason from the transformational point of view why it is so difficult for the writer to play the role of a reader. The structural linguist's view of the "chain of speech" was that the speaker encoded his message into language and transmitted the language through some physical vehicle—sound waves or marks on paper, as the case may be. The hearer/reader decoded the language from the vehicle in some inductive way and then discovered the message from the language.

The transformationalists, however, offer a completely different view of operations that the hearer/reader go through. Lester argues that

> the vehicle does not contain enough information to allow the receiver to abstract the language from the vehicle inductively.

Instead, they argue that the hearer/reader must impose an interpretation on the vehicle by some kind of matching process, that is, the hearer/reader matches his expectations, both linguistic and nonlinguistic, against the sound or marks he perceives. When his interpretation coincides with his preception of the vehicle, the resulting match is taken as the speaker's intended message. The key point here is that the role of the hearer/reader is not passive, but quite active. He is continually unconsciously testing and adjusting his own understanding. As a consequence of this view,

> when the sender and receiver are one and the same, the matching process is completely short-circuited; he does not need to perceive the words because he already knows the meaning. This is why it is almost impossible for a writer to see his essay the same way any other reader will. For the writer, the transitions are not abrupt, the pronoun references are perfectly clear, the organization is transparent, and there is no unintended ambiguity because he knows perfectly well what the sender's exact message is.

Lester closes the essay with a suggestion for a classroom trick to get across to students the magnitude of the problem of seeing their own writing as the reader will see it.

The value of transformational grammar as a theory of language is great and consequently it is a legitimate field of study in its own right. However, it is a moot question as to whether it has any direct value per se in the teaching of composition. We would all agree that the goal of composition teaching is to enable the student to write better. The value of transformational grammar must be measured in terms of that goal.

The fact that a goal is universally applauded does not, unfortunately, mean that it is universally understood. In fact, I see two quite different meanings of "better writing." One is better grammatically, that is, a paper that has fewer grammatical errors than a second paper is better written than the second. The other meaning is better stylistically, that is, if two papers are equally free from grammatical error, the one that is better organized and more fluent is better written than the other.

Composition classes often separate these two goals completely. Unfortunately, the first tends to drive out the second by a kind corollary to Gresham's Law: the tangible is preferred to the intangible. We have all had students in our freshman classes who got straight A's in their high school composition courses solely through the negative virtue of being able to write a sentence free of mechanical error. The fact that the students' papers were banal in content and incoherent in organization was never noticed by the harassed teacher who considered the assignment a success if the bulk of the essays were written on one side of the page.

Most teachers would justify teaching grammar on the grounds that its study would improve the student's ability to write a grammatical sentence. Unlike its predecessors, transformational grammar has been very wary about making any such claim. Eighteenth-century Latin grammars, nineteenth-century historical grammars, and twentieth-century structural grammars all claimed salutary benefits. These claims, however, when put to the test, have all proven false. There simply appears to be no correlation between a writer's conscious study of grammar and his ability to write. The claim is obviously false, for, if it were true, then all linguists would be great writers.

It could be argued, as each of the above grammars did about its predecessor, that because the newest form of grammar is so superior to the bad old grammars it will succeed where the others have failed. Having been led down the garden path three times before by linguists, I think composition teachers have the right to be suspicious of claims of utility until the usefulness has actually been demonstrated. Frank Zidonis at Ohio State University has been studying the effect of transformational grammar on the writing of junior high school children. His findings are encouraging, but far from conclusive.

On the college level, "better writing" generally means better stylistically. In the area of stylistic analysis, transformational grammar promises exciting things. Richard Ohmann's article in the December 1964 issue of *Word*, "Generative Grammars and the Concept of Literary Style," is impressive. In this article, Ohmann differentiates the style of several modern writers in terms of the characteristic way each combines kernel sentences. Henry James, for instance, relies on a self-embedding process, while D. H. Lawrence relies on deletion and

Faulkner on a piling up of kernel and near kernel sentences. In the following excerpt, Ohmann summarizes the basic idea of his approach.

> A generative grammar with a transformational component provides apparatus for breaking down a sentence in a stretch of discourse into underlying kernel sentences (or strings, strictly speaking) and for specifying the grammatical operations that have been performed upon them. It also permits the analyst to construct, from the same set of kernel sentences, other non-kernel sentences. These may reasonably be thought of as *alternatives* to the original sentence, in that they are simply different constructs out of the identical elementary grammatical units. Thus the idea of alternative phrasings, which is crucial to the notion of style, has a clear analogue within the framework of a transformational grammar.

Does the application of transformational grammar to stylistic analysis justify the study of grammar in the composition class? I think that the answer must be No. Last year I was allowed to conduct an experimental class of first semester Freshman English using transformational grammar. At the end of the semester, I reluctantly reported that the experiment should not be repeated because, while in some ways the operation was a success, the patient had died.

The main difficulty with the course was a mechanical one: I was forced to use two-thirds of the semester teaching grammar. This did not leave much time to explore the applications of transformational grammar to grammatical and stylistic problems. By the ordinary measure, my students could not organize and write a theme as well as students in a rhetorically oriented section because we were left with almost no time to deal with rhetorical problems. The course was a success in that the students seemed to enjoy it, and they felt that they had gained a great deal from it in terms of their understanding of language. The fact remains that, however pleasant the side effects, the study of transformational grammar as an aid in teaching composition could not justify itself in terms of the time expended on the grammar.

Mechanical problems are amenable to mechanical solutions. The applications of transformational grammar could be studied in Freshman English if the responsibility for teaching it were pushed off onto the high school, the universal cure for all our problems. The high schools are, of course, totally unprepared to assume such a burden, and are so naive as to look to the colleges and universities for guidance.

Before committing ourselves to a massive retraining program of all English teachers, I think it is important to examine more carefully (1) what the basic concepts of transformational grammar are and

(2) what implication these concepts have for the pedagogical application of transformational grammar in general.

For the transformational grammarian, the study of language falls under the model of scientific explanation that has been called the "covering law model" by its originator, Rudolf Carnap. The essence of the covering law model is that an assertion can be proved only by its ability to predict data. Einstein verified his general theory of relativity by predicting that when a solar eclipse took place, the stars next to the sun, normally invisible because of the sun's light, would appear to shift over a few seconds of a degree.

The covering law model is essentially a deductive theory. Einstein deduced that, if his theory was correct, light would have mass and, as a further consequence, light would bend in the gravitational field of the sun. The covering law model says nothing about methods of data collection, nor does it inquire how the scientist got his idea in the first place. It may seem pointless to labor the definition of a deductive theory, but linguistics up to the publication of Chomsky's *Syntactic Structures* was dominated by a rigorously inductive model of scientific explanation. The profound differences between these two approaches to scientific theory are discussed brilliantly in Michael Polanyi's *Personal Knowledge*.

What a grammatical theory of a language must predict is the totality of all the grammatical sentences in the language, along with an analysis of each that can account for a native speaker's ability to recognize ambiguity and paraphrase. To do this, the transformational grammarian predicates the existence of a small number of element-like units, such as noun phrase, verb phrase, and transitive verb, which can combine in a large number of ways to form molecular units, or sentences.

The implications of this theory of grammar bear directly on the teaching of composition. For a child to learn to speak, he must have the innate capacity of building a theory of his own language that enables him to generate and understand an infinite number of new sentences. This theory is built without conscious effort, without external rewards or punishments, and without any necessary instruction from the adult community. This amazing linguistic capacity or competence is apparently the birthright of every normal child.

Miller, Galanter and Pribram in their highly respected book, *Plans and the Structure of Behavior*, argue that our conscious minds are almost totally ignorant of how or by what steps or processes we perform any complex process or skill. In other words, the performance of a skill involves innate competencies beyond our conscious knowledge and control. A poet can no more describe how he actually writes a poem than Willie Mays can tell how he actually hits a curve ball. This strongly suggests that there is little hope that by teaching a student conscious grammatical rules we can affect his unconscious grammatical processes.

Transformational grammar has thus clearly separated innate language competence from actual language performance. Only the performance is tangible. In composition classes we can discuss it, evaluate its success or failure, and compare it with similar performances. This seems to me the proper study of composition. Competence, on the other hand, like the part of the iceberg below the surface, is always there, but is never visible.

All too often, however, composition classes try to deal with competence. Students are assigned books of logic in order that they may learn to think straight. They are given rhetorical forms in which to channel their thoughts (which have assumedly already been properly straightened by the study of logic). They are given methods of composing, such as outlining their essays before they begin writing. The fallacy here, of course, is that logic and rhetoric are conscious processes of analysis that can be applied only to the performance *ex post facto*.

Assuming that the logical and rhetorical faults in the student's performance have been called to his conscious attention, we cannot thereby guarantee that this conscious instruction will in any way affect the student's basic competence. And unless the level of competence is altered, the student's performance next week will be about the same as it was this week. It may seem the counsel of despair to say that, if we cannot improve the student's writing, at least we do it no harm, but even this sorry consolation may not be true. Albert Kitzhaber reported in his book *Themes, Theories, and Therapy: The Teaching of Writing in College* that college sophomores at Dartmouth, on the average, wrote slightly worse than they did as entering freshmen, but by the time they had become seniors their writing had noticeably deteriorated from its pre-college peak. The point, stated more seriously, is that the complexity of human language competence is so vast that we can hardly expect our petty tinkering with the surface of performance to produce lasting results.

There is at least one area, nevertheless, where I think transformational grammar can be very helpful to the composition teacher. We have all noticed that the level of some students' verbal performance is much higher than the level of their written performance. This seems all the more puzzling since we have assumed that the same basic language competence underlies both.

From the standpoint of the communications engineer, however, the two situations are quite different. In conversation the speaker's language is riddled with abrupt transitions, vague pronoun references, poor organization, unintended ambiguity and all the other faults we find in his written work. Unless the speaker is grossly inept, this verbal stumbling does not block communication; in fact, the hearer usually notices very little of it. What makes communication possible in this situation is the ability of the speaker to gauge the reaction of the hearer. He can tell when the hearer is puzzled and can make further explanations. He continually readjusts the rate of information. In short, he relies on the phenomenon called feedback.

In writing, the situation is reversed. The writer has the opportunity to pick and choose his words at leisure, to rewrite as much as he wants; but he has no feedback from the reader at all. The task of the writer, then, is to compensate for his loss of feedback by anticipating the reader's reactions. This in turn demands that the writer can see his performance as the reader will see it. I believe that the writer's inability to project himself into the role of a reader is the single most important cause for the difference in levels of verbal and written performances.

Transformational grammar offers some suggestion why this role reversal is so difficult for the writer. All grammatical theories agree, at least in general, that the communication process involves a message, a language of some sort, a vehicle to carry the language, a sender and a receiver. There is also a general agreement about the sender's part of the communication process. The sender encodes the message into language and then encodes the language onto some physical vehicle— usually either sound waves or marks on paper. This is a model of behavior; the actual process, of course, is almost totally unconscious.

There is no general agreement on the model for the process that the receiver uses to decode the message. Structural linguistics committed itself to a model that predicates a sequential decoding. That is, the receiver completely decoded the language from the vehicle before decoding the message from the language. Transformational grammarians have gone to a great deal of effort to prove that this inductive model cannot be literally true. Chomsky, it seems to me, has demonstrated beyond doubt that the vehicle does not contain enough information to allow the receiver to abstract the language from the vehicle inductively.

The transformationalist's model is that the receiver continually operates both inductively in stripping the language from the vehicle and deductviely in generating the language from what the receiver predicts the message to be. Thus there is a kind of matching process in operation at the level of language: the receiver fits together the information from the vehicle and the information from the supposed message. When the fit is poor, the receiver must readjust either his understanding of the vehicle or his projection of the message, or both. This model is important for the composition teacher because it casts the reader into a very active role; he must continually match expectation against perception. As Kant said, "Ideas without content are empty, observations without concepts are blind."

The pedagogical corollary of this theory is that when the sender and receiver are one and the same, the matching process is completely short-circuited; he does not need to perceive the words because he already knows the meaning. This is why it is almost impossible for a writer to see his essay the same way any other reader will. For the writer, the transitions are not abrupt, the pronoun references are perfectly clear, the organization is transparent, and there is no unintended ambiguity because he knows perfectly well what the sender's exact message is.

I might mention here a classroom trick that seems helpful in getting students to realize the magnitude of this problem. I present a student essay one sentence at a time. I then ask members of the class to predict what the next sentence will be about and how he is able to make that prediction. Then I show the sentence the student actually wrote. The frequent contrast between prediction and reality is a source of fruitful discussion. I hope by this means to enable the class to see each sentence as a link in a gradually unfolding chain of ideas and relations. In a good essay each sentence adds to the reader's store of information and enables him to predict even more accurately the next sentence.

To return to the original question of this paper, the study of transformational grammar in a composition class cannot be justified until it can be demonstrated that the study of grammatical competence will affect grammatical performance. I have also suggested some reasons why this demonstration may be a long time in coming. The application of transformational grammar to stylistic analysis is promising, but the exploitation of this possibility is entirely dependent upon the study of transformational grammar in high school.

The great value of transformational grammar, it seems to me, is not for the student, but for the teacher of composition. Every decision the teacher makes is a reflection of an assumption that the teacher has tacitly made about the nature of language. The more the teacher is made aware of these assumptions and of their consequences the better he can assess their validity. Without this assessment, the teacher is condemned to a treadmill existence: forever changing texts and techniques, but never getting anywhere.

LEONARD NEWMARK

Grammatical Theory and the Teaching of English as a Foreign Language

INTRODUCTION

Newmark begins by drawing a distinction between two different ways of language teaching. In one way, the teaching material is organized and taught on the basis of the structure of the language. The other way, the "natural" or "direct" way, subordinates linguistic concerns to teaching "natural utterances that living people would use to say what they actually might want to say."

We tend to think of traditional language teaching as belonging to the first way and the linguistic approach to language teaching as belonging to the second. Newmark points out that as time has past, the language materials produced by structural linguists have become more and more concerned with structural habits and less and less concerned with language in context. The result, according to Newmark, is that

> both traditional and structural textbooks select and organize material in the interests of a particular view of the principles governing linguistic form, and both isolate linguistic forms from natural contexts.

Reprinted with permission of the author from *The 1963 Conference Papers of the English Language Section of the National Association for Foreign Affairs*, ed. by David P. Harris, pp. 5–8.

With the advent of transformational grammar, language teachers have a powerful new view of the structure of English, and are tempted to employ this new view in their textbooks. Newmark suggests three ways in which transformational grammar tempts the language teacher.

1. Transformational grammar, at least in some areas, offers a description of English which is a genuine explanation rather than a display of data, and consequently the language teacher is tempted to include these areas in his teaching. Also, since transformational grammar is able to deal with more than just surface structures, it has a great advantage in constructing contrastive grammars to explain the differences and similarities between the first and second languages.

2. It is a temptation for the structure of a transformational grammar to be used as a model for the organization of the language course. For example, the sequence of material taught might follow the order of the rules in the grammar. Specifically, the language course might (a) teach kernel sentences first, and then the ways that kernels can be expanded; (b) teach new vocabulary only in the kernel sentence, since that is the entry point for lexical items in the grammar; and (c) delay teaching phonology, the last stage in the cycle of rules in a transformational grammar, until a relatively late point in the language program.

3. The language teacher is tempted to use transformational grammar because its psychological and pedagogical implications seem desirable. Newmark gives three instances: (a) transformational drills are easy to write and easy to use in the classroom; (b) transformational grammar does not place such great emphasis on the sound system per se. In particular, this allows the language teacher to de-emphasize the role of suprasegmental features; and (c) the transformational grammarian is interested in the same thing that the language teacher is—"the intuitive ability of the speakers of a language to generate new sentences." Furthermore, the rules of a transformational grammar are "dynamic and prescriptive, in a sense acceptable to language teachers."

Newmark concludes the article by returning to his original point: the duty of a language teacher is to teach the student to use the language in a natural way, not to teach linguistic forms in a synthetic way. Consequently, Newmark warns the language teacher against the temptation of misusing transformational grammar the way structural linguistics was misused. Newmark says that "the whole question of the utility of grammatical analysis for language teaching needs to be reopened." He concludes with three facts that support his position: (1) systematic attention to grammatical form is neither necessary nor sufficient for successful language learning; (2) teaching language in meaningful and usable contexts is both sufficient

and necessary for successful language learning; and (3) the formal properties of sentences do not reflect "relationships of meaningful use," and consequently, teaching formal relations is "incompatible with the only necessary
and sufficient method we know has succeeded for every speaker of a
language."

A great contribution of linguists to the teaching of foreign language
was made by the "liberal" nineteenth- and twentieth-century grammarians like Otto Jespersen who taught us to view natural languages
freshly as worthy objects of teaching: the liberal grammarians freed
us from a tradition of teaching artificial sentences constructed and
studied as illustrations of rules of formal grammar, and they urged
that we teach natural utterances that living people would use to say
what they actually might want to say. Various "natural" or "direct"
methods had grown and continued to grow out of such discontent with
traditional language teaching. When structural linguists first faced the
problem of developing methods to teach exotic languages, and later
languages like English, they maintained this "natural" emphasis on
teaching concrete uses of language.

But as structuralists grew more and more confident about the "scientific" analysis of language, they modified their teaching programs more
and more to reflect these analyses: phonemic drills and structural pattern drills were increasingly elevated from the minor role they played
in the early Army language courses to the major role they play in, say,
the Michigan English Language Institute textbooks or in recent FSI
books. This increase in pattern drill is an index of the return from
"natural" material to grammatical-illustration material.* In the traditional textbook the examples seem to be given largely for the sake of
an intellectual understanding of the formulated rules, while in the
newer structural textbook the examples are practiced on to instill
implicit "habits" whose formulation in rules may not even be presented
explicitly; but both traditional and structural textbooks select and

---

*I am, of course, aware of the vast differences between the older tradition and
the newer structural tradition in the number and selection of the illustrative
examples, the use to which these examples are put, and the underlying grammar
which the examples are selected to illustrate. Nevertheless, I see an important
similarity in the kind of systematicness which both orthodoxies take as being the
guiding principle of language teaching: whether given the name "structural
habits" or "rules of grammar," the systematicness is primarily one of formal construction rather than appropriateness of use.

organize material in the interests of a particular view of the principles governing linguistic form, and both isolate linguistic forms from natural contexts.

Now that we have a new view—that presented by transformational grammars—of the principles (or, if you like, the habits or rules) governing the formal properties of English sentences,† there are great temptations to write new language textbooks to reflect this view. The temptations tempt in several ways:‡

First, on the premise that the best description of a language affords the best base upon which to build a language-teaching program, the transformational grammar of English should appeal to authors of TEFL materials. In an important sense transformational grammar is the most promising response we have to our common desire for descriptions that explain rather than merely display language data. For example, the transformationalist's derivation of imperative sentences from underlying strings with *you* as subject and *will* as the modal auxiliary makes possible an explanation of many things—from the traditional intuition about the understood *you* in imperatives to the fact (unexplained by orthodox structural linguists) that the "interrogative tags" on the imperative are *won't you* or *will you*. In general, the transformationist's analysis of verb phrase constructions, beginning with Chomsky's simple C(M) (have + en) (be + ing) V formula, brings startling simplicity and clarity to our understanding of the

---

† What I have to say bears most clearly on English, since that is the language for which the most detailed set of generative rules has been formulated, but I see no particular characteristics of other languages that would militate against the validity of the position I take in the following discussion.

‡ The most recent statement of the attractions of transformational grammar as a base for teaching foreign languages has been made by Karl V. Teeter in his review of Elinor C. Horne's *Beginning Javanese* in *Language* 39.146–151 (1963). Other tentative suggestions about the bearing of transformational grammar on the learning of languages have been offered by Yehoshua Bar-Hillel, "Third Lecture: Language and Speech; Theory vs. Observation in Linguistics," in *Four Lectures on Algebraic Linguistics and Machine Translation* (an unpublished series of lectures given in July 1962, before a NATO Advanced Summer Institute on Automatic Translation of Languages in Venice, Italy), Noam Chomsky, "Explanatory Models in Linguistics," *Logic, Methodology and Philosophy of Science: Proceedings of the 1960 International Congress*, edited by E. Nagel, P. Suppes, and A. Tarski, 1962, pp. 529–531, Richard Gunter, "A Problem in Transformational Teaching," *Language Learning* XI. 119–124 (1961), Mary S. Temperley, "Transformations in *English Sentence Patterns*," *Language Learning* XI. 125–134 (1961), to mention only a few. Textbooks in the teaching of English as a foreign language have been written and used by B. Kirk Rankin, III, and John J. Kane, Jr., *Review Exercises in English Grammar*, Washington, D. C., 1962, and Paul Roberts (reported in *The Linguistic Reporter* IV, No. 6, December 1962). I have not had the opportunity to examine the latter, but the former makes the application I allude to below.

grammatical structure of a number of discontinuous and elliptical verb constructions; transformational grammar seems to offer suggestions neatly and precisely for what a program for teaching English verb structure would have to include.

If contrastive grammars of native language with target language are assumed to be required for optimal planning of EFL materials, then it should seem obvious that the explicitness of generative grammars for each language is necessary for making explicit comparisons between two languages. A generative grammar has the advantage of showing not only the direct and superficial, physically manifest similarities and differences between two languages, but also the more profound differences and similarities between languages that appear when the rules of sentence formation are required to be explicitly formulated.

The second temptation I want to talk about derives from the fact that the grammar of English contains an *ordering* of rules. It seems to follow naturally that a teaching program follow the order of the rules, so that a student would learn grammatically prior rules (or habits) before grammatically later ones. Thus, he might learn the rules that generate sentences with noun objects (e.g. *I like her cake*) before he learns rules that generate sentences with nominalizations as objects (e.g. *I like her singing*); or he might learn in a general way that verbs may have objects before he learns the rules which permit him to distinguish which classes of verbs may have which classes of objects.

On a grander scale, we might even suggest specifically that an elementary EFL course limit itself to teaching only kernel sentences and that only in intermediate and advanced courses would sentences involving optional transformations be introduced. The pedagogical rationale here would be that teaching should proceed from grammatically simpler to more complex, inasmuch as this can be expected to agree with the psychological direction of less difficult to more difficult; few educators would disagree that progression from easy to difficult is important to gain efficiency in learning and to reduce the frustration of failure. That grammatical simplicity might be an index of psychological easiness has been suggested by a number of respectable linguists and psychologists.[§]

§ See Bar-Hillel, *op. cit.*, "Second Lecture: Syntactic Complexity"; Noam Chomsky and George Miller, "Finitary Models of Language Users," *Handbook of Mathematical Psychology* (in press), cited in Bar-Hillel lecture above; and Teeter, *op. cit.* and references cited in these articles for discussion of the suggestion.

Such a precise non-arbitrary notion of what constitutes simplicity in language would afford an attractive alternative to the superficial kind of grading of teaching materials that we have seen so often in textbooks. The ordering of rules and sets of rules that characterize a transformational grammar seems to offer for the first time a grammatically motivated principle for ordering the presentation of sentences.‖

Three particular ordering characteristics of present transformational grammars have especial appeal for English language teachers:

a. The position of transformational rules after phrase-structure rules in the grammar suggests the possibility of teaching a finite manageable set of elementary constructions first, then teaching the ways in which modification and combination of these elementary constructions can add the infinite set of possible sentences that any speaker of a language has at his disposal.

b. Since lexical vocabulary is introduced in a transformational grammar by phrase-structure rules only, an apparent theoretical justification seems to be offered for teaching new vocabulary in simple kernel sentences, without complicating the teaching of vocabulary by teaching new sentence patterns at the same time, and vice versa. The grammatical and semantic properties (e.g. mass vs. count nouns) of vocabulary, then, might be introduced economically at one time, and only for the simplest constructions.

c. The fact that the detailed phonological rules# come late in the grammar suggests that attention to the details of pronunciation might be left until relatively late in a foreign language teaching program. Note that such delay in teaching "a good accent" is at sharp variance with the attitudes of most applied linguists today, but is in good agreement with our common sense feeling that it is more important to be able to speak a language fluently and to say a lot of things in it than to have marvelous pronunciation but not know what to say. The relative lateness of phonological rules in a transformational grammar helps account for the fact that we can often understand a foreign speaker even when he lacks most of the phonological habits of English; if we

‖ The grading referred to in such techniques as those summarized in Anne Cochran, *Modern Methods of Teaching English as a Foreign Language*, Washing-D.C., 1952, Chapter 5, has largely been based on frequency counts, and those mostly of vocabulary. Frequency counts, if they have any application at all to language teaching, reflect degree of usefulness rather than degree of difficulty. For example, notice that students have very little difficulty learning taboo words in a language, in spite of their low frequency of use.

Not the morpheme-structure rules, however, which may precede the transformational rules. See M. Halle, "Questions of Linguistics," *Nuovo Cimento* XIII 494–517, (1959), and N. Chomsky, "Explanatory Models in Linguistics."

attempt to follow the order of grammatical rules in teaching simple before complex sentences, by the same token we should teach meaningful sentences before we worry much about teaching their proper pronunciation.

The third set of reasons for finding transformational grammar attractive for language teaching are psychological and pedagogical.

a. Most obvious, transformational drills are easy to construct and easy to operate in class. The fact that the transformational grammar of English calls for the derivation of, for example, interrogatives from underlying statements seems to justify the conversion practices that have been with us since traditional days.

b. In the treatment of phonological facts, transformational grammars have a strong appeal to the practical language teacher, in a way that orthodox structural grammars could not match. For one thing, the psychological reality of phonemes has been more convincingly demonstrated for phonemes thought of in the Sapir-Chomsky sense than in the Twaddell-Bloch sense; language teachers will appreciate that somehow the phonemes that represent sentences may be present in a student's rendition even when their proper allophones are not, and this seems more in accord with a theory that presents phonemes as indices of higher grammatical strings rather than as classes of physical phenomena. Language teachers will probably also welcome the transformational deemphasis of suprasegmental features which Trager-Smith structuralists have considered so basic for syntactic analysis and for teaching languages.

c. Less obvious, the goals of generative grammar themselves seem to offer more to the language teacher than those of orthodox structuralism do. Language teachers will be particularly sympathetic to the desire of the generative grammarian to explain the intuitive ability of the speakers of a language to generate new sentences. The generative grammarian tries to state explicitly what constitutes the *Sprachgefühl* of the native speaker; what is "ungrammatical" about utterances to a generative grammarian is roughly equivalent to what is "foreign" to a language teacher.

His interest in the generation of new sentences leads the generative grammarian to present his description of a language as a set of rules for the composition of sentences. The attention paid to *sentences* rather than to *words* is much welcomed by the language teacher, who has known for a long time about the practical necessity to teach the language in units of usable size, but who has had to use grammars whose descriptive strength all lay in their morphology and phonology, rather than syntax, sections. And the presentation of a grammar as an ordered set of rules is a welcome relief from the collections of inventories that constitute an orthodox structural grammar; the rules of generative grammar seem dynamic and prescriptive, in a sense acceptable to language teachers, rather than statically descriptive, as the taxonomic schemes of orthodox structural grammars are.

Since my purpose here was to sketch the appeals of transformational theory, I have not and will not go into a long excursus on why I think all these appeals are deceptive, all wrong, for the language teacher, but I must say at least a few words here on the matter. If the assumptions that underlie the application of grammatical description of languages to the teaching of those languages are granted—and they have never even been stated in a testable form—then I think some of the characteristics I have alluded to above afford legitimate reasons for preferring transformational over orthodox structural grammars.** But I would maintain that those assumptions should not be granted, and that the whole question of the utility of grammatical analysis for language teaching needs to be reopened. I want only to suggest here how I expect the question to be answered.

From the largest body of empirical evidence we can imagine—take all native learners vs. all "taught" learners—we can induce three evident facts.

1. Systematic attention to the grammatical form of utterances is neither a necessary condition nor a sufficient one for successful language learning. That it is not necessary is demonstrated by the native learner's success without it. That it is not sufficient is demonstrated by the typical classroom student's lack of success with it.

2. Teaching particular utterances in contexts which provide meaning and usability to learners is both sufficient (witness the native learner) and necessary (witness the classroom learner). Until meaning is associated with the utterance, the learner cannot use what he has learned. And when he has meaningful control over particular utterances, he will extend that control to new utterances without benefit of much practice.

3. Systematic teaching of formal relations (e.g. question-underlying statement [rather than question-answer] or active-passive) does not

** Even if we were to grant those assumptions we should suspect the kinds of direct application of grammatical theory to language teaching that were implied in my preceding discussion. For example, the ordering of rules in a generative grammar does not correspond in any obvious way to the production of speech. In fact we would find it silly indeed to delay teaching a student to produce an actual sentence until we had taught him the very great number of rules (including the final phonological rules) that a transformational grammar would claim to underlie that sentence.

reflect relationships of meaningful use. Thus, planning of lessons that is based on formal properties of sentences is incompatible with the only necessary and sufficient method we know has succeeded for every speaker of a language.

Transformational grammar offers the best account to date of the formal properties of sentences. When we make statements about those formal properties of English I think we are well-advised to make use of the insights offered by transformational grammar. But as TEFL's we should not allow *any* analysis of the formal properties of language to take priority over our duty to teach our students to use a language. Like the liberal grammarians before us, we should liberate language teaching from grammatical theory, and should teach the natural use of language rather than the synthetic composition of sentences.

LEONARD NEWMARK

How Not to Interfere
with Language Learning

INTRODUCTION

The main theme of the article is that much language teaching emphasizes the mastery of linguistic form at the expense of the purpose of learning a foreign language in the first place: the ability of the learner to say what he wants in the second language. According to Newmark, modern foreign language teaching has been dominated by two sets of ideas: (1) structural linguistics and (2) reinforcement theory psychology. Applied linguistics has made much of the importance of language interference. In this view, the linguistic habits the speaker has learned for his first language will interfere with his establishing the new habits necessary for speaking a second language. As Newmark puts it

> linguists . . . consider the task of learning a new language as if it were essentially a task of fighting off an old set of structures in order to clear the way for a new set.

Reinforcement theory psychology has led

Reprinted with permission of the author from the *International Journal of American Linguistics*, Vol. 32, No. 1, Part II (January), 1966, pp. 77–83.

to programmed instruction, step-by-step instruction based in practice on the identification of what are taken to be the components of the terminal verbal behavior.

Newmark describes modern language teaching as

the marriage of linguistics and psychology in the programmed instruction of foreign languages, with linguistics providing the "systematic specification of terminal behaviors" and psychology providing "the techniques of the laboratory analysis and control of those behaviors."

In reply to the linguist's concern with language interference, Newmark argues that first language interference or a "foreign accent" is the natural result of the speaker's lack of knowledge about English. The learner is being asked to perform before he is able to control English, and consequently he pads his performance with material "from what he already knows, that is, his own language." Newmark concludes the argument on this point by saying,

seen in this light, the cure for interference is simply the cure for ignorance: learning. There is no particular need to combat the intrusion of the learner's native language—the explicit or implicit justification for the contrastive analysis that applied linguists have been claiming to be necessary for planning language-teaching courses.

In reference to the views of reinforcement-theory psychology, Newmark says that the consequence of this position is that English is taught as if it were "additive and linear," that is, each item is taught one at a time in contrastive drills, proceeding from the simplest to the complex, and each connected to a specified stimuli. Newmark argues that if this were really an accurate picture of the way we learn, "the child learner would be old before he could say a single appropriate thing and the adult learner would be dead." Furthermore, such teaching ignores the need of the user to speak correctly, but with understanding.

. . . we want the learner to be able to use the language we teach him, and we want him to be able to extend his ability to new cases, to create new utterances that are appropriate to his needs as a language user.

Newmark argues that language acquisition is not simply "additive and linear"; language is learned in whole chunks in a real context. He says that

we have always known how to teach other human beings to use a language: use it ourselves and let them imitate us as best they can at the time . . . language is learned a whole act at a time rather than learned as an assemblage of constituent skills.

Newmark then shows what a program based on the principles would look like. One way to put language into a real context is to create a dramatic situation in the classroom. The teacher can introduce variation into the situation. The variation will cause the situation to be re-enacted, for instance, a student could play the role of being a dissatisfied customer rather than a satisfied one.

In the applied linguistics of the past twenty years much has been made of the notion of first-language interference with second-language learning. Our dominant conception of languages as structures and our growing sophistication in the complex analysis of these structures have made it increasingly attractive to linguists to consider the task of learning a new language as if it were essentially a task of fighting off an old set of structures in order to clear the way for a new set. The focal emphasis of language teaching by applied linguists has more and more been placed on structural drills based on the linguist's contrastive analysis of the structures of the learner's language and his target language: the weight given to teaching various things is determined not by their importance to the user of the language, but by their degree of difference from what the analyst takes to be corresponding features of the native language.

A different analysis of verbal behavior has been motivated in psychology by reinforcement theory; the application of this analysis has led, of course, to programmed instruction, step-by-step instruction based in practice on the identification of what are taken to be the components of the terminal verbal behavior. What could be more natural than the marriage of linguistics and psychology in the programmed instruction of foreign languages, with linguistics providing the "systematic specification of terminal behaviors" and psychology providing "the techniques of the laboratory analysis and control" of those behaviors.*

If the task of learning to speak English were additive and linear, as present linguistic and psychological discussions suggest it is, it is difficult to see how anyone could learn English. If each phonological and syntactic rule, each complex of lexical features, each semantic value and stylistic nuance—in short, if each item which the linguist's analysis leads him to identify had to be acquired one at a time, pro-

---

* Harlan Lane, "Programmed Learning of a Second Language," IRAL 2. 250, 1964.

ceeding from simplest to most complex, and then each had to be connected to specified stimuli or stimulus sets, the child learner would be
old before he could say a single appropriate thing and the adult
learner would be dead. If each frame of a self-instructional program
could teach only one item (or even two or three) at a time, programmed language instruction would never enable the students to use
the language significantly. The item-by-item contrastive drills proposed by most modern applied linguists and the requirement by programmers that the behaviors to be taught must be specified seem to
rest on this essentially hopeless notion of the language learning
process.

When linguists and programmers talk about planning their textbooks, they approach the problem as if they had to decide what structural features each lesson should be trying to teach. The whole program will teach the sum of its parts: the student will know this structure and that one and another and another. . . . If the question is put
to him directly, the linguist will undoubtedly admit that the sum of
the structures he can describe is not equal to the capability a person
needs in order to use the language, but the question is rarely put to
him directly. If it is, he may evade the uncomfortable answer by
appealing to the intelligence of the user to apply the structures he
knows to an endless variety of situations. But the evasion fails, I think,
against the inescapable fact that a person, even an intelligent one, who
knows perfectly the structures that the linguist teaches, cannot know
that the way to get his cigarette lit by a stranger when he has no
matches is to walk up to him and say one of the utterances "Do you
have a light?" or "Got a match?" (Not one of the equally well-formed
questions, "Do you have fire?" or "Do you have illumination?" or "Are
you a match's owner?").

In natural foreign language learning—the kind used, for example,
by children to become native speakers in a foreign country within a
length of time that amazes their parents—acquisition cannot be simply
additive; complex bits of language are learned a whole chunk at a
time. Perhaps by some process of stimulus sampling[†] the parts of the
chunks are compared and become available for use in new chunks.
The possible number of "things known" in the language exponentiates
as the number of chunks increases additively, since every complex
chunk makes available a further analysis of old chunks into new elements, each still attached to the original context upon which its
appropriateness depends.

[†] I take the term and notion from W. K. Estes, "Learning Theory," *Annual
Review of Psychology* 13. 110, 1962.

It is not that linguists and psychologists are unaware of the possibility of learning language in complex chunks or of the importance of learning items in contexts. Indeed it would be difficult to find a serious discussion of new language teaching methods that did not claim to reform old language teaching methods in part through the use of "natural" contexts. It is rather that consideration of the details supplied by linguistic and psychological analysis has taken attention away from the exponential power available in learning in natural chunks. In present psychologically oriented programs the requirement that one specify the individual behaviors to be reinforced leads (apparently inevitably) to an artificial isolation of parts from wholes; in structurally oriented textbooks and courses, contrastive analysis leads to structural drills designed to teach a set of specific "habits" for the well-formation of utterances, abstracted from normal social context.

Our very knowledge of the fine structure of language constitutes a threat to our ability to maintain perspective in teaching languages. Inspection of language textbooks designed by linguists reveals an increasing emphasis in recent years on structural drills in which pieces of language are isolated from the linguistic and social contexts which make them meaningful and useful to the learner. The more we know about a language, the more such drills we have been tempted to make. If one compares, say, the Spoken Language textbooks devised by linguists during the Second World War with some of the recent textbooks devised by linguists,‡ he is struck by the shift in emphasis from connected situational dialogue to disconnected structural exercise.

The argument of this paper is that such isolation and abstraction of the learner from the contexts in which that language is used constitutes serious interference with the language learning process. Because it requires the learner to attach new responses to old stimuli, this kind of interference may in fact increase the interference that applied linguists like to talk about—the kind in which a learner's previous language structures are said to exert deleterious force on the structures being acquired.

Consider the problem of teaching someone to say something. What is it we are most concerned that he learn? Certainly not the mere mouthing of the utterance, the mere ability to pronounce the words. Certainly not the mere demonstration of ability to understand the utterance by, say, translation into the learner's own language. Even the combination of the two goals is not what we are after: it is not

‡ For example, see Dwight L. Bolinger et al., *Modern Spanish*, Harcourt, Brace & Co., 1960; L. B. Swift et al., *Igbo: Basic Course*, Foreign Service Institute, 1962; John J. Gumperz and June Rumery, *Conversational Hindi-Urdu*, n.p., 1962.

saying *and* understanding that we want but saying *with* understanding. That is, we want the learner to be able to use the language we teach him, and we want him to be able to extend his ability to new cases, to create new utterances that are appropriate to his needs as a language user.

Recent linguistic theory has offered a detailed abstract characterization of language competence; learning a finite set of rules and a finite lexicon enables the learner to produce and interpret an infinite number of new well-formed sentences. Plausible detailed accounts also abound in the psychological and philosophical literature to explain how formal repertoires might be linked referentially to the real world. But the kinds of linguistic rules that have been characterized so far (syntactic, phonological, and semantic) bear on the question of well-formedness of sentences, not on the question of appropriateness of utterances. And the stimulus-response or associational- or operant-conditioning accounts that help explain how *milk* comes to mean "milk" are of little help in explaining my ability to make up a particular something appropriate to say about milk—such as *I prefer milk*—in a discussion of what one likes in his coffee, and even less my ability to ignore the mention of milk when it is staring me in the face. An important test of our success as language teachers, it seems reasonable to assert, is the ability of our students to choose to say what they want. It has been difficult for linguists and psychologists to attach any significance to the expression "saying what you want to say"; our inability to be precise about the matter may well have been an important reason for our neglect of it in language teaching. But importance of a matter is not measured by our ability at a given moment to give a precise description of it: we can be precise about the allophones of voiceless stops in English after initial /s/, but it seems absurd to claim that it is basically as important—some textbooks imply *more* important—to teach students to make these allophones properly as it is to teach them, for example, how to get someone to repeat something he has just said.

The odd thing is that despite our ignorance as experts, as human beings we have always known how to teach other human beings to use a language: use it ourselves and let them imitate us as best they can at the time. Of course, this method has had more obvious success with children than with adult learners, but we have no compelling reason to believe with either children or adults that the method is not both necessary and sufficient to teach a language.

If we adopt the position I have been maintaining—that language is learned a whole act at a time rather than learned as an assemblage of constituent skills—what would a program for teaching students to speak a foreign language look like?[§]

For the classroom, the simple formulation that the students learn by imitating someone else using the language needs careful development. Since the actual classroom is only one small piece of the world in which we expect the learner to use the language, artificial means must be used to transform it into a variety of other pieces: the obvious means for performing this transformation is drama—imaginative play has always been a powerful educational device both for children and adults. By creating a dramatic situation in a classroom—in part simply by acting out dialogues, but also in part by relabeling objects and people in the room (supplemented by realia if desired) to prepare for imaginative role-playing—the teacher can expand the classroom indefinitely and provide imaginatively natural contexts for the language being used.

The idea of using models as teachers is hardly new in applied linguistics; and nothing could be more commonplace than the admonition that the model be encouraged to dramatize and the student to imitate the dramatization of the situation appropriate to the particular bit of language being taught. The sad fact is, however, that the drill material the model has been given to model has intrinsic features that draw the attention of the student away from the situation and focus it on the form of the utterance. Instead of devising techniques that induce the model to act out roles for the student to imitate, the applied linguist has devised techniques of structural drill that put barriers in the way of dramatic behavior and a premium on the personality-less manipulation of a formal repertoire of verbal behavior.

If what the learner observes is such that he cannot absorb it completely within his short-term memory, he will make up for his deficiency if he is called on to perform before he has learned the new behavior by padding with material from what he already knows, that is, his own language. This padding—supplying what is known to make up for what is not known—is the major source of "interference," the major reason for "foreign accents." Seen in this light, the cure for interference is simply the cure for ignorance: learning. There is no particular need to combat the intrusion of the learner's native language—the explicit or implicit justification for the contrastive analysis

§ I shall restrict myself here to the question of teaching a spoken foreign language. How one teaches people to read and write a foreign language depends on their literacy in another language and on their mastery of the spoken language in which they are learning to be literate. The problems involved would take me too far afield of the subject I am discussing here.

that applied linguists have been claiming to be necessary for planning language-teaching courses. But there is need for controlling the size of the chunks displayed for imitation. In general if you want the learner's imitation to be more accurate, make the chunks smaller; increase the size of the chunks as the learner progresses in his skill in imitation. We do not need to impose arbitrary, artificial criteria for successful behavior on the part of the learner. If we limit our demand for immediate high quality of production, we may well find that his behavior is adequately shaped by the same *ad hoc* forces that lead a child from being a clumsy performer capable of using his language only with a terribly inaccurate accent, and in a limited number of social situations, to becoming a skillful native speaker capable of playing a wide variety of social roles with the appropriate language for each.

To satisfy our requirement that the student learn to extend to new cases the ability he gains in acting out one role, a limited kind of structural drill can be used: keeping in mind that the learning must be embedded in a meaningful context, the drill may be constructed by introducing small variations into the situation being acted out (e.g., ordering orange juice instead of tomato juice, being a dissatisfied customer rather than a satisfied one, changing the time at which the the action takes place) which call for partial innovation in the previously learned role. In each case the situation should be restaged, reenacted, played as meaning something to the student.

The student's craving for explicit formulization of generalizations can usually be met better by textbooks and grammars that he reads outside class than by discussion in class. If discussion of grammar is made into a kind of dramatic event, however, such discussion might be used as the situation being learned—with the students learning to play the role of students in a class on grammar. The important point is that the study of grammar as such is neither necessary nor sufficient for learning to use a language.

So far, I have been talking about the use of live models in language classrooms. How can such techniques be adapted for self-instruction? The cheapness and simplicity of operation of the new videotape recorders already make possible a large portion of the acquisition of a language without the presence of a model; it has been shown convincingly that under the proper conditions it is possible for human students to learn—in the sense of acquiring competence—certain very complex behaviors by mere observation of that behavior in use.‖

‖ For an excellent discussion of the roles of imitation and reinforcement in the acquisition and performance of complex behavior, see Albert Bandura and Richard H. Walters, *Social Learning and Personality Development,* Holt, Rinehart and Winston, 1963.

Acquiring the willingness to perform—learning in a second sense—seems to depend to a greater extent on reinforcement of the student's own behavior and is thus not quite so amenable to instruction without human feedback at the present time. However, extension of techniques (originally developed to establish phonological competence in step-by-step programmed instruction)# for self-monitoring to cover whole utterances with their appropriate kinetic accompaniment may suffice in the future to make the second kind of learning as independent of live teachers as the first and thus make complete self-instruction in the use of a language possible.

For example, the techniques used in Stanley Sapon's *Spanish A*, in the TEMAC series for Encyclopedia Britannica Films, 1961.

LEONARD NEWMARK
DAVID A. REIBEL

Necessity and Sufficiency in Language Learning

INTRODUCTION

This article is divided into two sections. In Section I the authors take the position that the adult learner of a second language acquires the second language in much the same way that he acquired his first language. In Section II the authors present and discuss four possible arguments against their position.

Section I begins with the assertion that linguists have shifted the emphasis in language teaching "from mastery of language use to mastery of language structure." Consequently, the linguist has assumed that learning takes place because of the contribution of the structuring of the material. The authors take the view that the learner's contribution to his own learning has been neglected. They feel that the preoccupation with control of structure has

> distracted the theorists from considering the role of the learner as anything but a generator of interference; and preoccupation with linguistic structure has distracted them from considering that learning a language means learning to use it.

Reprinted with permission of the authors and publisher from the *International Review of Applied Linguistics in Language Teaching*, Vol. VI, No. 2, 1968, pp. 145–164.

In the next paragraph the authors present what they consider to be both the necessary and sufficient conditions in language acquisition:

> a language will be learned by a normal human being if and only if *particular, whole instances of language use are modeled for him and if his own particular acts using the language are selectively reinforced.* The critical point here is that *unless* a learner has learned instances of language in use, he has not learned them as language, and that if he has learned enough such instances, he will not need to have analysis and generalization about those wholes made *for* him.

The authors take as a case in point the most successful instance of language learning—the child's acquisition of his first language. Since the child is not instructed in his language and yet in a short period of time is able to produce "intelligent, appropriate speech" we must conclude that

> the child proceeds in an incredibly short time to induce a grammar of the language far more complex than any yet formulated by any linguist. We must, therefore, assume that the child is somehow capable of making an enormous contribution of his own. We may call this contribution his *language learning capability.*

The authors argue that this capability must organize and store the structurally diverse data of the language in such a way that it will be available for future use. Since language exists, not for the sake of form or structure, but for the sake of use, the organization of the sentences of his language must be "in terms of the situation they share (that is, their functional *use*) rather than the form they share."

The authors point out that teaching material is organized on exactly the opposite principle: control of linguistic form at the expense of situation or use. The authors stress that "the example of the child indicates that situational rather than grammatical cohesion is what is necessary and sufficient for language learning to take place."

The main argument in Section I rests on the assumption that the process of second language acquisition is essentially the same as first language acquisition. In Section II the authors defend this assumption against four possible counter arguments:

1. "The child's brain is different from the adult's. The adult has lost the neurological ability to infer general linguistic laws from particular instances." The authors grant that the adult does not usually acquire the second language as perfectly as a child acquires his first, but they argue that the difference in degree of skill is no argument for the adult and child being "qualitatively different *kinds* of learners."

2. "The child has much more time to learn the language." The authors reply that it is difficult to say how much time the child actually spends in language learning. They insist that it is not the time spent that gives a child an advantage over the adult learner, but his

opportunity to put his knowledge to practical use, while on the other hand, "the classroom student's 'knowledge' of the language may allow him to do everything with the language except use it."

3. "The child is much more strongly motivated to learn his first language than the adult is to learn a foreign language." The authors point out that there are several possible interpretations of what the term "motivation" means. Nevertheless, they think that in any strict psychological interpretation of "motivation," the adult is as well motivated and rewarded as the child, perhaps even more so.

4. "The child offers a *tabula rasa* for language learning. The adult's native language will interfere with his acquisition of a foreign language." The authors grant that there is such a thing as second language interference, but deny that this is of any significant importance to the process of learning. The interference results from the student's inability to produce correct forms in the second language. When the learner outstrips his knowledge of the second language, if he is to talk at all, he must fall back on what he does know, namely, his first language. Thus, first-language interference is not a hindrance to be overcome by contrast analysis, rather it is a negative thing to be overcome by more knowledge of the second language.

In a strict psychological sense, "interference" means that learning one set of responses to a set of stimuli may interfere with learning a new set of responses to the same stimuli. The authors suggest that the danger of interference in this sense may be minimized if the learning situations are clearly separated. They also point out that if this model were really true, the learning of the new set of "habits" for the second language should have a corresponding weakening effect on the habits of the first language. Obviously, however, learning a second language does not necessarily in itself reduce our ability to use our native language. The authors conclude with the observation that adults do acquire "new abilities that could never have been taught them by mere summation of the formal exercises to which they may have been exposed."

✳

ABSTRACT

In present-day "linguistically-oriented" language teaching literature the underlying principles and pedagogical recommendations drawn from them seem either supererogatory or logically and empirically inadequate to provide a plausible foundation for the teaching programs they claim to justify.

From a consideration of successful vs. unsuccessful cases of language learning, we assert three propositions:

1. Systematic organization of the grammatical form of the language material exposed to the learner is neither necessary nor sufficient for his mastery of the language.

2. Presentation of particular instances of language in contexts which exemplify their meaning and use is both sufficient and necessary.

3. Systematic teaching of structure (as in structural drills) imposes formal rather than useful organization of language material. To plan teaching programs on the basis of formal properties of sentences is thus incompatible with the only necessary and sufficient method known for learning a language.

SECTION I

In his zeal to teach language students to produce well-formed sentences, the language teacher is in great danger of underestimating the importance of teaching students to use the language. This is as true in the 20th century with its linguistically enlightened methods as it was in the 19th century for methods that men like Gouin, Sweet, and Jespersen were reacting against.* The growing emphasis during the past twenty years on the improvement and expansion of techniques of structural drill represents a corresponding de-emphasis on techniques of teaching language use. In constructing language textbooks and language teaching programs, linguists have—for good professional reasons but bad pedagogical ones—increasingly shifted from a reliance on the simple, direct technique of teaching language use by presenting for imitation instances of the language in use to a reliance on the complex, indirect technique of preparing the learner for language use by means of structural drills based on the linguist's expert contrastive analysis of the native and target languages.† With this shift in emphasis from

* François Gouin, *The Art of Teaching and Studying Languages* (London, 1892) (English translation by Howard Swan and Victor Bétis of Gouin's *L'Art d'enseigner et d'étudier les langues,* Paris, 1880); Henry Sweet, *The ractical Study of Languages* (London, 1899); Otto Jespersen, *How to Teach a Foreign Language* (London, 1904).

† A whole conference, for example, was devoted to this topic; see Francis W. Gravit and Albert Valdman, eds., *Structural Drill and the Language Laboratory, IJAL* XXIX, No. 2 (April, 1963), Part III (=IURCAFL Publication 27).

The importance that linguists ascribe to contrastive analysis is typified by the following from the "General Introductions," by Charles F. Ferguson, General Editor, to the monographs in the *Contrastive Structure Series* (Chicago, University of Chicago Press, 1962):

"The Center for Applied Linguistics, in undertaking this series of studies, has

mastery of language use to mastery of language structure, language pedagogy has gradually lost much of the value contributed to the design of language teaching materials by American linguists during the Second World War.‡

An examination of the literature on second language teaching written either by linguists or by teachers who claim a linguistic orientation will reveal a certain typical uniformity in the structure of the theoretical statements that seek to justify their choice of method and selection of material. In some cases, the theoretical discussion may be as short as two or three paragraphs, e.g. in an article in *Language Learning* or *IRAL*, or as long as whole chapters of books. In other cases, of course, the argument will not be explicitly formulated, but will be implied at various critical points in the discussion. Whatever the format selected for the presentation of the theoretical background, whether explicit or implicit, its structure can be resolved into two parts.

The underlying principles which form the first part are presented as propositions alleged to form part of linguistic science. These propositions are taken either as fundamental assumptions of linguistic science itself or as findings of linguistic science, although in just what sense they can be taken to be one or the other is not usually spelled out. A statement such as "Language is structured" may in one set of underlying principles figure as an assumption while in another discussion it seems to be claimed as one of the findings of linguistics.§

---

acted on the conviction held by many linguists and specialists in language teaching that one of the major problems in the learning of a second language is the interference caused by the structural differences between the native language of the learner and the second language. A natural consequence of this conviction is the belief that a careful contrastive analysis of the two languages offers an excellent basis for the preparation of instructional materials, the planning of courses, and the development of actual classroom techniques."

‡ For the nature of this contribution, see William G. Moulton, "Linguistics and Language Teaching in the United States 1940–1960," in Mohrmann, Sommerfelt and Whatmough, eds., *Trends in European and American Linguistics*, 1930–1960 (Utrecht, 1961), pp. 82–109 (also IRAL I (1963), pp. 21–41); but note especially pp. 86–90 (IRAL, pp. 24–27), where he particularly mentions the role of drill, and pp. 97–98 (IRAL, pp. 32–33) where he quotes C. C. Fries about the contributions of linguists to language teaching programs. See also Mary R. Haas, "The Application of Linguistics to Language Teaching," in A. L. Kroeber, ed., *Anthropology Today* (Chicago, 1953), pp. 807–818.

§ Not at all unrepresentative is the following from Jeris E. Strain, "Teaching a Pronunciation Problem," *Language Learning*, XII (1962), pp. 231–240.

"Our task is to teach the sound system of a foreign language. To do so we attempt to bring as much linguistic knowledge as possible to bear on the 'what' of our task and complement it with the best 'how' ideas that are known to us.

The second part of the theoretical discussion typically consists of statements concerning principles or details of pedagogical practice, alleged to be the logical consequences of the underlying principles. A number of these pedagogical recommendations and the teaching programs they claim to justify seem to us logically and empirically faulty. We can put our objections succinctly:

1. The pedagogical recommendations do not follow logically from the underlying principles upon which they are claimed to be based.

2. The recommended pedagogical procedures themselves can be shown to be neither necessary nor sufficient for the learning of a language.

For example, we may find as an underlying principle a statement like:

1. "Linguistic theory tells us that the ability to speak a language is fundamentally a vast system of habits—of patterns and structures used quite out of awareness."||

"In defining our task, we take certain propositions for granted, propositions based on conclusions [N.B.] reached in the scientific study of language; namely:

a. that the sound system of a language is made up of a certain rather small set of elements which function significantly as carriers of the message (usually called phonemes).

b. That the sound systems of two languages are never the same.

c. that pronunciation problems can be predicted at least in part by comparing the native-language sound system with that of the target language.

d. that skill in pronunciation consists of a set of automatic habits involving the hearing organs and the speech organs, plus the ability not only to recognize significant sounds in a stream of speech but also to react to them in an acceptable manner.

e. that a prerequisite to developing the ability to produce significant sounds is development of the ability to recognize the significant sounds.

f. that learning to speak a language should precede learning to read and write it."

Or the following from Albert Valdman, "Breaking the Lockstep," in F. W. Gravit and A. Valdman, *op. cit.*, p. 147:

"Scarcely anyone in this audience would quarrel fundamentally with the basic assumptions [N.B.] of the New Key:

(1) Language is primarily speech and writing is its secondary derivative; (2) Foreign language instruction should progress in the sequence listening, speaking, reading, and writing; (3) Language consists of a complex set of habits learned through practice and analogy; (4) The acquisition of foreign language habits is considerably accelerated by structuring the subject matter and ordering it in a series of graduated minimal steps; (5) Practice is more effective if reinforced by rewarding desired terminal responses; (6) Foreign language learning will be substantially increased if positive motivational factors are present in the teaching situation."

|| William G. Moulton, "What is Structural Drill?," in F. W. Gravit and A. Valdman, *op. cit.*, p. 5.

And its putative pedagogical consequence:

1a. Structural drill is an important component of any efficient foreign language teaching program.[#]

Or the principle:

2. An important cause of difficulty in second language learning is the set of structural non-congruencies between the learner's native language and the target language.[**]

Followed by the claim that:

2a. Only materials based on a contrastive analysis can most efficiently overcome the interference in the foreign language behavior caused by the native language speech habits.[††]

The logical flaw arises in such instances when the linguist attempts to draw simple and direct conclusions about the manner of acquisition of language from his knowledge of the abstract structure of language, and claims that the success or failure of language teaching programs depends to a large extent on the degree to which the language course

---

[#] Cf. Nelson Brooks, *Language and Language Learning* (Second Edition) (New York, 1964), p. 146:

"Pattern Practice is a cardinal point in the methodology proposed in this book. Pattern practice (or structure drill, as it is sometimes called), contrary to dialogue, makes no pretense of being communication. It is to communication what playing scales and arpeggios is to music: exercise in structural dexterity undertaken solely for the sake of practice, in order that performance may become habitual and automatic. . . ."

[**] Cf. for example the following from Robert L. Politzer and Charles N. Staubach, *Teaching Spanish, A Linguistic Orientation* (Revised Edition) (New York, 1965), p. 22:

"Our appraisal of second language learning must take into account three important facts which inevitably determine much of the learning process:

1. Language is an elaborate system, full of analogical forms and patterns.
2. Language is habit, or a complex of habits.
3. The native language (an established complex of habits) interferes with the acquisition of the habits of the new language."

Subsequent pages (23–32) develop these notions in terms of drill designed to prevent, avoid, or mitigate various kinds of interference (transfer) from native language patterns or imperfectly learned second language patterns.

[††] *Ibid.*, p. 32: "For the time being, intensive drill at the points of interference remains our most practical tool in overcoming the obstacles created by the native language habits of the mature speaker."

Cf. also the following from Emma Marie Birkmaier, "Extending the Audio-Lingual Approach: Some Psychological Aspects," in Edward W. Najam, ed., *Language Learning: The Individual and the Process*, IJAL XXXII, No. 1 (January, 1966), Part II (=IURCAFL Publication 40), p. 130:

"There is an automatic transfer in the learning of a second language of which the teacher must be aware, namely, the interference of the speech patterns of one's native language. Interference can be negligible in a bilingual who learns his language during childhood. This fact speaks for the introduction of foreign languages at an early age level, since the adolescent and adult will find this interference a considerable handicap.

"The teacher must constantly be aware of and give special emphasis to the

writer or language teacher orders his pedagogical material to reflect a theoretically sound description of the native and target languages.‡‡ The excessive preoccupation with the contribution of the teacher has then distracted the theorists from considering the role of the learner as anything but a generator of interference; and preoccupation with linguistic structure has distracted them from considering that learning a language means learning to use it.

Our contention is that to be effective language teachers, we need not wait for the development of a theory of language acquisition based on a theory of the structure of language. We believe that the necessary and sufficient conditions for a human being to learn a language are already known: a language will be learned by a normal human being

---

points of interference. *The automatic transfer of the learner's native speech habits must be drilled out of him.* This is really the foreign language teacher's chief job." (Emphasis added.)

The modern ancestor of such formulations is evidently the following oft-quoted summary statement by C. C. Fries, *Teaching and Learning English as a Foreign Language* (Ann Arbor, 1945), p. 9: "The most efficient materials are those that are based upon a scientific description of the language to be learned, carefully compared with a parallel description of the language of the learner."

‡‡ Fries, *op. cit.*, p. 5: "But the person who is untrained in the methods and techniques of language description is not likely to arrive at sound conclusions concerning the actual practices of the native speakers he observes. He will certainly not do so economically and efficiently. And the native speaker of the language, unless he has been specially trained to analyze his own languages processes, will be more likely to mislead than to help a foreigner when he tries to make comments about his own language. On the other hand, the modern scientific study of language has within the last twenty years developed special techniques of descriptive analysis by which a trained linguist can efficiently and accurately arrive at the fundamentally significant matters of structure and sound system amid the bewildering mass of details which constitute the actual rumble of speech. If an adult is to gain a satisfactory proficiency in a foreign language most quickly and easily he must have satisfactory materials upon which to work— i.e. he must have the really important items of the language selected and arranged in a properly related sequence with special emphasis upon the chief trouble spots. . . The techniques of scientific descriptive analysis . . . can provide a thorough and consistent check of the language material itself and thus furnish the basis for the selection of the most efficient materials to guide the efforts of the learner."

Further, p. 7: "it is the practical use of the linguistic scientist's technique of language description in the choice and sequence of materials and the principles of the method that grow out of these materials that is at the heart of the so-called 'new approach' to language learning."

Statements with the import of those just quoted from Fries are repeated almost ritualistically in foreign language methodology textbooks and articles that adopt his point of view. Our objection to this point of view stems from its uncritical equation of "the really important items" with "the chief trouble spots." W. F. Mackey's book *Language Teaching Analysis* (London, 1965) is a good example of the attempt to define the components of the language teaching program in terms of an analysis of the components of language structure. See also M. A. K. Halliday and Peter Strevens, *Linguistics and Language Teaching* (London, 1965).

if and only if *particular, whole instances of language use are modeled for him and if his own particular acts using the language are selectively reinforced.*§§ The critical point here is that *unless* a learner has learned instances of language in use, he has not learned them as language, and that if he has learned enough such instances, he will not need to have analysis and generalization about those wholes made *for* him. If our contention is correct, there is a heavy—and we think impossible—burden of proof on anyone who insists (1) that language is most efficiently taught if structure is taught separately from use (as implied by structural drills) or (2) that the organization of language material for the student should follow a scheme dictated by the comparative structures of the language to be learned and the language of the learner.

Let us consider the obvious fact that in just that case where the most successful language learning takes place—namely, in the child—the linguistic material displayed to the learner is not selected in the interest of presenting discrete grammatical skills in an orderly fashion. On the contrary, the child is exposed to an extensive variety and range of utterances selected for their situational appropriateness at the moment, rather than to illustrate a particular grammatical principle. The child proceeds in an incredibly short time to induce a grammar of the language far more complex than any yet formulated by any linguist. We must, therefore, assume that the child is somehow capable of making an enormous contribution of his own.‖ ‖ We may

---

§§ Cf. the following from Albert Bandura and Richard H. Walters, *Social Learning and Personality Development* (New York, 1965), p. 106:

"Relevant research demonstrates that when a model is provided, patterns of behavior are typically acquired in large segments or in their entirety rather than through a slow, gradual process based on differential reinforcement. Following demonstrations by a model, or (though to a lesser extent) following verbal descriptions of desired behavior, the learner gradually reproduces more or less the entire response pattern, even though he may perform no overt response, and consequently receive no reinforcement, throughout the demonstration period. Under such circumstances, the acquisition process is quite clearly not as piecemeal as is customarily depicted in modern behavior systems."

Note their finding that the acquisition of behavior need not be accompanied by any overt response by the subject whatsoever, something which they demonstrate in a large number of varied learning situations. "While immediate or inferred response consequences to the model have an important influence on the observer's [i.e. learner's] *performance* of imitative responses, the *acquisition* of these responses appears to result primarily from contiguous sensory stimulation [i.e. observation]." (p. 107) (Authors' emphasis.) All this strikes hard at the psychological base of the linguist who adopts an analytic, stimulus-response model for language teaching, with its consequent emphasis on the accumulation of a repertory of language behavior bit by bit via structural drill.

‖ ‖ Cf. N. Chomsky, *Aspects of the Theory of Syntax* (Cambridge, Mass., 1965), p. 25:

"Clearly, a child who has learned a language has developed an internal repre-

call this contribution his *language learning capability*, by which we mean simply whatever it is that makes it possible for a child to observe a number of particular acts of speech in context and then to perform new acts of speech that will seem to the observer to imply that the child has formed general rules for producing intelligent, appropriate speech. It is still unknown what neurological mechanisms account for his linguistic accomplishment; but the fact that the child can produce new intelligent speech after observing only particular language acts of varied linguistic structure in contextual wholes seems indisputable.##
This capability, among other things, accomplishes what it is assumed the course writer tries to accomplish for the adult learner: it organizes and stores a wealth of structurally diverse input language data in such a way as to be available for future language use in thinking, speaking, hearing, reading and writing.

Since any successful language learning program must ultimately

---

sentation of a system of rules that determine how sentences are to be formed, used, and understood. Using the term 'grammar' with a systematic ambiguity (to refer, first, to the native speaker's internally represented 'theory of his language' and, second, to the linguist's account of this), we can say that the child has developed and internally represented a generative grammar, in the sense described. He has done this on the basis of observation of what we may call primary linguistic data. This must include examples of linguistic performance that are taken to be well-formed sentences, and may include also examples designated as non-sentences, and no doubt much other information of the sort that is required for language learning, whatever this may be. . . . On the basis of such data, the child constructs a grammar—that is, a theory of the language of which the well-formed sentences of the primary linguistic data constitute a small sample. To learn a language, then, the child must have a method for devising an appropriate grammar, given primary linguistic data."

On the nature of the child's accomplishment vis-à-vis that of the linguist, cf. the following from H. E. Palmer, *The Principles of Language Study* (new edition: London, 1964), pp. 4–5:

"In English we have a tone-system so complicated that no one has so far discovered its laws, but little English children observe each nicety of tone with marvelous precision; a learned specialist in 'tonetics' (or whatever the science of tones will come to be called) may make an error, but the little child will not. . . .

"When, therefore, we find that a person has become expert in a difficult and complex subject, the theory of which has not yet been worked out, nor yet been discovered, it is manifest that his expertness has been acquired otherwise than by study of the theory."

Cf. C. F. Hockett, "Linguistic Ontogeny," *A Course in Modern Linguistics* (New York, 1958), pp. 356–357:

"In the communicative economy of the child at the earliest speech stage, his vocal signals are not words in this sense, but the indivisible and uncompoundable signals of a closed repertory: each utterance from the child consists wholly of one or another of these signals. Each signal has been learned as a whole, in direct or indirect imitation of some utterance of adult language. For a while the repertory is increased only by the holistic imitation of further adult utterances. This does not 'open' the closed system, but merely enlarges it.

"In time, the child's repertory includes some signals which are partially similar in sound and meaning. Suppose, for example, that the child already uses prelin-

teach the *use* of sentences, if the adult learner can, like the child, contribute a knowledge of the *form* of sentences from his knowledge of the form of previously learned sentences, a presentation of sentences organized in terms of the situation they share rather than the form they share would seem clearly the more efficient one.

In discussions of modern language teaching methodology, it has been argued that structural randomness in teaching materials makes language learning excessively difficult; a sufficient demonstration of the invalidity of this contention as a general principle for language teaching is the fact of the child's easy success in learning a language— whether it is his first or second one—from just such materials. Furthermore, in practice the design of teaching material to minimize *grammatical* randomness seems to maximize situational randomness. A set of successive items in a typical structural drill normally have in common *only* their shared grammatical properties—not their relatedness to a given situation. On the other hand, the successive utterances in a normal discourse, say in a dialogue or piece of connected text, rarely share the same grammatical structure, but nevertheless exhibit a highly structured situational or contextual cohesion. And the example of the child indicates that situational rather than grammatical cohesion is what is necessary and sufficient for language learning to take place.

We are saying that a chunk of language is most efficiently learned as a *unit* of form and use. This has an important implication on language pedagogy: structural drills, in which the student practices switching quickly from an utterance appropriate for one situation to another utterance appropriate for quite another situation, are ineffective in principle. They force the student to produce utterances whose use is made difficult to grasp, unless he has the rare skill (there may be a small number of learners who apparently can learn to use a language from structural drill alone) of imagining a whole fresh situation for every utterance, while keeping up with the mechanical requirements of the exercise.

How can the evident success of the child's language learning method be realized for foreign language teaching to adults?*** The proponents

---

guistic equivalents of adult /³mámɔ¹ ↓ / and /³mámɔ² ↑ /, and of /³dǽdij¹ ↓ /, but not, it so happens, of /³dǽdij² ↑ /. The adult forms are structured: each consists of a recurrent word plus a recurrent intonation. The child's analogs, at the moment, are unitary signals. But then comes the most crucial event in the child's acquisition of language: he analogizes, in some appropriate situation, to produce an utterance matching adult /³dǽdij² ↑ /, which he has never heard nor said before."

*** Arguments concerning language learning abilities in the adult on the analogy of those of the child are used explicitly—albeit inconsistently—in works like the

of the various "direct methods" have developed numerous techniques that attempt to do this; and linguists have done even better than the more physicalistic of the direct methodists, by utilizing the powerful tool of dialogue memorization, which at its best provides less limiting and more realistic contexts for learning than can be provided if the strictures (e.g., no translation, structurally limited lessons) of the more rigid of the direct methodists are adhered to.

The pedagogical implication of our position is that we abandon the notion of structural grading and structural ordering of exercise material in favor of situational ordering. That is, we need to devise no more structural drills like that illustrated in Appendix I. Through the materials we would propose instead (see Appendix II for an example of one kind), the student would learn situational variants rather than structural alternants independent of a contextual base. The principal motivation for providing contextual and psychological reality for dialogues in a believable manner is not, as is so often objected, to provide the learner with something to say for a particular, necessarily limited situation. Rather, it is to present instances of meaningful use of language which the learner himself stores, segments, and eventually recombines in synthesizing new utterances appropriate for use in new situations.†††

In our language teaching research we need to pay more attention to improving and making more effective our presentations of language

---

ones cited in Note * above. Cf. for example the following from H. E. Palmer, *op. cit.*, p. 7: "We may well ask ourselves whether the forces which were operative in the case of [the acquisition of] our first language are available for the acquisition of a second, third, or fourth language." After a detailed discussion and analysis of the relevant possible differences, he concludes, p. 11: "No reasonable doubt remains: we are all endowed by nature with certain capacities which enable each of us, without exercise of our powers of study, to assimilate and to use the spoken form of any colloquial language, whether native or foreign. We may avail ourselves of these powers by training ourselves deliberately to utilize them, or, having more confidence in our studial efforts, or for some reason of special expediency, we may choose to leave our spontaneous capacities in their latent state and make no use of them. We cannot, however, afford to ignore them, and it would be foolish to deny their existence."

††† Our use of the terms segment, store, recombine, etc., should not be taken to mean that we have in mind some particular taxonomic or stimulus-response model of grammatical structure or language use. Modern grammatical theory makes it clear that such models could not in themselves be adequate representations of the nature of the language learning process. Cf. N. Chomsky, *op. cit.*, pp. 47–59, especially p. 57; also T. G. Bever, J. A. Fodor and W. Weksel, "On the Acquisition of Syntax," *Psychological Review* LXXII (1965), pp. 467–482. What is important is our claim that, whatever the nature of this process, it is carried out by the learner rather than being performed vicariously for him by the teacher.

For further discussions of these topics, see the following: Leonard Newmark,

in use. For example, we need careful studies to tell us what dosage
of conversational material will maximize the ratio of amount retained
to amount of time spent in acquisition;‡‡‡ we need to devise and
employ exercises that will extend the applicability of material already
learned to new situations—for instance, we may give students practice
in substituting new items in previously learned dialogues, corresponding to slight changes they wish to introduce into the situation, as in
Appendix II; and we need to learn to manipulate the relationship
between model and observer in such a way as to increase the likelihood
that the student will imitate the language behavior of his teacher.

SECTION II

Now, against the assertion that first language learning provides
instructive insights for planning second language teaching programs,
it is easy and usual to object that the adult is not a child and that the
process of second language learning must therefore be different from
that of first language learning (and then to construct teaching programs which will guarantee that the adult is *made to be* a different
kind of learner from the child). It is denied that an adult can effectively be taught by grammatically unordered materials, which seem
so sufficient for the child's learning (we repeat, the *only* learning
process which we know for certain will produce mastery of the language at a native level).

Several serious arguments for treating the adult as a different kind
of learner from the child have been advanced. We may take four to
be representative:

Jerome Mintz and Jan Ann Lawson, *Using American English* (New York, 1964),
Introduction, pp. 3–18, by Leonard Newmark; David A. Reibel, "The Contextu-
ally-Patterned Use of English: An Experiment in Dialogue Writing," *English
Language Teaching* XIX (1964), pp. 62–71; Leonard Newmark, "How Not to
Interfere with Language Learning," E. W. Najam, *op. cit.*, pp. 77–83.

‡‡‡ For example, we know that it would be easy to learn a two-word dialogue
very well in an hour—"Hello." "Hello."—but little would be gained for the hour's
work; on the other hand, a great deal of language might be exposed in a forty-line
dialogue, but the effort to memorize the dialogue would not be worth the gain,
and little of it would be retained and reemployed by the student. How long should
a dialogue be in order to gain maximal retention per unit of time spent in learning? Experience in language teaching suggests that a dialogue of perhaps four to
six lines—two or three short utterances per participant—for each learning dose
may be optimal. This length sharply contrasts with the length of dialogues in
many "linguistically oriented" textbooks.

Argument 1: The child's brain is different from the adult's. The adult has lost the neurological ability to infer general linguistic laws from particular instances.§§§

While we recognize the psychological and neuro-pathological evidence for positing differences between child and adult brains, we cannot consider this evidence to be decisive on the question of whether the adult is capable of linguistic inference. Healthy adult brains do enable adults to make various other kinds of generalizations from particular instances—e.g., adults can gain the general skill of driving, and can use that skill in new instances, on unfamiliar roads, in a new car, etc. We are unaware of any empirical evidence for saying that it is exactly the ability to make new applications of linguistic material to new instances that is lost in adulthood.‖ ‖ ‖

---

§§§ This is the implication, for example, of this statement by Karl Teeter in his review of E. C. Horne, *Beginning Javanese, Language* XXXIX (1963), p. 147; "First of all, it needs to be clearly recognized that adults learn languages differently from children. They have lost, at least in large part, the ability to make that remarkable induction that all children, independently of intelligence, make with such speed when they learn a language."

‖ ‖ ‖ W. Penfield and L. Roberts, *Speech and Brain-Mechanisms* (Princeton, 1959)—see also Lenneberg's review in *Language* XXXVI (1960), pp. 97–112—offer physiological evidence for cortical specialization during childhood development, with resulting inability later in adult life to recreate lost speech mechanisms in new areas of the brain after trauma.

The fact that the speech mechanism must be developed in childhood if the individual is to speak at all does not *a priori* preclude the possibility that, once developed, it can be applied later in adult life to the learning of new languages. Cf. especially Penfield and Roberts, *op. cit.*, pp. 251–254, where they discuss the case of the bilingual child learning through the "direct" or "mother's" method, or the adult learning through the "indirect" or "secondary" method. Penfield discusses Joseph Conrad's success in learning English as an instance of the application of the direct method to adult language learning (*op. cit.*, pp. 241–242), but he fails to draw the proper general pedagogical conclusions from the case. Thus the possibility is left open that, despite the loss of certain kinds of plasticity in the brain of the adult as the combined result of maturation and learning, new learning in later life is still possible, provided that the basic mechanisms are laid down in early life. The allegation that language learning capability has been lost in the adult—on the grounds of the neurological evidence—fails to recognize the possibility that so long as the *mechanism* for learning language exists, language learning may proceed as with the child. For example, Penfield elsewhere suggests that bilingual experience in childhood, where two languages (or dialects) are learned under different conditions of use, provides the child with a learning strategy that he can apply later in life either in reactivating and extending his now dormant secondary childhood language, or in acquiring additional languages:

"I suspect that the basic units of second languages are hidden away in the brain during the childhood of those who grow up in lands where many languages echo in playground or home. This it is, perhaps, that makes the Pole and the Swiss and the Hollander better language students. I suspect, further, that the child who has the basic units of French and English hidden away in his brain

The difficulty with a statement such as Penfield's:

> When new languages are taken up for the first time in the second
> decade of life, it is difficult, though not impossible, to achieve a good
> result. It is difficult because it is unphysiological.###

is that it seems to contain a self contradiction: if it is "unphysiological"
for an adult brain to learn a new language, how are we to account for
the fact that it is possible at all? What could an "unphysiological"
mechanism be that would explain language learning in adults? In fact,
many adult learners do learn new languages very well. What is usually
taken as evidence against their ability to learn as a child learns is the
fact that they speak the new language with an accent. But our point is
that they do learn to speak it and that the amount of skill they often
acquire far exceeds in amount and importance the amount of skill they
seem not to acquire. The neurophysiological evidence may be used to
argue that adults are quantitatively inferior to children as language
learners; it cannot be used to argue that they are qualitatively different
kinds of learners. We submit that the same language learning capability exists in both child and adult, quite possibly in different degrees,
and that the extraordinary efficiency of the "method"**** by which
children learn can and should be taken advantage of in teaching adults.

Argument 2: The child has much more time to learn the language.††††

---

finds it easier in later life to take up a third language, for example, German, even
by the indirect method. He has a double number of basic units to call on. And
they are similar, at least in part, to those needed." "Learning a Second Language,"
The Second Career (Boston, 1963), p. 135.
Speech and Brain-Mechanisms, p. 255. Penfield does not seem here to be
exercising the same caution as when he says (p. 249):
"Returning to the act of speaking: We control voice and mouth by following
the verbal motor units formed and fixed by early practice. It is difficult to make
any certain statement on the question of accents by reference to physiological
evidence alone. One may say that children have a greater capacity for imitation
than adults. That seems to be a fact, but it is not an explanation of what happens
in later life."
**** *Op. cit.*, p. 254.
†††† Cf. William G. Moulton, *A Linguistic Guide to Language Learning* (Modern Language Association of America, 1966), p. 2: "One of the most striking
aspects of a child's language learning is the fact that he spends so much time at it.
He talks with his parents, he talks with his brothers and sisters, he talks with his
playmates; if no one else is around, he even talks himself. It is a little sad to
realize that the child practices so much, because this is something which no adult
language learner can ever hope to match—he has too much else to do."
The argument has been made earlier: "The learning of vernacular sounds by
imitation is a slow and difficult task, but the conditions of beginning in infancy,
having nothing else to do, and, above all of the mind being unhampered by conflicting associations with the sounds of other languages, are so favorable, and the

This argument is difficult to evaluate, since we do not have reliable information about how much time the child actually does spend in learning a language. From casual observation, however, it does not appear that the young child spends as much time in language contact as would be required to explain the vast differences between the language-using abilities of native four-year-old children and those of college students after two years of language courses. The small child is busy with many things—including sleeping and solitary playing—other than language, and it is the rare mother who can bear to keep a one-way conversation going without long breaks during her periods of contact with the child.‡‡‡‡ There is also some question whether the adult might not gain as much from his ability to focus his attention over a period of time as the child gains from longer, but less concentrated contact with the language.

More important, there is a striking difference between the *kind* of linguistic proficiency children have immediately and that of classroom students (including those under the tutelage of a linguist), a difference that has nothing to do with the amount of time spent in contact: what the child knows of the language he can use (perhaps only in listening and comprehending, perhaps also in his own speech), while the classroom student's knowledge seems all too often to be unavailable for his own immediate use. To put it in other terms, the child is fluent in his language very early, increasing his fluency in direct proportion to his knowledge of the language, while the classroom student's "knowledge" of the language may allow him to do everything with the language except use it.§§§§ And notice that the classroom student does not need

---

inducements to learn are so strong, that the initiation is in most cases practically perfect." (Emphasis added.) Henry Sweet, *The History of Language* (London, 1900), p. 19. Incidentally, note also Sweet's modern-sounding references to interference ("conflicting associations") and motivation ("inducements").

‡‡‡‡ Cf. the following observation of Otto Jespersen's relevant to the passage from Sweet quoted in Note ††††: "Sweet ([*History of Language*] 19) says among other things that the conditions of learning vernacular sounds are so favourable because the child has nothing else to do at the time. On the contrary, one may say that the child has an enormous deal to do while it is learning language; it is at that time active beyond belief: in a short time it subdues wider tracts than it ever does later in a much longer time. The more wonderful is it that along with those tasks it finds strength to learn its mother-tongue and its many refinements and crooked turns." *Language, Its Nature, Development and Origin* (London, 1922), p. 141.

§§§§ Cf. also the following from Jespersen, *op. cit.*, p. 142–143: "The child has another priceless advantage: he hears the language in all possible situations and under such conditions that language and situation ever correspond exactly with one another. Gesture and facial expression harmonize with the words uttered and keep the child to a right understanding. Here there is nothing unnatural, such as is often the case in a language-lesson in later years, when one talks about

an inordinate amount of time to learn things he sees immediate use for; e.g., he quickly learns to say and respond to short greetings or to utter curses and dirty words in the new language, though from the linguistic analyst's point of view, these may be quite complex structurally. Psychological factors seem to be at least as crucial as structural ones in determining how much time is needed to learn utterances.

> Argument 3: The child is much more strongly motivated to learn his first language than the adult is to learn a foreign language.

If we take "motivation" here to imply something like "need" or "deprivation," it is not at all clear that the child does so poorly without language. In our culture, as in many others, a crying, inarticulate baby has his needs rather well taken care of: it is not until he develops language, as a matter of fact, that he seems to need what he can get only through language. And it is not clear that motivation in this sense has much to do with adult learning of language: there are cases galore of immigrants whose very livelihood depends on their mastering a language which nevertheless largely eludes them, and not a few cases of good language learners whose general reward will be no greater than one more A in a language course.

If on the other hand we take "motivation" to mean something like "effective reward," there is no theoretical, and little practical difficulty in constructing teaching programs for adults which are at least as efficient in their selective reinforcement as that which most native learners receive for their linguistic efforts. Indeed, any imputation of some general, motivational differences between first and second language learning will fail to account for the observable success of children becoming bilingual in learning a second language.

There is another equivocation often concealed in the use of the term motivation. Suppose we replace motivation with the expression "wanting to." Then saying that someone "wants to" learn a language can be taken to mean either that he wants to be in possession of the skill, or that he "wants to" do the things that will lead him to acquire it. Clearly the former should, but does not automatically, imply the latter. Thus we can explain the paradox of the person who says he "wants to" be able to play the oboe, but never learns, because he doesn't like to practice.

---

ice and snow in June or excessive heat in January. And what the child hears is just what immediately concerns and interests him, and again and again his own attempts at speech lead to the fulfillment of his dearest wishes, so that his command of language has great practical advantages for him."

In arguing for the relevance of motivation in accounting for observably different degrees of success in language learning, we seem to be led ultimately to the circularity—apparently inescapable outside of controlled laboratory conditions—of positing motivation in exactly those cases where successful learning has taken place and denying its presence in unsuccessful cases.

> Argument 4: The child offers a *tabula rasa* for language learning. The adult's native language will interfere with his acquisition of a foreign language.‖ ‖ ‖ ‖

No one can doubt the reality of the phenomena that are referred to by the term *interference*, but the metaphor implied by the term is unfortunate and misleading in discussions of language learning. It is true, indeed obvious by now, that learners will speak a foreign language with many errors which the observer can identify with characteristics in the learner's own language. But it seems to us that the pedagogical implications drawn by linguists have depended on an inadequate analysis of the term interference as applied to those phenomena.

The term "interference" is appropriately used to describe a phenomenon observable in psychological experiments in which different sets of responses are to be learned to the same set of stimuli or, more generally, when one set of behaviors is supposed to *replace* another set. In that case (when the stimulus set is held constant) the previous

---

‖ ‖ ‖ ‖ Cf. Robert L. Politzer, Foreign Language Learning, A Linguistic Introduction (Preliminary Edition) (Englewood Cliffs, N. J., 1965). p. 8:

"But the most essential difference between learning the native language and a foreign language lies in the simple fact that when you learn the foreign language you have already learned (consciously or subconsciously) a set of rules—namely the set that governs the system of the native language. If you learn a foreign language while you are still young, at an age at which the patterns and rules of your native language are still comparatively new to you, the interference that comes from the rules of the native language is likely to be small. But the older you become, the more practice you have had in speaking the native language, the more the rules and system of the native language are likely to interfere with learning the system of the foreign language. Once you are in your teens it is no longer possible to learn the foreign language in exactly the same way in which you learned your native language. The mere fact that you already have a native language that will interfere with the foreign language makes second language learning and first language learning quite different processes."

We would argue that if it were in fact true that "the mere fact that you already have a native language . . . makes second language learning and first language learning quite different processes," then bilingualism would be impossible for the child as well as for the adult, something that runs contrary to the observation that children can acquire one or more second languages with comparative ease and little or no interference.

learning of a certain set of responses may have a detrimental effect on the learning of a new set. The problem of interference in language study arises genuinely under conditions in which two different sets of responses are to be learned to the *same* set of stimuli, or more generally, in the same stimulus field. Such conditions are met in certain traditional translation-grammar procedures, but they are also met in courses devised by linguists in which the student's attention is called explicitly or implicitly to a contrast between the native and target language.#### What linguists (in common with traditional teachers) have typically *not* done consistently in planning language courses is to minimize the conditions that lead to interference by doing for the adult learner what is typically done for the child who is learning a second language: namely, using one language in a set of circumstances consistently distinguished from the set of circumstances in which the other language is used. The example of bilingual children who learn and use one language at home and another at school—without suffering enormous difficulties of interference—should induce language

---

Cf. the following very cogent remarks by Roger L. Hadlich, "Lexical Contrastive Analysis," *Modern Language Journal* XLIX (1965), pp. 426–429:

"Thus, paradoxically, when pairs of words which are known traditionally and shown analytically to be a problem are placed in juxtaposition, explained, contrasted and drilled, students tend to continue confusing them; when they are presented as if no problem existed students have little or no difficulty." (p. 426)

"The point is that 'problem pairs' [such as Spanish *salir* and *dejar*] are nonnative. The relation between the members of each pair is extraneous to the language being studied and is thus an artificial and perhaps unnecessary constriction, imposed on the foreign language from without." (p. 427)

"In [contrastive] drill of this type [i.e. on pairs such as *salir* and *dejar*], even if students are somehow prevented from making associations based on the implicit English language criteria, they are nevertheless being taught that *salir* and *dejar* are easily confused in Spanish and must be used with care. Awareness of the possibility of erroneous substitution fosters in itself the substitution it is designed to forestall and so defeats its own purpose. Thus contrastive drill is a self-fulfilling prophesy, and problem pair confusions are the result." (p. 427)

"If we ignore all problem pairs and treat the words separately, in the terms of the foreign language, general lexical interference will be reduced and confusion avoided." (p. 429)

Applying these considerations in developing materials for teaching Spanish (*A Structural Course in Spanish*, New York, 1963), Hadlich and his colleagues D. L. Wolfe and J. G. Inman concluded:

"No effort was made, in the elaboration of the materials, to apply the contrastive analysis techniques on the vocabulary level. . . . Our students' control of the pairs was markedly better than that of the usual first year Spanish students. No confusions were made; the students we questioned were not aware of any problem; they were even surprised to find later that, in translating sentences containing these words, two different words in Spanish were represented by only one in English." (p. 426)

Equally important here as their informal finding is the clear formulation of the possible and actual effect of contrastive drill on the student's performance.

teaching planners to spend their ingenuity in devising language teaching situations that differ grossly from situations in which the native language is used, rather than devising means of calling students' attention to fine distinctions between the native and foreign language.*****

But how can we understand the phenomenon of foreign accent without resorting to the notion of interference? Our account is something like this: A person knows how to speak one language, say his native one. Now he tries to speak another one; but in his early stages of learning the new one, there are many things he has not yet learned to do; that is, he is grossly undertrained in the new one. But he is induced to perform ("perform" may mean understand, speak, read, or write) in that new one by an external teacher or by his internal desire to say something. What can he do other than use what he already knows to make up for what he does not know? To an observer who knows the target language, the learner will seem to be stubbornly substituting the native habits for target habits. But from the learner's point of view, all he is doing is the best he can: to fill in his gaps of training he refers for help to what he already knows. The problem of "interference" viewed thus reduces to the problem of ignorance, and the solution to the problem is simply more and better training in the target language, rather than systematic drill at the points of contrast between the two languages in order to combat interference.

The child is developing his intellect simultaneously with his language and can "want to say" only what he is learning to say. The adult, on the other hand, can want to say what he does not yet know how to say, and he uses whatever means he has at his disposal. It is easy to see how the phenomenon of interference can result from his attempts to do more than he has yet learned to do in the new language. This seems to us sufficient explanation of how interference comes about, without the unnecessary hypostacization of competing linguistic systems, getting in each other's way or taking pot shots at one another.

There is much evidence to support our view. For example, if already learned habits exerted force against learning a new language (as implied by active metaphorical extension of the term "interference") we would expect the strongest habits to exert the greatest force: specifically, if a person knows imperfectly another foreign language in addition to the one he is trying to learn, we should expect his second

***** Cf. Penfield's observation (*Speech and Brain-Mechanisms*, p. 251–255) that no interference phenomena ("confusion" is his term) are noticeable in the speech of multi-lingual children who have learned several languages by either the "direct" or "mother's" method, different languages being learned under different circumstances.

language to be unable to compete with the native one in interfering with the third one. But in fact, it is commonly observed that the two imperfectly learned languages may infect each other to a greater degree than the native language will infect either one.

Again, if learning a new language followed the psychological laboratory model of learning a new set of "habits," we should expect interference in both directions: any reduction of interference (which in the view we oppose is held to be proportional to the increase in skill in the new language) should be accompanied by a weakening of the habits in the native language. But in fact we observe no direct, necessary ill effects on native habits as a result of increased learning of a second language.†††††

Finally, if every individual point of difference between native and new language had to be taught to adults through carefully constructed drills devoted to that point, it would be as impossible to learn a new language as it would be to learn one's native language one bit at a time. The observable fact is that adults do learn new languages— acquiring new abilities that could never have been taught them by mere summation of the formal exercises to which they may have been exposed. And they do learn remarkably well—remarkably, if the doctrine of the mature "frozen brain" were accepted. Linguists have been so eager to display their expertise in pointing to the minor ways in which foreign accent distorts performance in the new language that they have underestimated the enormous amount of mastery of language structure that the foreign speaker is exhibiting when he is using long utterances to say something. If the mistakes are to be scored against the learner's brain, then the successes must be scored for it; on balance, the adult must be appreciated to be a potentially magnificent learner of language.

To sum up, a minimal viable theory of foreign language learning assumes a language learning capability qualitatively the same—though perhaps quantitatively different—in the adult and in the child. This capability enables the learner to acquire the general use of a foreign language by observation and exercise of particular instances of the language in use. Such observation and exercise is necessary, because without it, language cannot be learned as language; sufficient, because the learner can do the analysis for himself. The main control the

---

††††† There may be indirect ones. If as a person learns a second language he abandons the situations in which he speaks his native one, he may actually forget the latter. But such loss of native habits is like any other loss of skills which are not exercised: the proper learning of new skills—in contexts sharply set off from those appropriate for the old ones—does not interfere with the old ones.

teacher needs to exert over the materials to be studied is that they be graspable as usable items by the learner. The language learning capability of the student will gradually take care of the rest.

APPENDIX I

(To review the use of ME, TO ME, FOR ME, etc.) Listen to the words and the statements. Include the words in the statements. For example:

Me She talked about music.
   SHE TALKED ABOUT MUSIC TO ME.
Them He asked some questions.
   HE ASKED THEM SOME QUESTIONS.
John The teacher pronounced the word.
   THE TEACHER PRONOUNCED THE WORD FOR JOHN.

1. Us. He talked about Ann Arbor.
2. Me. He visited in Miami.
3. Them. They waited.
4. Me. He told a story.
5. John. She made a cake.
6. Her. He explained the program.
7. Him. I asked for a cigarette.
8. Mary. John pronounced the sentence.
9. Him. We bought a present.
10. Me. John did the work.
11. Bill. Mary introduced us.
12. Them. He got some pencils.
13. His mother. He wrote a letter.
14. The class. He is going to speak about language.
15. Her. He always says a kind thing.‡‡‡‡‡

APPENDIX II

PRÉTEXTES

Galathée et son amie sont au restaurant universitaire et Galathée voit Hector qui la cherche. Elle est en colère contre lui, et ne veut pas lui parler.

‡‡‡‡‡ Robert Lado and Charles C. Fries, *English Sentence Patterns* (Ann Arbor, 1957), p. 94.

1.

Galathée (à voix basse):	Fais semblant de ne pas voir!
L'amie (étonnée):	Pourquoi? Je ne vois personne.
Galathée (insistante):	Il y a Hector qui me cherche et je ne veux pas lui parler.
L'amie:	De toute façon je ne crois pas qu'il nous aperçoive.

2. Même que 1.

Galathée (chuchotant):	Fais semblant de ne pas entendre.
L'amie (étonnée):	Pourquoi? Je n'entends rien!
Galathée (avec urgence):	Il y a Hector qui m'appelle et je ne veux pas le voir.
L'amie:	De toute façon je crois qu'il nous aperçoit.

3. En classe. Galathée n'écoute pas et le professeur la regarde d'un mauvais oeil. Hector essaie de la rappeler à l'ordre.

Hector (sans en avoir l'air):	Fais semblant d'écouter.
Galathée (baillant):	Pourquoi? Je suis trop fatiguée.
Hector (avec urgence):	Il y a le professeur qui te regarde et il voit bien que tu ne sais pas.
Galathée (indifférente):	De toute façon il ne croit pas que je sois très intelligente.

4. A la bibliothèque. Hector et son copain voient Galathée qui vient dans leur direction. Le copain d'Hector ne peut pas sentir Galathée et veut l'éviter.

Le copain (avec urgence):	Vite, fais semblant d'étudier.
Hector (étonné):	Pourquoi? C'est bien ce que je fais.
Le copain (avec insistance):	Il y a Galathée qui approche et je ne veux pas qu'elle vienne ici.
Hector:	De toute façon je ne crois pas qu'il y ait de place libre.

PRETEXTS

Galathea and her friend are at the cafeteria and Galathea sees Hector looking for her. She is mad at him and doesn't want to speak to him.

1.

Galathea: (in a low voice)	Pretend that you don't see anyone.
Friend: (surprised)	Why? I don't see anyone.
Galathea: (impatiently)	Hector's looking for me, and I don't want to talk to him.
Friend:	Well, anyway, I don't think he will notice us.

2. Same as 1.

Galathea: (whispers)	Pretend that you don't hear anything.
Friend: (surprised)	Why? I don't hear anything!
Galathea: (urgently)	Hector's calling me and I don't want to see him.
Friend:	In any case, I think that he's noticed us.

3. During class, Galathea is not listening and the teacher is glaring at her. Hector tries to get her to pay attention.

Hector: (out of the side of his mouth)	Hey, pretend to be listening.
Galathea: (yawning)	Why? I'm too tired.
Hector: (urging)	The teacher is looking at you and he can see you are not paying attention.
Galathea: (indifferent)	Well, anyway, he doesn't think I'm very intelligent.

4. At the library. Hector and his buddy see Galathea coming in their direction. Hector's buddy can't stand Galathea and wants to avoid her.

Buddy: (urgently)	Quick, pretend that you're studying.
Hector: (surprised)	Why? That's what I am doing.
Buddy: (insisting)	Galathea is coming this way and I don't want to talk to her.
Hector:	Well, anyway, I don't think there's any room.

After his performance of the dialogue-variants has become fluent and natural, the learner is encouraged to make new uses and new combinations of the language he has acquired, as in conversations like the following. The indirect cues mitigate the compulsion to translate from English into the foreign language. The learner supplies some of the language needed to perform the conversations from previously learned dialogues. Short conversations allow the situation to be comprehended quickly and without effort.§§§§§

CONVERSATION 1

You are on the bus with a friend and spot Jules to whom you owe some money. Your friend is about to call over to Jules.

You . . . . . . Tell your friend to pretend that he is looking out of the window.

He . . . . . . Asks you why, he's about to call over to Jules.

You . . . . . . Tell him that Jules is looking for you, that you owe him money.

He . . . . . . Says O.K., but not to worry, Jules has probably not noticed you.

CONVERSATION 2

You and your boy friend are at a night club, and you spot your ex-fiancé across the room.

You . . . . . . Tell your boy friend to pretend to be talking to you.

He . . . . . . Says that that is exactly what he's doing.

You . . . . . . Say that an old friend of yours is sitting across the room, and you don't want him to notice you.

He . . . . . . Says not to worry, in any case it is too dark here to see anything.

§§§§§ An explicit use of this device is also to be found in the exercises called "Conversation" in the old *Spoken Language Series* (ca. 1945) now published by Holt, Rinehart and Winston, Inc., New York. Cf. the following from Jeannette Dearden and Karin Stig-Nielsen, *Spoken Danish* (Book One) (New York, 1945), p. v.:

"The Conversation Practice represents the central aim of the course. Situations will be outlined which will give you the setting for your conversations. Here you will be able to use all the material that you have learned up to this point."

LEON JAKOBOVITS

Implications of Recent Psycholinguistic Developments for the Teaching of a Second Language

INTRODUCTION

This paper is divided into two large sections. The first is concerned with the child's acquisition of his first language. The second section deals with second language learning. Jakobovits differentiates between learning theory and the new view originated by Chomsky in terms of the explanation of how a child acquires his first language. He characterizes the two positions in terms of the relation of *surface* and *base*:

> (in learning theory) the process of acquisition was from surface to base; that is, the knowledge represented by language learning at all levels—phonological, semantic, syntactic—was entirely based on the relations contained in the overt speech of the parents. The new approach . . . can be characterized by saying that it reverses this order; that is, the burden of acquisition is now placed on the child with relatively minor importance attached to the environment as a *reinforcing* agency. Furthermore, it minimizes the relations contained in the surface of language, attributing the significant information to be acquired to the underlying structure of language which is not contained in the surface input.

Reprinted with permission of the author from *Language Learning*, Vol. XVIII, Nos. 1 and 2 (June), 1968, pp. 89–109.

Jakobovits then points out and discusses three specific inadequacies of the older view: (1) "The acquisition of phonology," (2) "The acquisition of meaning," and (3) "The acquisition of syntax." In the view of learning theory, the child learns the identity of the sound elements of the adult language by the process of association. Jakobovits argues that the structure of the sound system of the adult language is not just a series of elements: "the 'cracking' of the phonological code of a natural language involves a process of pattern recognition and equation, not simply learning the identity of constituent elements."

From the standpoint of learning theory, the meaning of words is learned by association. This in turn leads to the view that "words tag things." Jakobovits points out that this conception of meaning is inadequate to explain our capacity to extend the meanings of words, as, for instance, the *eye* in *the eye of the needle* because learning theory can only specify the nature of the extension after it has happened, that is, it has no predictive power. As the author puts it, "the creative and novel use of words which is so characteristic of language remains completely beyond its explanatory range."

The learning theory view of syntax was that a sentence is composed of a sequence of words learned in terms of the sequential probabilities of the items. Jakobovits rejects this view on the grounds that sentences, in fact, are much more complex than that. He demonstrates this by citing several sets of sentences whose relationships with the other sentences within their set could not be accounted for by simply viewing a sentence as a sequence of items in a certain fixed pattern.

Since, according to Jakobovits, the traditional view of first language acquisition seems inadequate, "it is necessary to start anew right from the beginning." The author turns his attention to the study of how children first begin to combine words into two-word sequences (beginning at about 1½ years). The two-word combinations are neither random groupings nor the result of direct imitation of adult sentences. The two-word combinations have their own special structure consisting of what is called a "pivot" class and an "open" class of words. As the child matures, the pivot class gradually subdivides into further classes. The important point here is that children do not discover word classes by rearranging the elements they hear in adult speech in some trial-and-error way, as learning theory would suggest. Instead, the child seems predisposed to "look for" certain kinds of relationships. Thus the child's ability to discover these grammatical categories must be based on "linguistic universals that are part of the child's innate endowment" (quoting McNeill). A second kind of grammatical category, also innate, is transformational rules. However, as the author points out, "the early stages of child language competence does not apparently include the ability to perform transformations."

In the second section, the author examines "the implications for language teaching of the views outlined earlier on the language acquisition process." The author discusses these three topics in reference to second language teaching: (1) "The role of practice and imitation," (2) "The distinction between competence and performance," and (3) "The nature of skills involved in foreign language acquisition."

1. "The role of practice and imitation." In the view of the Behavioral school, practice and imitation were essential steps in the learning process. It is only through practice that a novel form becomes "stamped in." In reply, Jakobovits argues that children do not readily mimic a form that they do not already possess, and in fact regularize the forms of the adult language to fit their own generalizations. As Jakobovits says, "concept attainment and hypothesis testing are more likely paradigms in language development than response strength through rote memory and repetition."

2. "The distinction between competence and performance." If one basic language competence underlies all language performance, why does "one type of performance, understanding, appear to develop before another type of performance, speaking"? After discussing a possible solution that McNeill proposes, Jakobovits advances the theory that understanding and speaking employ different kinds of capabilities or processes: understanding is essentially analytic while speaking is synthetic. "It may be that for humans, analytic processes are easier than synthetic ones. One might say that it is easier to learn the art critic's job than the artist's."

3. "The nature of skills involved in foreign language acquisition." Jakobovits points out some differences between first language learning and second language learning: (1) an adult's cognitive development is more advanced than a child's, and (2) the fact that the adult already knows one language will facilitate the learning of the second through transfer of skills and concepts acquired in the first language. In reference to the first point, Jakobovits points out that language acquisition is an innate endowment, and consequently it is not clear that advanced age and cognitive development will help. In reference to the second point, Jakobovits argues that while in some areas at least it is possible to make predictions about what features of English a learner of English will have special difficulty with, this gives us no insight into how he will eventually overcome the difficulty. For instance, the fact that we can predict that a Japanese will have trouble with /l/ and /r/ does not suggest how we should teach him to make the distinction.

Jakobovits closes the article with a discussion of four specific topics in the teaching of a second language. (1) "Teaching the knowledge of structure." Since knowing a language means knowing sets of relations "rather than constituent elements, the usefulness of efforts to teach the latter is in doubt." (2) "Teaching successful strategies of acquisition." Following Carroll, it is possible to identify strategies that successful language learners employ. It is possible that these strategies may be teachable. (3) "Teaching habit integration and automaticity." Here Jakobovits proposes teaching exercises based on meaning (for example, families of transformational rules and vocabulary organized in semantic clusters) rather than on surface forms and patterns. (4) "On semi-grammatical sentences." In fluent speech semi-grammatical sentences are as common, and perhaps even more common, than well-formed sentences. Children seem able to use semi-grammatical sentences as the base for acquiring the rules governing the creation of well-formed sentences. "The logical implication of this would be that no language teacher should ever force his pupils to use only well-formed sentences in practice conversations."

This paper attempts to summarize some recently developed notions about the language acquisition process and makes some preliminary suggestions about the implications of these ideas for the problem of teaching a second language.* The original impetus in demonstrating the shortcomings of traditional psychological and linguistic theories in the understanding of the processes of language structure and language acquisition must be credited to Chomsky (1957; 1959) who also developed new theories to cope with the problem. Subsequent writers have elaborated upon this new outlook pointing out the various specific inadequacies of the earlier notions and making concrete suggestions for new approaches (see Miller, 1965; Katz, 1966; McNeill, 1966; Lenneberg, 1967; Slobin, 1966; and several others; see the contributions in Bellugi and Brown, 1964). To appreciate fully these new developments it is necessary to consider briefly the nature of the inadequacy of the earlier notions on the language acquisition process.

FROM SURFACE TO BASE

The traditional psychological approach to the language acquisition process was to view it within the framework of learning theory. The acquisition of phonology was viewed as a process of shaping the elementary sounds produced by the infant through reinforcement of successive approximations to the adult pattern. Imitation of adult speech patterns was thought to be a source of reward to the babbling

---

* This is an invited address to the 1968 convention of TESOL (Teachers of English to Speakers of Other Languages) delivered in San Antonio, Texas, March 9, 1968. The two sources to which I am most indebted in the preparation of this paper are McNeill (1966) and Lenneberg (1967) whose stimulating ideas it is a pleasure to acknowledge.

infant and repeated practice on these novel motor habits was thought to serve the function of "stamping in" and automatizing them.

From these elementary phonological habits the words of the language were thought to emerge through parental reinforcement. It was said that the child could better control his environment by uttering words to which the parents responded by giving the child what it wanted. The child learned the meaning of words through a conditioning process whereby the referents which the word signalled appeared in contiguity with the symbol thus establishing an association. The acquisition of grammar was conceptualized as learning the proper order of words in sentences. Generalization carried a heavy theoretical burden in attempts to explain novel uses of words and novel arrangements of sentences. Perceptual similarity of physical objects and relations, and functional equivalence of responses was thought to serve as the basis for generalizing the meaning of previously learned words. Similarly, generalization of the grammatical function of words was thought to account for the understanding and production of novel sentences.

Two aspects of this approach are noteworthy. One is that the burden of language acquisition was placed on the environment: the parents were the source of input, and reinforcement was the necessary condition for establishing the "habits." The child was merely a passive organism responsive to the reinforcement conditions arranged by agencies in the environment. The second aspect to be noted was the relatively simplistic conception of the knowledge to be acquired: sentences were conceived as an ordering of words, arranged in sequential probabilities that could be learned then generalized to novel combinations. A general characterization of this overall approach would be to say that the process of acquisition was from surface to base; that is, the knowledge represented by language learning at all levels—phonological, semantic, syntactic—was entirely based on the relations contained in the overt speech of the parents. The new approach to be discussed below can be characterized by saying that it reverses this order; that is, the burden of acquisition is now placed on the child with relatively minor importance attached to the environment as a *reinforcing* agency. Furthermore, it minimizes the relations contained in the surface of language, attributing the significant information to be acquired to the underlying structure of language which is not contained in the surface input. However, before taking up this new approach, it is necessary to point out the specific inadequacies of the earlier approach.

The acquisition of phonology.   The notion that the child first learns the constituent elements of the adult phonemic structure and then produces speech by associating these elements appears to be contrary to fact. In the first place, it is doubtful that speech is made up of a concatenation of physically unique sound elements. A sound typewriter which would convert each physically different sound into a different orthographic type would not produce a very readable record (Lenneberg, 1967). The reason for this is that speech recognition is not simply a process of identifying physical differences in sounds. In fact, it requires overlooking certain acoustic differences as unimportant and paying attention to certain other features in relation to the acoustic context in which the sound is imbedded. In other words, the "cracking" of the phonological code of a natural language involves a process of pattern recognition and equation, not simply learning the identity of constituent elements. The first recognizable words of a child are not composed of acoustically invariant speech sounds (see Lenneberg, 1967). Therefore, a description of phonological acquisition in terms of learning individual speech sounds which are then combined into words, must be false. Furthermore, it is not clear how a notion of shaping by successive approximation can ever account for the acquisition of sound pattern recognition and the discovery by the child of phonological structure of a hierarchical nature.

The acquisition of meaning. It is an indication of the simplistic character of previous behavioristic views of language that they have concerned themselves with the problem of reference to the almost total exclusion of the semantic interpretation of utterances. Reference deals with the relation between words and objects or aspects of the environment. Psychological theories of meaning (or reference) were based on a philosophical system of conceptualization which now appears to be false; namely the notion that "words tag things" in the physical environment. The adoption of such a view led to elementary descriptions whereby a particular combination of sounds (a word) was conditioned to an object or set of objects. When a new object having certain physical similarities to the one previously conditioned was encountered, the learned verbal response was said to have generalized to this new instance. More elaborate versions of this form of theorizing were developed to account for the obvious fact that familiar words would be used in connection with objects or situations which had no physical similarity to the originally conditioned object. However, due to the requirements imposed by viewing meaning as a conditioned response to a stimulus, these later elaborations merely pushed back the locus of the similarity from the external physical object to an internal (even though functional) representation of that object. Thus an individual's capacity to understand the extension of the word *eye* in *the eye of the needle* was thought of as arising from the fact that the internal conditioned responses elicited by the word *eye* in the above phrase are similar in some (unspecified) manner to the responses originally conditioned to the word *eye* in such instances as *this is your eye, these are my eyes, this is the doggy's eye,* etc. The total inadequacy of this kind of approach as an explanatory device is this: it leaves obscure the specific nature of the similarity of the conditioned response from the original to the extension, it is incapable of specifying the nature of the extension and cannot predict it until after it has occurred. Thus the view of reference as a conditioning process has the same shortcomings for semantics as the view of conditioning of sequential probabilities of parts of speech has for syntax. That is, the creative and novel use of words which is so characteristic of language remains completely beyond its explanatory range.

The difficulties attached to these behavioristic explanations of meaning can be resolved by abandoning the notion that "words tag things" in favor of the view that "words tag the processes by which the species deals cognitively with its environment" (Lenneberg, 1967, p. 334). This view reverses the order between the object-stimulus and its conditioned response-process. That is, rather than saying that the concept-meaning involved in the use of the word *eye* is a conditioned process (external, internal, or cortical) developed as a result of tagging various objects having certain characteristics and experiences relating to them, this view says that the word *eye* tags a class of cognitive processes developed through a categorization and differentiation process which is independent of verbal labeling. When a child (or adult for that matter) is confronted with a new word it acquires meaning only in the sense that it comes to refer to a class of cognitive processes already possessed by the individual. Novel uses of words, such as metaphoric extensions are understandable to others by virtue of the fact that human categorization and differentiation processes are similar across the species, the word merely serving as a convenient tag whereby these processes can be labeled. The language of stimulus-response theory does not seem to offer any particular advantages when conceptualizing the problem in this fashion.

A conception of meaning such as the one just outlined, has certain implications for a theory of semantics which it might be important to state explicitly. Meaning becomes a purely cognitive concept (as linguists of a generation ago used to believe) and semantics represents the linguistic expression of these cognitive operations. The problem of the development of meaning becomes the problem of cognitive development, which is to say that the dimensions of meaning—how the human species categorizes and differentiates the universe—*ante-date* the dimensions of semantics—how cognitive categories and relations find expression in linguistic terms. An adequate theory of meaning must be able to characterize the nature of this relation, namely the mapping of cognitive to linguistic processes. Note that this includes not only lexical (vocabulary) items, but also the morphophemic and inflectional system of language, since the latter contain cognitive differentiations such as present vs. past, animate vs. inanimate, definite vs. indefinite, mass vs. count, male vs. female, plural vs. singular, and so on. It follows that an adequate theory of semantics must concern itself not only with the vocabulary of a language and the relation between words and things (reference) but also with the manner in which the syntactic component of a language allows the expression of cognitive relations (meaning). While the first aspect may be conceptualized as a closed system such as that represented by a dictionary of a language, the second aspect is an open system that cannot be described by a taxonomy of properties or relations. In other words, while it is possible to make an inventory of all the words in a language, it is impossible to make an inventory of all the possible usages of any single word (with the exception perhaps of most function words). An adequate semantic theory must therefore contain at least the following two things: (a) a model of human cognition specifying a finite set of dimensions or features, probably in the form of a generic hierarchy of increasing inclusiveness as we move up the tree, and (b) a set of finite rules (or transformations) specifying the possibilities of manipulations of the elements in the tree. The description of (a) must be a general psychological theory and is made up of "psychological or cognitive universals" as defined by the biological capacity of the human species. The description of (b) must be a cultural and individual psychological theory as defined by individual differences in general intelligence and in personal experiences.

The acquisition of syntax. The failure of behavior theory to account in any significant manner for the problem of the acquisition of syntax can be interpreted as stemming from a failure to recognize the complexity of the syntax of language. As long as sentences are viewed as a sequential ordering of words or categories of words and the phenomenon to be explained as a problem in the learning of sequential probabilities of items or classes of items, no meaningful progress can be made. The relations among the following eight sentences taken from Lenneberg (1967, p. 273–275) illustrate the complexities of the problem to be dealt with:

1. colorless green ideas sleep furiously
2. furiously sleep ideas green colorless
3. occasionally call warfare useless
4. useless warfare call occasionally
5. friendly young dogs seem harmless
6. the fox chases the dog
7. the dog chases the fox
8. the dog is chased by the fox

If one compares sentence (1) and (2) it is evident that (1) is grammatical while (2) is not. The difference cannot be entirely in their meaning for, although sentence (1) is more likely to have some meaning than sentence (2), nevertheless sentence (1) will be judged more grammatical than sentence (2) even by the most prosaically inclined person. Nor can it be said that the reason sentence (1) is more grammatical than sentence (2) is that it is more familiar, since both sentences had a frequency of zero until linguists began to use it a short while ago to make the kind of point that is being made here. The ungrammatical string (4) has the same order of parts of speech as the grammatical string (1), namely (adjective + noun + verb + adverb). Similarly, the grammatical and semantically interpretable sentence (3)† has the same order of parts of speech as the ungrammatical and semantically uninterpretable string (2), namely (adverb + verb + noun + adjective). This shows that the transitional probability of parts of speech in a sentence cannot account for either their grammaticality or their susceptibility to semantic interpretation. The same is true for the order of morphemes in the sentence as shown by the fact that sentence (5) which is both grammatical and meaningful uses the same order of bound morphemes (-ly, -s, -ly) as sentence (2) which is neither grammatical nor meaningful. Sentences (6) and (7) demonstrate that the particular words used offer no clue to the meaning of the sentence. Sentence (8) can be recognized as having the same meaning as sentence (6) even though the order of subject and object is the same as that of sentence (7) showing that directional associations between the ordered elements are irrelevant to the understanding of the sentence.

These various examples should suffice to convince one that the process of acquiring language must involve a much more complex analysis procedure than that offered by such surface relations of sentences as order of elements and word-associations. As if this were not

---

† Sentence (3) might occur, as Lenneberg points out, "in an instruction booklet on pacifist rhetoric" (1967, p. 274).

enough, we are confronted with the added complication that the child is continuously exposed to both well-formed and semi-grammatical sentences in the ordinary speech of adult speakers. Out of this confused input, it has to be able to separate out the false clues from the correct ones, yet it demonstrates this ability and succeeds in the relatively short period of 24 months (roughly from age one-and-a-half to three-and-a-half). Let us now turn to these newer formulations of child language acquisition.

FROM BASE TO SURFACE

If we discard earlier theories of language acquisition as unproductive, it is necessary to start anew right from the beginning. The study of the acquisition of grammar usually begins when the child is at about a-year-and-a-half, the time when he begins to use two word combinations. Prior to that it is difficult to study the child's grammatical competence since he uses single words, and techniques have not as yet been developed to study the child's grammatical comprehension at that early age. Speech records of a child over successive periods offer a picture of a changing grammar which the psycholinguist attempts to characterize in formal terms by giving a description of its structure at each period. This approach is necessarily limited since an inference of grammatical competence must be made from the child's speech performance, the latter being affected by a number of variables that are not directly relevant to grammatical competence (e.g. memory span, temporal integration, inattention, etc.). Given this limitation, we can nevertheless inquire as to the kind of developmental picture that emerges.

Differentiation of generic classes. Children's earliest utterances of two words (or more) exhibit non-random combinations of some words. Some examples from the speech of three children reported in the literature are the following (McNeill, 1966, Table 1): *big boy, allgone shoe, two boot, that baby, here pretty*. Distributional analysis of these two-word combinations reveals that the words the child uses at this earliest stage fall into two categories in terms of their privileges of occurrence. One of the two classes contains a small number of words each having a relatively high frequency of occurrence. Examples of this class include *allgone, big, my, see* in one child's speech, *my, two, a, green,* in a second child's speech, and in a third, *this, a, here*. The second class contains a larger number of words and additions of new words to this class occur at a higher rate (some examples are: *boat, Mommy, tinkertoy, come, doed*). Words in this second class occur by themselves or in combination with words from the first class, while words in the first class never occur by themselves. For these reasons, the first class was named the "pivot" class (P) while the second class was named the "open" class (O). A shorthand expression of these facts can be represented by the following notation:

$$S \longrightarrow (P) + O$$

This notation implies that the child's competence includes a rule which says that a sentence, S, can be produced by combining any two words from class P and class O (in that order) or, alternately, by using any single word from class O. The rule excludes such sentences made up of two words from the same class, or a sentence made up of a single word from the P class.

It is to be noted that the rule[‡] for constructing this earliest sentence cannot have been developed as a result of direct mimicking of adult sentences. Many of the two-word combinations that this rule generates are in the wrong order from the point of view of adult speech (e.g. *allgone shoe* vs. the likely adult model of the *shoe is allgone*). In addition, it permits combinations that are unlikely to occur in adult speech at all (e.g. *big milk*). Such novel (and non-adult) combinations and the ready substitutability of words within each category are convincing arguments that these word combinations could not be memorized imitations of adult speech.

Distributional analysis of successive speech records of the children that have been studied shows that the words in the original pivot class begin to subdivide into progressively more differentiated categories in a hierarchical manner that can be represented as follows (based on McNeill, 1966, Fig. 1):

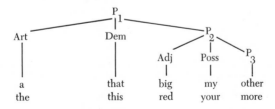

This representation shows that the original pivot class (P_1) subdivided into three classes of words: Articles, Demonstrative Pronouns, and all

‡ The concept of a grammatical "rule" as used in generative transformational linguistics in no way implies that the individual is consciously aware of what he is doing. "Rule" is to be understood in its formal (mathematical) sense as an expression that generates a set of operations of defined elements.

the rest (P_2). Subsequently, P_2 subdivided into three further classes: Adjectives, Possessive Pronouns, and all the rest (P_3).

The implications of this picture are extremely important. Note that there is no logical necessity for the development of grammatical distinctions to assume this particular form of development. The child could have made up categories of words on a trial and error basis, continually rearranging them on the basis of evidence contained in adult speech. He could thus isolate a category of words that correspond to adjectives, or articles, or possessives, until he gradually homes in on the full fledged adult pattern. However, instead of making, as it were, a distributional analysis of adult speech, he seems to have come up with a progressive differentiation strategy that has the peculiar property of being made up of a *generic* class at each point: that is, the original pivot class must already honor in a generic form all the future distinctions at level 2; the undifferentiated pivot class at level 2 (P_2) must contain in a generic form all the future distinctions at level 3, and so on. In other words, the child seems to honor grammatical distinctions in advance of the time they actually develop. How is this possible?

McNeill's conclusion is as bold as it is inevitable: the hierarchy of progressive differentiation of grammatical categories "represents linguistic universals that are part of the child's innate endowment. The role of a universal hierarchy of categories would be to direct the child's discovery of the classes of English. It is as if he were equipped with a set of 'templates' against which he can compare the speech he happens to hear from his parents. . . . We can imagine, then, that a child classifies the random specimens of adult speech he encounters according to universal categories that the speech exemplifies. Since these distinctions are at the top of a hierarchy that has the grammatical classes of English at its bottom, the child is prepared to discover the appropriate set of distinctions" (McNeill, 1966, pp. 35–36).

The assumption of innate language universals is sure to be unacceptable to current behaviorist theories. Someone is bound to point out that one doesn't explain the "why" of a complex phenomenon by saying it is innate. The fact of the matter is, however, that the complex behavior system of any organism is bound to be dependent upon the structural and functional properties of its nervous system. Language is a product of man's cognition, and as Lenneberg (1967, p. 334) points out, "man's cognition functions within biologically given limits." Granting the innateness of language universals, the task of explaining the "how" of language acquisition is still ahead of us. The scientific investigation of language, both from the linguist's and the psycholinguist's point of view, is to give an adequate characterization of the structure of the child's innately endowed "language acquisition device," the nature of its universal categories and their interrelations.

The development of transformations. The ability to manipulate transformations constitutes an essential part of linguistic competence according to the generative linguistics developed by Chomsky, and Lenneberg (1967) argues convincingly that transformations are an essential aspect of categorization processes of all biological organisms. An insight into the nature of linguistic transformations can be gained by considering the manner by which the following two sentences are understood by an adult speaker (based on Lenneberg, 1967, pp. 286–292):

> 1. they are boring students
> 2. the shooting of the hunters was terrible

Both sentences are semantically ambiguous. The ambiguity in sentence (1) can be resolved by a process of "bracketing" which reveals that its constituent elements can be broken up into two different "phrase markers,"[§] as follows:

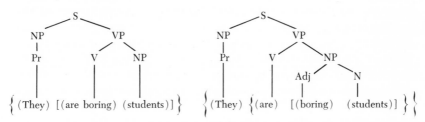

This phrase marker shows that the ambiguity of the sentence lies in the fact that the word *boring* functions in one case as an inflected verb-form, and in the other case, as an adjective modifying the word *students*. Now consider sentence (2): it is ambiguous in at least two ways (one could say that either the hunters need more practice or they need a funeral!). Only one phrase marker description is possible for this sentence, so we need some other process to explain its ambiguity. One interpretation is related to the sentence *hunters shoot inaccurately*, the other, to the sentence *hunters are shot*. The reason we understand the ambiguity of sentence (2) may thus be

§ A phrase marker is simply a graphic representation of the constituents of a sentence. "Bracketing" shown at the bottom of this figure is an alternative method of accomplishing the same thing.

attributed to the fact that we are able to recognize the relation between it and two other sentences each of which has its own distinct
phrase marker. This is the essence of transformations: they are laws
that control the relations between sentences that have "grammatical
affinity."

The early stages of child language competence does not apparently
include the ability to perform transformations, according to McNeill
(1966) who relates the impetus for acquiring transformations to the
cumbersomeness of having to manipulate the elementary forms of
sentences in the underlying structure of language ("base strings").
(More extensive discussion on the development of transformations is
not possible here. The reader is referred to McNeill, 1966, pp. 53–65).

IMPLICATIONS FOR SECOND LANGUAGE TEACHING

The view on language acquisition that has been outlined may at
first appear frustrating to those whose inclination and business it is to
teach language. The claim that a child has achieved linguistic competence by age three-and-a-half is likely to be scoffed at by the elementary school teacher in composition. At the claim that grammatical
rules are discovered by the child through linguistic universals, the
foreign language teacher is likely to wonder what happened to this
marvelous capacity in the foreign language laboratory. In this section,
I would like to examine the implications for language teaching of the
views outlined earlier on the language acquisition process. I shall discuss a number of topics including the role of practice and imitation,
the distinction between competence and performance, and the nature
of skills involved in foreign language acquisition.

The role of practice and imitation. The assumption that practice
plays a crucial role in language acquisition has been central to earlier
speculations. To Behaviorists it is almost an axiom not to be questioned. This view rests on the basic assertion that there exists a fundamental continuity between language acquisition and the forms of
learning studied in the psychological laboratory. Chomsky (1959),
Miller (1965), Lenneberg (1967), and others have questioned this
view on general grounds and McNeill (1966) questions it on more
specific and reduced grounds. Granting the language acquisition
process is guided by the child's innate knowledge of language universals, does practice theory explain how children go about finding out
the locally appropriate expression of the linguistic universals?

Practice theory leads to two possible hypotheses about language
acquisition: one is that when the child is exposed to a novel gram-

matical form, he imitates it; the other is that by practicing this novel form it becomes "stamped in." The evidence available indicates that both hypotheses are false. A direct test of children's tendency (or ability) to imitate adult forms of speech shows that children almost never repeat the adult sentence as it is presented. A child does not readily "mimic" a grammatical form that is not already in his repertoire as evidenced by his own spontaneous utterances. Direct attempts at imitation of adult sentences end up being recoded by the child, as the following examples taken from Lenneberg (1967, p. 316) illustrate:

Model Sentence	*Child's Repetition*
Johnny is a good boy.	Johnny is good boy.
He takes them for a walk.	He take them to the walk.
Lassie does not like the water.	He no like the water.
Does Johnny want a cat?	Johnny wants a cat?

It has been estimated that only about ten percent of a child's "imitations" of adult speech are "grammatically progressive" (that is, embodying a form novel to the child).

Whatever the means by which novel forms enter the child's speech, does practice strengthen these responses? The evolution of the child's command of the past tense of verbs provides negative evidence to this question. In the child's early language, the past tense of the irregular strong verbs in English (*came, went, sat*) appear with high frequency relative to the regularized /d/ and /t/ forms of the weak verbs. Thus, we would expect that these much practiced irregular forms would be highly stable, more so than the regular forms. Yet evidence shows that they are in fact less stable than the less practiced regular form, as indicated by the fact that at a certain point in the child's development he suddenly abandons the irregular form in favor of the regularized form and produces *comed, goed, sitted*. This kind of discontinuity shows that the practice model is not applicable here; rules that the child discovers are more important and carry greater weight than practice. Concept attainment and hypothesis testing are more likely paradigms in language development than response strength through rote memory and repetition.

This realization ought not to lead to pessimism about the potential usefulness of language *teaching*. There is strong evidence that the attainment of grammatical rules can be facilitated by proper presentation of speech materials. Observation of children's speech during play interaction with an adult (usually the mother) shows that up to half of their imitations of adult "expansions" of children's speech are grammatically progressive (McNeill citing data by Slobin, 1966, p. 75). An expansion is an adult's "correction" of the child's utterance. The advantage expansions seem to hold over other samples of adult speech may be attributable to the fact that expansions exemplify a locally appropriate expression of a linguistic universal at a time when the child is most ready to notice such a distinction. For example, if the child says *Adam cry*, and the mother expands this by saying *Yes, Adam cried* (or *Yes, Adam is crying*—depending on her understanding of what the child intends), the child is thereby given the opportunity of discovering the specific manner in which the past tense form (or progressive form) is expressed in English at a time when this distinction is maximally salient to him. The faster development of language in children of middle-class educated parents may be attributable to a tendency on the part of these mothers to expand to a greater extent than other parents. However, this hypothesis needs further investigation.

On the distinction between competence and performance. This distinction has been recognized by all psychological theories, including behavioristic ones (see Hull's, 1943, distinction between $_sE_R$ and $_s\bar{E}_R$). A confusion that may arise in language behavior comes from the fact that *understanding* is usually (if not always) superior to *speaking* and one might want to equate understanding with competence and speaking with performance. However, this cannot be the case. Both understanding and speaking must be viewed as performance variables since the non-linguistic variables that affect speaking (e.g. memory span, temporal integration, inattention, etc.) are equally likely to affect understanding. We are thus confronted with the fact that one type of performance, understanding, appears to develop before another type of performance, speaking. What may be responsible for this?

McNeill (1966) examines the specific claim that every grammatical feature appears first in understanding and second in speaking and is led to the conclusion that the overall parameters of conversion from competence to performance are simpler, less complex, easier in the case of understanding. In order to account for this fact, he postulates three kinds of memory span of different size or length, in the following order of decreasing magnitude: phonological production, grammatical comprehension, and grammatical production. This is intended to account for some data by Fraser, Bellugi, and Brown (1963) showing that a child can repeat a longer sentence than it can either understand or produce spontaneously, and also that it can understand a longer sentence than it can produce spontaneously. The difficulty with Mc-Neill's hypothesis is that it equates sentence length with sentence complexity. It would seem that it is easier to understand a long but simple sentence than a short but involved one. It would also appear that one can understand a sentence too long to be repeated. Children show evidence of having understood sentences they cannot (or will not) repeat (see Lenneberg, 1967, p. 316). The problem may be conceptualized in a different way, as illustrated by the following diagram:

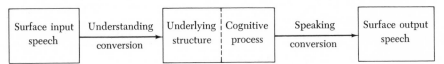

The asymmetry between the capacity to perform the understanding conversion as opposed to the speaking conversion may be related to the fact that the former requires an analytic approach while the latter demands a synthetic capability. It may be that for humans, analytic processes are easier than synthetic ones. One might say that it is easier to learn the art critic's job than the artist's.

The acquisition of foreign language skills. Let us raise the question of the specific relevance of our discussion on first language acquisition for an understanding of second language learning and teaching. What are the parallels to be considered? First, let us look at the argument for the differences. Assuming second language acquisition which takes place after the age of four, one may point out the following: (i) the individual's cognitive development is at a later and more advanced stage; (ii) he is already in possession of the grammatical structure of a language which may serve to facilitate the acquisition of a second one through transfer; (iii) he already possesses concepts and meanings, the problem now being one of expressing them through a new vocabulary.

The importance of the first argument would seem to depend on the relevance of cognitive development for the acquisition of language. The view outlined in this paper is that the necessary knowledge for language acquisition cannot be gained from experience with the outside world, that language acquisition is dependent on an innate endowment which constitutes the knowledge of language universals. Hence, the imputed advantage of advanced age and cognitive development is a dubious proposition. The two other arguments are based on the assumption of the operation of transfer in grammatical structure and in reference (vocabulary). What is the evidence in support of this assumption? It is necessary to distinguish between two claims about transfer theory. One refers to the general expectation that new forms of learning do not go on independently of what the organism has learned before. The truth of this statement would seem fairly obvious and need not concern us further. The second and specific claim expresses the expectation that the learning of certain specific and identifiable elements in Task B are facilitated (or hindered) by the previous learning of certain specific and identifiable elements in Task A. The status of this strong claim for any type of complex learning outside the laboratory is unknown. A serious test of it in second language acquisition would require the prior analysis of the two languages in a form which would identify the specific elements to be transferred at the grammatical and lexical levels. On *a priori* grounds we would expect negative transfer as much as positive transfer, assuming that transfer is relevant to the problem. Carroll (1966b) claims that the Modern Language Aptitude Test designed for English speakers predicts success in a foreign language equally well irrespective of the particular language involved. This is difficult to explain if transfer has any overall relevance to the language acquisition process. Nevertheless, some phonological studies on contrastive analysis reviewed by Carroll (1966a) would seem to indicate the operation of negative transfer effects. He cites Suppes *et al.* (1962) who "claim to be able to predict quite precisely from mathematical learning theory what [phoneme] discrimination problems will arise" (Carroll, 1966a, p. 16).

The problem is complicated still further by the possibility that transfer effects might effect performance and competence factors in different ways. Or, the various performance factors themselves (understanding, speaking, reading, writing) may be affected to different degrees. The same comment might be made for different levels of performance, that is phonology, vocabulary, and syntax. A further aspect to this problem is the consideration of whether transfer effects are necessary processes or whether the extent of their operation is dependent on the strategy with which the learner attacks the new task. An individual who tries to "fit in" the dimensions of the new task into the old structure may encounter different problems from the individual who inhibits the interaction of the two tasks, assuming that the latter strategy is possible. Finally, the fact that it is possible to predict errors of confusion, as in contrastive analysis of phonology, is not necessarily an indication that transfer effects will operate in the acquisition of the new task. Thus, the fact that the /l/ and /r/ sounds are predictable areas of confusion for a Japanese learning English says nothing about the way in which he will eventually learn the distinction. It is unlikely that this distinction is learned in isolation. Instead, it is more likely that the confusion will disappear when the overall structure of English phonology is internalized.

The above considerations lead to a number of implications for the teaching of a second language which I shall now take up.

1. *Teaching the knowledge of structure*: since it is clear that knowledge of language at all levels consists of knowing patterns of relations rather than constituent elements, the usefulness of efforts to teach the latter is in doubt. Examples of such efforts include teaching specific sound discriminations, "shaping" of phonological production, vocabulary acquisition through association of translation equivalents, and practice of specific morphological and inflectional examples. Pointing to individuals who successfully acquired a foreign language in a course using these methods has no force of argument, for it is quite possible that their success occurred despite these methods rather than because of them.

2. *Teaching successful strategies of acquisition*: Carroll (1962) has isolated a number of factors which are predictive of success in a foreign language. These may offer clues about the strategies that a successful learner uses with the possibility that such strategies may be taught to those who normally make no use of them. One of the abilities Carroll has identified deals with verbalization of grammatical relations in sentences. The successful foreign language learner is apparently capable of the following task: given a word underlined in one sentence (e.g. "The man went into the *house*") he can identify that word in another sentence which has the same grammatical function (e.g. picking one of the underlined words of the following sentence: "The *church* next to the *bowling alley* will be built in a new *location* next *year*"). We know of course that the individual is capable of recognizing the grammatical relations in the second sentence (otherwise he could not give it a semantic interpretation), so the ability must be one of explicit verbalization of implicitly known rules and relations.‖ Using, perhaps, linguistic theories of transformational grammar the teaching of such verbalizations therefore ought to facilitate foreign language acquisition.

Another variable identified by Carroll "is the ability to 'code' auditory phonetic material in such a way that this material can be recognized, identified and remembered over something longer than a few seconds" (1962, p. 128). We do not know at present the specific strategy that may be employed in facilitating this kind of coding. Whatever it may be, it seems unlikely that the superior person in this task derives

‖ Verbalizing a grammatical relation can take two forms; one refers to the type of statement that can be found in a grammar book that includes technical terms (relative clause, head noun, modifier, predicate phrase, etc.); the second refers to a statement of equivalence or relation expressed in any convenient way using whatever terms are available to the individual, whether technically correct or not.

his advantage from a special innate capacity. In the first place, it is not related to the ability to perceive phonetic distinctions, and second, given the biological foundations of language capacity (see Lenneberg, 1967) it would seem unlikely to expect innate differences in the general capacity of coding phonological material.

Contrastive analysis of grammatical structure would not seem to offer particular advantages beyond those provided by verbalization of grammatical relations and drawing attention to a grammatical distinction at a time of saliency (see the effects of *expansion,* discussed above). The expectation that the advantage of contrastive analysis lies in making the *contrast per se* is based on the assumption of transfer for which the evidence is lacking. At any rate, the pointing up of the *contrast* may just as well lead to negative transfer by facilitating the assimilation (or "fitting in") strategy. I know of no evidence that emphasizing distinctions of incompatible responses, especially those that are automatized, leads to a decrease in incompatibility.

3. Teaching habit integration and automaticity: temporal integration of phonological skills, whether at the understanding or production side, is a problem independent of the knowledge of the phonological structure and transformations of a language. It would seem likely that sensory and motor integrations of this type can be automatized through practice and repetition. The more interesting problem would relate to the time at which automaticity practice is likely to be valuable and the form it is to take. Reading represents a different aspect of phonological production skill than speaking, as is well known, and practice on reading does not represent a sufficient or necessary condition for achieving automaticity of phonological production in speaking.

The factors that enter into the problem of automatizing grammatical habits are not very clear. Tests of speech comprehension under conditions of noise (see for example Spolsky *et al.,* 1966) seem to be quite sensitive to the level of automaticity and degree of integration achieved by a foreign language speaker. They show that the problem of integration goes deeper than high proficiency in understanding and speaking demonstrated under ordinary conditions. At the moment we do not have available a psychological theory of sentence understanding or production. The relevance to this problem of recent experiments on latency of various grammatical manipulations still remains to be shown. Many language teachers seem to be convinced that pattern drills serve to automatize grammatical habits. However, it is difficult to justify this expectation on theoretical grounds. As was discussed earlier in this paper the semantic interpretation of a sentence cannot be viewed as a process of sequential analysis of categories of words. Thus, pattern drills, at best, can only serve to automatize phonological production skills, and for this latter purpose, other methods may prove equally, if not more effective. At any rate, if the pattern drill argument is taken literally, namely that the structure is automatized through practice of the specific pattern that is being repeated, then the learner could never achieve automatized speech. This follows since in ordinary speech we use an infinite variety of patterns, and therefore since the second language learner couldn't possibly be drilled on an infinite variety of patterns he could never develop automatized speech. Hence pattern drill cannot possibly do what it is supposed to be doing.

From a theoretical point of view, development of grammatical competence should be facilitated by getting the learner to perform a set of transformations on families of sentences (e.g. "I cannot pay my rent because I am broke"; "If I weren't broke I could pay my rent"; "Given the fact that I have no money, I cannot pay my rent"; "How do you think I could possibly pay my rent if I am broke"; "Since I am broke, the rent cannot be paid"; "To pay the rent is impossible given the fact that I have no money"; etc.).# The distinction between this, which we may refer to as perhaps "transformation exercises" and "pattern drill" is that the first deals with the competence involved in deep structure while the second focuses on surface structure. As Rutherford** has shown in his paper earlier at this meeting, surface structure similarities are completely unenlightening as to the semantic interpretation of sentences.

The notion of transformation exercises is equally applicable to phonology and vocabulary. DeCamp has given us some examples of practice exercises in phonological transformations in his paper read earlier at this Convention.†† Exercises in vocabulary transformations are more difficult to specify at this stage of our knowledge, but from our discussion on meaning earlier we can perhaps anticipate giving the student a task of this kind: "Change the following list of words using the sex transformation: boy, father, bull, sun"—which might yield: "girl, mother, cow, moon." Or, to give another example: "Change the following list of verbs by effecting a perfective transformation: to drown, to love, to switch on the light, to talk"—which yields: "to eat, to play

One of the films shown at the Convention had a demonstration of just this idea. It was made by the Ontario Citizenship Branch. The instructor, Ray Santon, referred to this technique as "structure drill" (in opposition to "pattern drill").
** "Deep and surface structure and the language drill," a paper delivered by William Rutherford of the University of California at Los Angeles.
†† "The current discrepancy between theoretical and applied linguistics" by David DeCamp of the University of Texas.

chess, to sleep, to read."‡‡ Semantic relations of this kind may be responsible for the well-known psychological fact that in memory words are organized in clusters (see, for example, Deese, 1965).

4. *On semi-grammatical sentences*: the fluent speech of most native speakers does not consist totally (or even in the majority of instances) of well-formed sentences. One would imagine that the imposition of a requirement to utter exclusively well-formed sentences would seriously hinder the fluency of most native speakers. The logical implication of this would be that no language teacher should ever force his pupils to use only well-formed sentences in practice conversation whether it be in the classroom, laboratory or outside. This conclusion is not as odd as it might seem on first account. After all children seem to acquire the competence of well-formed sentences despite the semi-grammaticality of the adult speech to which they are continually exposed. It is important to note that semi-grammaticality does not mean randomness. The reason that in most instances we are able to give a semantic interpretation of semi-grammatical sentences lies in the fact that we have the capacity of relating these semi-sentences to their well-formed equivalents. There must therefore exist lawful transformations between semi-sentences and well-formed ones. This is also the reason why we are able to understand the speech of children: the grammar of their utterances is generic of the later grammar of well-formed sentences. If this were not the case, we would not be able to expand (hence, understand) their utterances.

An important question poses itself at this juncture, and it is this: should second language teaching take specific account of the developmental stages that are likely to mark the acquisition of a language? By "specific account" is meant at least the following two things. First, to recognize and allow the production of semi-sentences on the part of the learner. Second, to expose the learner to utterances that are grammatically progressive at each stage but short of having the full complexity of well-formed sentences. The first proposition may already be the policy in some modern and intensive audio-lingual methods which encourage active speech production "at any *cost*" (sic). The second proposition is sure to be resisted by most teachers, yet the fact of the matter is that all "natural" language acquisition situations expose the learner to semi-grammatical sentences more often than not. We do not know whether this is a facilitative or retarding situation. Some parents tend to talk to their children by attempting to imitate their speech and

‡‡ The "perfective" aspect of verbs can be determined by placing the verb in a frame such as this: "If I have _____ but was interrupted, have I _____?" If the answer is "Yes" (e.g. *to talk*), the verb in question has the perfective aspect.

it is sometimes said that this kind of "baby talk" retards acquisition. The evidence on this is simply lacking. It may be, of course, that the fastest method of acquiring a second language need not be one that replicates the conditions existing under "natural" language acquisition. In fact various claims for highly intensive language courses followed by individuals with high foreign language aptitude put the time requirement for the acquisition of a foreign language between 250 and 500 hours of study (Carroll, 1966a, b). Compare to this figure a minimum estimate of 3,000 hours for first language acquisition.[§§] Of course, the two situations are not directly comparable and the level of competence achieved may be different (especially by measures of automaticity and background noise, see Spolsky, *et al.*, 1966), nevertheless the comparison highlights the fact that the "natural" rate of language acquisition process can be greatly accelerated. It is important to note that although the language acquisition capacity *per se* must be viewed as an innate capability shared by all members of the species, the *rate* at which language is acquired, especially a second language, and the effectiveness with which language is used as a *communicative process* are performance factors that are affected by individual differences within the species (variations in general intelligence, in experiences, in physical health, in motivation, etc.). It is here that the concept of *teaching* may assume its full importance.

REFERENCES

Bellugi, Ursula and Brown, Roger (Eds.). The acquisition of language. *Monographs of the Society for Research in Child Development,* 29, 1964.

Carroll, J. B. Research in foreign language teaching: The last five years. In R. G. Mead, Jr., Editor, *Language teaching: Broader contexts, Northeast Conference on the teaching of foreign languages; Reports of the Working Committees.* New York: MLA Materials Center, 1966a.

————. Individual differences in foreign language learning. Paper presented at the Thirty-Second Annual Foreign Language Conference, New York University School of Education, November 5, 1966b.

————. The prediction of success in intensive foreign language training. In Robert Glazer (Ed.), *Training research and education.* Pittsburgh: University of Pittsburgh Press, 1962.

Chomsky, Noam. Review of Skinner's "Verbal Behavior." *Language,* 35, 26–58, 1959.

————. *Syntactic structures.* The Hague: Mouton, 1957.

Deese, James. *The structure of associations in language and thought.* Baltimore: The Johns Hopkins Press, 1965.

[§§] This rough figure is arrived at by estimating the total waking hours of a child up to age three-and-a-half and taking thirty percent of that as an estimate of the amount of exposure to language.

Fraser, C., Bellugi, Ursula and Brown, R. Control of grammar in imitation, comprehension, and production. *Journal of Verbal Learning and Verbal Behavior*, 2, 121–135, 1963.

Hull, C. L. *Principles of behavior*. New York: Appleton-Century-Crofts, 1943.

Katz, J. J. *The philosophy of language*. New York: Harper, 1966.

Lenneberg, E. H. *Biological foundations of language*. New York: John Wiley & Sons, 1967.

McNeill, David. Developmental psycholinguistics. In Frank Smith and G. A. Miller (Eds.), *The genesis of language: A psycholinguistic approach*. Cambridge, Mass.: The M.I.T. Press, 1966.

Miller, G. A. Some preliminaries to psycholinguistics. *American Psychologist*, 20, 15–20, 1965.

Slobin, D. I. The acquisition of Russian as a native language. In Smith and Miller (1966).

Spolsky, B., Sigurd, B., Sato, M., Walker, E. and Arterburn, Catharine. Preliminary studies in the development of techniques for testing overall second language proficiency. Indiana Language Program, Indiana University, Bloomington, Indiana, 1966 (mimeo.).

Suppes, P., Crothers, E., Weir, Ruth, and Trager, Edith. Some quantitative studies of Russian consonant phoneme discrimination. Stanford, Calif.: Institute for Mathematical Studies in the Social Sciences, Technical Report No. 49, 1962.

READING

NOAM CHOMSKY

Comments for Project Literacy Meeting

INTRODUCTION

Chomsky asserts that the study of language is concerned with the relation between sound and meaning. Both sound and meaning have a psychological reality which the grammar must reflect. In order to do this, the grammar must have at least two levels—a level of phonetic representation for sound and a level of structural representation (termed the structural description) which will be "adequate to express the semantic content of a sentence."

The structural description contains "a representation of the meaning-bearing units of which the sentence is composed and of the phrasing of the sentence." Chomsky illustrates the notion of structural description with the phrase "American history teacher." The "meaning-bearing 'units' " are word elements like *America* and the derivational suffix *-an*. In this case, the word *American* consists of two meaning-bearing units. By "phrasing of the sentence" Chomsky means the way that the units are to be related to each other. In the case of "American history teacher" there are two possible phrasings: a history teacher who is an American, and a teacher who teaches American history. The phrasing would have to indicate which of the two interpretations was intended in any given sentence.

Reprinted with permission of the author from *Project Literacy Reports No. 2,* September 1964, pp. 1–8.

The structural description of the sentences of a language is produced by the grammar of that language. The grammar contains three components: (1) a set of *syntactic rules*, (2) a *lexicon*, and (3) a set of *phonological rules*. The syntactic rules govern the phrasing of the sentence and the placement of the derivational affixes. These affixes are said to have "grammatical" as opposed to "semantic" meaning. For instance, the *-an* in *American* has the grammatical function of converting the noun *America* into an adjective. The lexicon introduces semantic units, like the noun *America*. The phonological rules convert the string of "meaning-bearing units" into the level of phonetic representation. In order for the phonological rules to operate properly, the rules must refer to the sentence phrasing (the product of the syntactic rules) and the nature of the representation of the "meaning-bearing units" (the product of the lexicon).

The phonological rules (like the syntactic) are highly abstract, general, and systematic. So much so, in fact, that speakers of a language are almost totally unaware of the existence of such rules. The operation of these rule systems accounts for the different pronunciations of the two meanings of "American history teacher." What is not predictable by general rule must be supplied by the lexicon; consequently the lexical representations of meaning-bearing units have a psychological reality that "is hardly open to question." To make the same point in different words, the lexicon provides a representation of the words of the language in a form which will provide the correct input to the phonological rules to guarantee the automatic production of the correct phonetic representations of the words.

Chomsky's key point in this essay is that the conventional orthography of English comes remarkably close to being an optimal lexical representation: it provides the information that a speaker of the language (that is, someone who knows the "rules" of the language) needs to know in order to pronounce the word. Notice, for instance, that in each of the three forms of the word set *telegraph, telegraphic, telegraphy* the main stress falls on a different syllable: in *telegraph* it falls on the first syllable with the vowel of the unstressed second syllable reduced to an uncontrastive "uh." In *telegraphic* the stress falls on the third syllable. In *telegraphy* the stress is on the second syllable with the first syllable now unstressed and consequently reduced to an uncontrastive "uh." The phonological rules (drawing on the information generated by the syntactic rules) govern the movement of stress from syllable to syllable and the degree of vowel reduction when stress is removed from the syllable. The lexicon must supply the placement of stress to begin with and also indicate the vowel each stressable syllable would have if the stress were to fall on it. As Chomsky puts it,

> the relation between conventional spelling and phonological representation is very close, and . . . conventional spelling is, by and large, a highly effective system for a wide range of dialects because it corresponds to a common underlying phonological representation, relatively invariant among dialects despite wide phonetic divergence.

> Let me emphasize again the advantages of phonological (i.e., essentially conventional orthographic) representation *for a speaker who understands the language.*

Chomsky raises two other main points in the balance of the essay: (1) the question of "phoneme-grapheme correspondence," and (2) some thoughts about the way children acquire the phonological rules. Chomsky discusses several definitions of "phoneme," and concludes that to recognize a separate phonemic level between the abstract representations in the lexicon and the very specific level of phonetic representation of sound is to establish "nothing more than a methodological artifact." Chomsky argues that the level of phonemic representation does not exist in a psychological sense and is unjustifiable in terms of linguistic theory. The question of "phoneme-grapheme correspondence" is thus a "pseudo-issue," and consequently Chomsky feels that

> the only reasonable way to study sound-letter correspondences seems to be to utilize the fact that orthography corresponds closely to a significant level of linguistic representation.

The essay closes with a discussion about the child's acquisition of the full set of phonological rules. Chomsky says that a child of 6 may not even have been presented with the evidence needed to determine the rules. A second point is that children may simply operate at less general levels than adults, that is, they might " 'hear phonetically' rather than phonologically." This suggests that

> the psychologically real representation for the child changes and deepens with age, approaching the adult phonology with increasing maturity and linguistic experience.

Morris Halle and I have been working for several years on a study of English sound structure, some aspects of which seem to me to touch on the concerns of this meeting—in particular, on questions of dialectal variation, the psychological reality of linguistic units, and the nature of conventional orthography and its relation to the sound system.

When we consider the structure of a language we are, fundamentally, concerned with a relation of sound and meaning. The rules of the language—the rules that the native speaker intuitively commands and that the linguist tries to discover and exhibit—relate certain physical signals to certain semantic interpretations; more precisely, they relate phonetic representations of sentences to their structural descriptions. Thus one level of representation that must have psychological significance, both on the perceptual and motor levels, is the level of phonetic representation; another is the level of representation that appears in structural descriptions.

The level of phonetic representation is fairly well understood. Structural descriptions are a more obscure matter. Clearly, a structural description (adequate to express the semantic content of a sentence) must contain, at least, a representation of the meaning-bearing units of which the sentence is composed and of the phrasing of the sentence (and, of course, much more which we here disregard). Thus the structural description of the Phrase "American history teacher" must contain the units *America, -an, histor-, -y, teach, -er*, and a bracketing indicating which of the two semantic interpretations is intended. Similarly, the word *theatricality*, for example, must be represented as a Noun derived from the Adjective *theatrical*, which is in turn derived from the Noun *theater*. Thus the grammar of a language must contain (at least) syntactic rules that determine phrasing and the placement of "grammatical" units such as *-er, -ity*, a lexicon that contains the semantically functioning units, and rules that convert structural descriptions to phonetic representations.

Consider now the character of the lexicon. It is easy to justify the requirement that each lexical item be represented as a sequence of *segments*. Each item, of course, has a unique such spelling—a single entry—in the lexicon. This spelling must contain all information not predictable by phonological rules (presupposing the rest of the structural description of the sentence in which the item is embedded). Thus the lexical representation of the common item of *histor-y, historical, historian,* or of *anxi-ous, anxi-ety,* or of *courage, courage-ous,* or of *tele+graph, tele+graph-ic, tele+graph-y,* etc., must be selected so as to contain just what is not predictable in the variant phonetic realizations of these items. The psychological reality of lexical representation, in this sense, is hardly open to question.

Observe that a lexical representation, in this sense, provides a natural orthography for a person who knows a language. It provides just the information about words that is not predictable by phonological rule or by the syntactic rules that determine the phrasing of the sentence in which the item is embedded. It provides just the information needed by a person who has command of the syntactic and phonological rules (up to ambiguity). Conventional orthography, in English, as in every case of which I have any knowledge, is remarkably close to optimal, in this sense. For example, the spellings *histor-, anxi-, courage, telegraph* are (minor notational conventions aside) essentially what would appear in the lexicon of spoken English. Conventional orthographies tend to differ *systematically* from lexical representation only in that true irregularities (e.g., *man-men, cling-clung*) are differently represented, as is quite natural. The symbols of conventional orthography correspond to feature sets, in the underlying sound system of the spoken language.

It seems fairly well established that the level of lexical representation is highly resistant to change, and is highly persistent over time (and hence over a range of dialects). Correspondingly, one finds that conventional orthographies remain useful, with minor change, over long periods and for a wide range of dialects.

As a result of our work, we have come to the conclusion that there is no linguistically significant (and, presumably, no psychologically real) level of systematic representation intermediate between the level of representation to which conventional orthographies closely correspond and (broad) phonetic representation. These underlying representations we call "phonological," following Sapir, our conclusions being closely akin in many respects to his views on the nature of sound pattern and phonological rules. Following this usage, we may say that the relation between conventional spelling and phonological representation is very close, and that conventional spelling is, by and large, a highly effective system for a wide range of dialects because it corresponds to a common underlying phonological representation, relatively invariant among dialects despite wide phonetic divergence. Let me emphasize again the advantages of phonological (i.e., essentially conventional orthographic) representation *for a speaker who understands the language*. In contrast, broad phonetic (or, possibly, so-called "phonemic") representation is the only kind that would be of any use for someone who knows nothing of the syntax of the language but who wishes to produce a noise which is close to the phonetic form of a sentence—for example, an actor who has to produce a sentence of a language that he does not know.

Consider, in contrast, phonemic representation in the modern (post-Sapir) sense. The phonemic system, in effect, extracts all regularities from the sound system that can be detected with no consideration (or, in some varieties, highly restricted consideration) of higher level structure. A priori, there is no reason to suppose that such a system exists. For example, it is obvious that a child does not first construct such a phonemic system and then proceed to the problem of acquiring syntax and semantics, and there is not the slightest reason to believe that there is a level of perceptual processing (or of motor performance) that corresponds to phonemic representation, in the modern sense.

Furthermore, we have offered several arguments in support of the conclusion that there is no linguistic justification for a phonemic level—
that is, it can be incorporated in a full grammar only at the cost of
otherwise valid generalizations. Consequently, it seems to me that
phonemics, in the modern sense, is perhaps nothing more than a
methodological artifact.

In considering problems of literacy, the questions of "phoneme-
grapheme correspondences" and of dialect variation naturally arise.
As to the latter, this is a problem only to the extent that dialects differ
on the syntactic and lexical level. Differences in phonological rules
are irrelevant, since orthography corresponds to a deeper level of
representation than (broad) phonetic. Hence the question raised
above (of uniformity of lexicon over time and dialect), and the
analogous question with respect to sameness of deeper structures in
syntax, becomes highly relevant. As to the question of "phoneme-
grapheme" correspondence, it may be that this is something of a
pseudo-issue, or more properly, a set of pseudo-issues, depending on
how exactly it is interpreted. If by "phoneme" is meant the unit constructed in accordance with modern principles, there is no reason to
expect any significant set of phoneme-grapheme correspondences,
since it seems that phonemes are artificial units, having no linguistic
status, whereas the "graphemes" of the conventional orthography do
correspond fairly closely to a linguistically significant level of representation. Hence it is not clear why one should investigate phoneme-
grapheme correspondence at all. (In passing, it should be noted that
so far as relevant information is now available, the same seems to be
true for other languages.) If the word "phoneme" is taken in the sense
of Sapir, and "phonological representation" is the level at which all
predictable differences are extracted, then the phoneme-grapheme
correspondences seem quite simple—they are very close to one-one,
given certain notational conventions and disregarding a class of true
exceptions. On the other hand, if we use the phrase "phoneme-
grapheme" correspondences to refer to the study of sound-letter correspondences, we are, in effect, simply doing phonology. Or, to be
more precise, the only reasonable way to study sound-letter correspondences seems to be to utilize the fact that orthography corresponds closely to a significant level of linguistic representation—
namely, phonological representation, in the sense used above—which
is, furthermore related to sound by general rules—namely, the rules
of the phonological component. Hence the study of sound-letter correspondences can be divided into three parts: phonology, the systematic (near one-one) relations between phonological segments and
letters (or conventional letter sequences), and a residue of exceptions

(some of which exhibit subregularities of various sorts). But the bulk of the study is simply investigation of the phonological pattern.

If this much is correct, then it would seem to follow that the rules of sound-letter correspondence need hardly be taught, particularly the most general and deepest of these rules. For these rules are in any event part of the unconscious linguistic equipment of the non-literate speaker. What he must learn (except for true irregularities) is simply the elementary correspondence between the underlying phonological segments of his internalized lexicon and the orthographic symbols.

However, there is one qualification that must be added to this remark. The conventional orthography corresponds closely to a level of representation that seems to be optimal for the sound system of a fairly rich version of standard spoken English. Much of the evidence that determines, for the phonologist, the exact form of this underlying system is based on consideration of learned words and complex derivational patterns. It is by no means obvious that a child of six has mastered this phonological system in full—he may not yet have been presented with all of the evidence that determines the general structure of the English sound pattern. It would not be at all surprising to discover that the child's intuitive organization of the sound system continues to develop and deepen until considerably later. Furthermore, it seems that children are much more attuned to phonetic nuance than adults—they "hear phonetically" rather than phonologically, to a considerable extent. Though I have no serious evidence, I have observed quite a few cases where children developing their own alphabet or learning to read insisted on a much narrower representation than would strike the adult ear as plausible. To take one extreme case, my oldest daughter at age five objected to using the same symbol for the two Stops in *cocoa*, as it turned out on investigation, because the difference in aspiration seemed to her sufficiently significant to require a different symbolization. Though this is hardly better than a guess, it is not particularly a surprising one. Thus it is a familiar observation that children can mimic and can acquire a new pronunciation much more readily than adults, and this may correlate with a more superficial (narrower) level of organization of the phonetic material. For various reasons, then, it may turn out that the psychologically real representation for the child changes and deepens with age, approaching the adult phonology with increasing maturity and linguistic experience. Serious investigation of these questions is far from easy, but it should shed much light on problems of speech perception and production and, perhaps indirectly on the problems of literacy as well.

DAVID W. REED

A Theory of Language, Speech, and Writing

INTRODUCTION

The subject matter of this article is the interrelation of language, speech, and writing. The traditional linguistic view of the relationship has been that "speech *is* the language" and that writing is a very imperfect reflection of speech. From this point of view, the initial teaching of reading was largely a matter connecting the orthographic representations with their spoken forms through the establishment of phonemic-graphemic correspondences.

Reed's first main point is that while speech is primary over writing in a historical and sociological sense, its chronological primacy in the individual is "not a necessary condition in the relationship of speech to writing." Reed points out that the deaf learn to write before they learn to speak. Furthermore, rapid readers read faster than they could possibly speak the material out loud.

A further implication of the above is that there is no direct correspondence between sound and symbol that would necessarily enable us to cor-

Reprinted with permission of the author and of the National Council of Teachers of English from *Elementary English*, Vol. XXXII, No. 8 (December), 1965, pp. 845–851. Part I appeared in *Elementary English*; Part II is from the original, unpublished manuscript by the author.

rectly pronounce a written word and correctly spell a spoken word. To establish this argument, Reed cites words like "read" which have two different pronunciations, in this case, depending on whether it is the past or the present tense of the verb. The converse would be homophones like /red/, which could be either the past tense of the verb or the name of the color. In other words, the speaker needs syntactic and semantic information in order to correctly relate sound and spelling.

Having attacked the basis for a phonic approach to teaching reading, Reed turns to the other extreme, the whole-word method. Reed argues that the whole-word method confuses "linguistic form" with the understanding of what that form means. The former is a specific relation between a word and its pronunciation. The latter is what dictionaries deal with. If reading means the recognition of meaning in this sense, then the child

> confronted with a string of graphic configurations, like "The dog ate the meat," could demonstrate his ability to read by uttering "The canine quadruped devoured the flesh," or some other suitable paraphrase.

In place of the phonic and whole-word approaches, Reed offers a different theory of the relation of language, speech and writing based on the notion of "linguistic form." A linguistic form is an abstraction which may be thought of

> as simultaneously having semantic and physical features, neither of which is paramount. This may be explained by the analogy of a coin on which "heads" represents the meaning, "tails," the physical representation. It would be absurd to speak of either side of the coin as the "real" coin.

The physical representation of meaning can be either spoken or written. Thus in any given linguistic form there is a direct relation between meaning on the one hand and the various representations in speech and writing on the other. The important point here is that speech and writing are not directly related to each other; they are only indirectly related through the meaning. Put another way, both speech and writing are physical representations of linguistic form, but neither are representations of each other. In normal children the linking between meaning and physical representation is made first through speech; in deaf children the first linking would be through writing. In either event,

> it follows that the learning of linguistic forms, which consists of the linking of a meaning or meanings with an arbitrary but wholly regular representational configuration, must at first consist of laborious trial-and-error imitation and memorization.

However, the child who acquires the *second* representational system already knows the linguistic forms, and consequently, does not have to go through the trial-and-error discovery stage. Instead, "he can begin to learn to associate graphic configurations with linguistic forms that he already knows."

Reed closes the article by suggesting "how the construction of reading materials should take advantage of the fact that the child is already a native speaker of English." He proposes a set of rules which would apply to a representation of the meaning of linguistic forms (the morphemes of English in ordinary orthography), determining their spoken representation. Reed points out, however, that such a rule system is not intended to be necessarily taught to the children. Rather, the set of rules would provide the optional structuring for elementary reading materials. What the optional form actually would be is an empirical question to be answered by psychologists and classroom teachers.

"Linguistic form," defined in this article, is a concept by which linguists may relate their scholarship to the process of reading. "Linguistic forms" are links between meaning and the symbol systems of writing and speaking but not to be exclusively identified with either meaning or symbol.

PART I

Recent awareness that the science of linguistics may be of considerable relevance to research in elementary reading instruction could produce very unfortunate effects if linguistics should be misunderstood as giving wholehearted support to phonic methods of teaching reading. It is true that during the thirties, forties, and fifties of this century most linguists emphasized the primary nature of speech and the secondary nature of writing. A few were incautious enough to state that writing is merely a secondary representation or identification of speech. Many non-specialists, in their efforts to apply the findings of linguistics to the accomplishment of practical ends, concluded that speech *is* the language. It will be demonstrated shortly that these more extreme positions about the primacy of speech over writing are patently absurd.

Linguistic statements, like other scientific statements, have to be understood in terms of the historical context that produced them. During most of the nineteenth century and until about 1925, the primary interest of linguists was in historical linguistics and in the reconstruction of prehistoric stages of descendant languages. This interest naturally led investigators to the written records of earlier periods as their primary source of information. Around 1925 several new interests combined to shift attention from writing to speech. Among these were interests in recording and analyzing the very large number of unwritten languages in the world, interest in more accurate descriptions of modern languages that have systems of written representation, and interest in the comparison of dialects of living languages. All of these interests fostered the development of phonetics and structural linguistics as more exact sciences. It was entirely natural that linguists would seek, during this period, to make supportable generalizations about the primacy of speech over writing. It was observed, for example, that even in historical linguistics it is necessary to interpret written records in terms of speech sounds before a systematic description of the historical development of the language can be given.

Although all the linguistic interests of recent decades have continued to the present day, it has come to be recognized increasingly since the late fifties that phonologically based grammars are incapable of producing adequate analyses of syntax. All of the newer theories of grammar, including the transformational, have in common the procedure from syntax to speech and writing rather than the other way around. And, as soon as one views speech and writing as the end products of grammar rather than as the starting point for grammatical analysis, it is inevitable that he will view the relationship of speech and writing to one another in a new light.

THE PRIMACY OF SPEECH REDEFINED

Speech is certainly primary and writing secondary in at least the following respects: (1) Speech in some form is probably more than a half million years old; writing is no more than one percent this age. (2) Every contemporary human society has one or more languages, but of the thousands of such now in existence, a large majority have no accepted system of writing. (3) The experience of individuals with unimpaired hearing, nervous systems, and vocal organs, who grow up in a society that has a system of writing, parallels the experience of the race, in that speech is acquired first and largely without conscious effort, whereas understanding of the writing system comes much later as a result of extended and intensive study. (4) In societies that have writing, all normal adults have a working command of the spoken language, but only a minority have a comparable command of the written language.

These statements might be summarized by saying that speech generally enjoys a chronological primacy over writing. But it is interesting to note that even this chronological primacy is not a necessary condition in the relationship of speech to writing. One who is totally deaf may be expected to learn to read and write before he learns to speak. Indeed, he may grow up as a deaf mute—one who never learns to speak and is thus exactly comparable to the adult illiterate, who never learns to read and write. In the very interesting case of Helen Keller, who was rendered deaf and blind by scarlet fever before she was two years old, the primary system of representing the English language was a tactile system, in which symbols identifying language are formed by the fingers of one person in contact with the hand of another. Braille became the secondary system, comparable in function to reading and writing for most people, and speech, which Miss Keller never acquired perfectly, was merely a tertiary system for representing English.

In short, the observed relationships between speech and writing will not justify our saying that speech *is* the language or that writing is merely a secondary representation of speech. If speech *were* the language, then deaf mutes would be people who have never learned a language—in spite of the obvious fact that some of them read and write English, others German, others French, and so forth. We should also be at a loss to explain how skilled readers can, within a given period of time, identify through reading, a string of linguistic forms that cannot possibly be uttered by the most rapid speaker in a comparable period of time.

THE LIMITS OF PHONEMIC-GRAPHEMIC CORRESPONDENCE REAPPRAISED

It is also easy to prove, in terms that would satisfy the most exact physical scientist or mathematician, that neither writing nor speech is a direct representation of the other. No set of rules of phoneme-grapheme correspondence, however numerous or complicated, can tell us how to pronounce all graphic configurations or how to spell all spoken forms. As an example of the former impossibility, consider <read> or <lead>. To read the first of these, we need to know whether it consists of verb + present, or verb + past. To read the second, we need to know whether it is a verb, or a noun. As an example of the other kind of impossibility, consider a homophone like /red/. One cannot write this correctly unless he knows it to be adjective or, alternatively, verb + past.

THE WHOLE WORD FALLACY IN READING

I have devoted so much time to refutation of what I shall call the phonic fallacy, because I believe that linguistics is popularly understood to support it. However, it would be most unfortunate indeed if the preceding remarks were understood to give aid and comfort to supporters of what I shall call the "whole word fallacy." This position is more ridiculous and more dangerous by far than the phonic fallacy. It is more ridiculous, because it is based on a more fundamental misunderstanding of the interrelations between language, speech, and writing than is phonics. It is more dangerous because it has been used for a longer period as one of the methods of the basal readers, which have been employed in the vast majority of instances in teaching American school children to read.

READING AND UNDERSTANDING

In its most extreme, or, shall I say, crudest, form, the whole word position is that the English system of writing represents whole words which are conceived of, not as linguistic forms, but as something called "meanings." Reading, then, is viewed as a process of identifying meanings from their written representations. If this hypothesis were valid, a child confronted with a string of graphic configurations like <The dog ate the meat.> could demonstrate his ability to read by uttering "The canine quadruped devoured the flesh," or some other suitable paraphrase. Obviously, if our hypothetical child were able to perform such feats consistently, we should be forced to conclude that he could read, but, at the same time, we should also have to say that he had not directly demonstrated his ability to read, but rather his ability to understand written English—a more complicated skill that is based on the ability to read. In fact, the only adequate response to <dog>, if one is to demonstrate that he can read it, is to identify the linguistic form it represents by producing the conventional sign for it in some other system of representation—as, for example, by uttering the syllable/dɔg/.

The whole word fallacy, then, is based on a confusion between reading and understanding. Reading is the identification of linguistic forms from strings of written configurations that represent them, as evidenced by producing the conventional signs for the *same* linguistic forms in some other system of representation. Understanding a passage of writing is the identification of the meaning of the linguistic forms that have been identified from the writing, as evidenced by producing, in any system of representation, the conventional signs for *different* linguistic forms that will be judged by native users of the language to have the same meaning. Anyone who has learned to read can read many sentences whose meanings are almost completely unknown to him. I shall now do so: "The theory of functions of a complex variable deals with the differentiability of complex functions, analytic continuation, the residue theorem, and conformal mapping." In reading this sentence, I had no difficulty whatever in identifying all the linguistic forms—both the words and the syntactic structures—but I would find it impossible to produce a paraphrase that would be remotely satisfactory to a mathematician. That is, I *read* this sentence but I don't understand it.

Before turning to more specific matters, I should like to clear up two possible misunderstandings that may derive from my effort to distinguish between reading and understanding. First, let me say that I think that understanding is of vital importance. If one assumes, as I do, that any normal or above average child should be able to learn to read within two years, then most of the reading that he does from the third grade to the end of his formal education and beyond ought to have as its purpose the improvement of his understanding. But I also believe that to introduce this second goal before he has learned to read can only confuse him and delay his progress in learning to read.

Second, there may be those who challenge the notion that different linguistic forms are judged by native users of the language to have the same meaning. Isn't it true, they may ask, that two formally different statements never have the same meaning? This objection may be categorically disposed of: No, it is not true. If it were true, human communication would be impossible. Consider the case of a college student who is asked on an examination to discuss the meaning of Hamlet's third soliloquy or any other passage from literature. If the objection expressed above were valid, the only correct answer to the question would be a verbatim and letter-perfect quotation of the passage. Consideration of this and similar examples may lead to the formulation of a revised and weaker hypothesis to the effect that, although two formally different statements always have different meanings, there is a wide range of variation in the degree of difference between statements. Although I believe in the validity of the qualification, its attachment to the false generalization will not enable us to account for examples of the type cited above, because, even though some paraphrases of Hamlet's third soliloquy might be judged superior to others, all paraphrases would still be judged inferior to a verbatim quotation.

In short, I believe that the correct hypothesis about meaning is that some formally different statements have the same meaning, whereas, among those that do not, there is a wide range of variation in the degree of difference in meaning. Only with some such assumption can we continue to grade examinations.

Probably some of you agree with my conclusions about the inadequacy of both the phonic and the whole word methods of teaching elementary reading, but would hasten to point out that these are only two among a number of methods of reading instruction employed in the basal readers. I am sorry to say that this argument reminds me of Stephen Leacock's description of an upright woman who raised her daughter according to the best Christian principles, then taught her Mohammedanism to make sure. The phonic and the whole word methods are contradictory. If one is right, the other must be wrong. To use both is to spend at least part of one's time teaching wrongly, so as to mislead and confuse the learner. If, as I hope I have demonstrated, both methods are based on fallacious theories, to use the two methods is to spend all of one's time teaching wrongly. What is needed at the outset is a better theory of the interrelationship of writing and speech.

LINGUISTIC FORMS VARIOUSLY REPRESENTED IN DIFFERENT SYMBOL SYSTEMS

In the theory I have been seeking to develop, the term *linguistic form* is of critical importance. It is certainly not original to me, having been used at least as early as in Bloomfield's *Language* in 1933. Bloomfield defined linguistic forms as the grammatical units of the language, consisting of morphemes (the smallest meaningful units) and what he called taxemes of order, selection (primarily of form classes and constructions), phonetic modification (by which the form of morphemes is modified when they enter into combination with other morphemes), and modulation (*i.e.*, intonation). Probably no linguist today would analyze grammar in strict Bloomfieldian terms. Phonetic modification, for example, would be analyzed not as part of the grammar itself, but as part of the transition from language to speech, known as morphophonemics; and modulation would have to be defined abstractly enough to permit its actualization as either intonation or punctuation. The significance of Bloomfield's analysis, however, lies not in such details but in the recognition of a linguistic, or grammatical, level, of which phonemic and graphemic representations make up no part. In the discussions that have raged over Bloomfield's chapter on "Meaning," the placement of that chapter in the total book has been generally overlooked. It comes immediately after the chapters devoted to phonetics and phonemics and immediately before the chapter devoted to morphology. Moreover, although many Bloomfieldians have sought to avoid meaning altogether in their linguistic analyses, Bloomfield is explicit on the point that meaning, regardless of how resistant it may prove to analysis, is an indispensable feature of every linguistic form.

A linguistic form, then, is a linking of a unit of meaning to a physical representation in terms of a conventional system such as speech or writing. Although some linguists have preferred to think of linguistic forms as physical units that signify meanings that are themselves non-linguistic, and others have thought of linguistic forms as semantic units that are identified by non-linguistic physical configurations. I am of the opinion that it is preferable to think of linguistic forms as simultaneously having semantic and physical features, neither of which is paramount. This may be explained by the analogy of a coin, on which "heads" represents the meaning, "tails" the physical representation. It would be absurd to speak of either side of the coin as the "real" coin, in contrast to the other face which is merely a secondary concomitant. To improve the analogy, we might imagine a country in which several national banks are authorized to strike coins. There is a prescribed national standard for the size, weight, and metallic content of each denomination of coin, but each bank may place its own design on the two faces, so long as these are always the same for one denomination struck by one bank and different for different denominations. We actually have something like this system, since the designs on our coins are changed from time to time. In any event, without laboring the analogy further, the variant designs on the obverse face of a given denomination would correspond to the variant meanings that may be associated with a given linguistic form, whereas the variant designs on the reverse face would correspond to variant representations of the same linguistic form in speech, writing, Braille, *etc.* Correct association of a written symbol with a spoken symbol is accomplished through identification of the linguistic form rather than the meaning, in the same way that, shown a coin with a picture of Monticello on it, one would know that there are other coins of the same value—nickels—that bear a corresponding picture of a buffalo. No knowledge would be required of what appears on the opposite face of either coin, although the ordinary user of American coins would presumably have such knowledge.

Further clarification of the concept, linguistic form, may be secured by comparing it to a related but different concept, commonly termed the "nonsense syllable." I must first comment on the singular ineptness with which these units have been named. The term *syllable* suggests that they are phonological units of a particular length, yet they may equally well be graphic configurations, and their length may range from less than a syllable to many syllables. The term *nonsense* indicates that they are devoid of meaning, but anyone who has encountered "burbled" or "snicker-snack" in "Jabberwocky" knows that this is not true. A better term than *nonsense syllable* might be *pseudo linguistic form*, since the term is meant to cover graphic or phonological configurations or sometimes graphic *and* phonological forms that are associated with one another, all of which are likely to be assigned to a common area of meaning by native users of the language, but have in common the fact that they do not represent any current linguistic form in a given language. Many non-English graphic configurations like <gough> do not correspond to anything in speech, since they have no linguistic form to serve as intermediary. We may imagine <gough> to be pronounced /guː/, /gau/, /gɔːf/, /gəf/, *etc.*, indifferently, on the analogy of *through, bough, cough,* and *tough*. Likewise, many non-English phonological configurations like /foːt/ have no graphic correspondent forms. We may think of /foːt/ as beginning with <f> or <ph>, with its vowel spelled <o ... e>, <oa>, and so forth. Furthermore, the semantic feature of a pseudo linguistic form is usually much less precise than that of a true linguistic form. It seems likely that many forms which finally attain linguistic status pass through a transitional stage as pseudo linguistic forms.

LINGUISTIC FORMS REGULARLY REPRESENTED IN ANY GIVEN SYMBOL SYSTEM

If both writing and speech are actualizations of linguistic forms and if neither is a representation of the other, just where does this leave us as regards the teaching of reading? In order to proceed, we need to take into account two apparently contradictory characteristics of representational systems: they are always absolutely regular and absolutely arbitrary in terms of the units represented. We are familiar with statements, that have often been ridiculed by linguists, to the effect that English is not a phonetic language. If this statement has any meaning at all, it should mean that the linguistic forms of English are not consistently represented in speech by phonological symbols. Given the knowledge that there is a linguistic form in English that means "canine quadruped," I might sometimes represent it as /hɔːrs/, sometimes as /nóːšən/, and sometimes as /muːn/. If this kind of irregularity existed, spoken communication in English would clearly be impossible. Parallel to the statement that English is not a phonetic language is the often-heard allegation that the English system of writing is highly irregular. Once again, if this statement were at all meaningful, it should mean that the linguistic forms of English are not consistently represented by graphic symbols. I might represent the linguistic form that means "canine quadruped" as <horse>, <notion>, or <moon>, as the spirit moved me. If this kind of irregularity existed, written communication in English would be impossible. In short, where the question of regularity is concerned, the only hypothesis that makes sense with reference to English speech and English writing is that both are absolutely regular representations of the English language. It does not follow that either is a regular representation of the other, although, as will be pointed out as soon as we have considered the arbitrariness of representational systems, since English writing is alphabetic, there is a degree of correlation between spoken and written symbols for the same linguistic forms.

LINGUISTIC FORMS AND LEARNING TO SPEAK AND TO READ

Readers of linguistic literature during the last forty years are probably more familiar with the concept that representational systems are arbitrary than that they are regular. There is nothing intrinsic in the linguistic form that means "canine quadruped" that makes it essential for me to pronounce it /dɔːg/ and spell it <dog>. Except for the arbitrary conventions of English, I might always pronounce it /muːn/ and spell it <tab>. It follows that the learning of linguistic forms, which, I must remind you, consist of the linking of a meaning or meanings with an arbitrary but wholly regular representational configuration, must at first consist of laborious trial-and-error imitation and memorization. This is what normal children do at the stage of learning to speak their native language, or what deaf children do in learning to read their native language. Gradually the child comes to recognize certain regularities within the grammatical system and the representational system—that, for example, there are a limited number of different sounds in speech and that they occur only in certain patterns. From this point on, his progress in learning improves, because he can call into play higher mental faculties than mere imitation and memorization.

The position of one who has already learned the grammar of a language through one of its representational systems and then turns to learning a second representational system for the same language he has been learning is quite different from the situation described above. The normal child who has learned to speak English and is proceeding to the study of reading and writing is in this second position. He can begin to learn to associate graphic configuration with linguistic forms that he already knows. Only after he has learned to read and write his own stock of linguistic forms should he be encouraged to make use of reading to learn further linguistic forms.

I had hoped to devote my major attention to a consideration of how the construction of reading materials should take advantage of the fact that the child is already a native speaker of English, but space will not permit any detail on that subject. Probably what I could have developed along those lines would have been incomprehensible without the theoretical background that has been presented. In the briefest possible terms, a set of rules can be devised, ordered from the most specific rules, that account for single morphemes, to the most general rules, such that, given the spelling of English morphemes, their spoken representations may be arrived at. The list of rules will be long, and it is not necessarily being urged that all or even any of these rules should be taught to the child. It is urged, however, that elementary reading materials should be structured in terms of the rules. This principle does not prescribe any particular structure: Two organizations, of which one is the exact reverse of the other, might both be structured in terms of the rules. Once the rules have been set forth, however, it will be the responsibility of psychologists and classroom teachers to determine which organization, deriving from the rules, is most conducive to learning. On this question, the linguist, as linguist, cannot be expected to have a valid opinion.

PART II

If we are to come to a better understanding of the complex relationship between speech and writing, we need to characterize as accurately as possible those particular linguistic forms that are actualized as English sounds and English letters. The *phoneme* of descriptive linguistics is entirely inappropriate for this purpose. Insofar as it may be useful at all, it is as a unit of speech rather than of language. Phonemes must bear a direct relationship to the sounds that one speaker of English

utters, and they cannot, by their very nature, account for the morphological structure of his language or for the relationships between his
speech and that of other speakers of the language, including that of
speakers of other dialects. *Graphemes,* as units of writing rather than
of language, are also inappropriate for similar reasons.

Let us consider, first, how morphological structure is a factor in the
determination of linguistic forms and therefore affects the relationship
between speech and writing. The words *metal, rebel, civil, Mongol,*
and *cherub* have the same vowel phoneme in their second syllables
in most, if not all dialects of English. Yet in English spelling the vowel
of these second syllables is represented by five different letters. If we
try to describe this situation in terms of direct phoneme-grapheme
correspondence, we shall need five rules—one each to explain the
spelling of the unstressed vowel in each of these words. There are
undoubtedly thousands of English words that present comparable
problems, so that the student of English reading who follows strictly
the method of phoneme-grapheme correspondence will have to memorize the spelling of thousands of apparently isolated examples. If,
however, we consider the following words that are derived from those
in the original list—*metallic, rebellion, civilian, Mongolian,* and
cherubic—it is obvious that they contain five different vowels that are
in a consistent relationship with the spelling. If we assume that *metal,*
for example, consists of the same linguistic forms (which would generally be called *morphophonemes*), regardless of whether *metal* has
/ə/ in its second syllable when it occurs alone or /æ/ in its second
syllable when it occurs as part of *metallic,* we shall be in a position
to account relatively simply for the spelling of the unstressed vowels
in these and thousands of other words. In terms of practical applications of this principle it is suggested that, wherever other considerations (such as unfamiliarity of the derived form) do not militate
against it, the longer derived form ought to be taught first, to exemplify
the basis for the spelling, before the shorter base form is taught.

Consider, next, such pairs of words as *defy, defies; rely, relied,* and
and any number of other words that are spelled with <y> in final position, but <ie> in medial position. In such cases it is clear that English *pronunciation* signals the linguistic identity of the forms /difáy/
and /riláy/, even though these forms are spelled differently as bases
and as part of derived forms in conventional English writing. The
method of phoneme-grapheme correspondence, which cannot take
account of the morphological identity involved, will require the memorization of long lists of words in which <ie> spells the diphthong
/ay/ of *defies* rather than the vowel /i:/ of *relieve.* Recognition of a

linguistic form (in this case a *morphographeme*) that occurs in *defy*, *rely*, and derived words that contain these and similar elements would obviate this difficulty. The practical application of this principle would be to teach base forms like *defy* and *rely* first; then to teach a simple rule by which derivatives are formed from such bases, rather than attempting to teach derivatives as independent, unrelated forms. The correct procedure has always been followed by reasonably intelligent teachers, but it is important to observe that it is an outright contradiction of the method of phoneme-grapheme correspondence.

From what has been noted up to this point, it should be obvious that the linguistic forms that are represented in English speech and writing consist in part of morphophonemes that are different from the phonemes employed by most if not all speakers in certain words, and in part of morphographemes that are different from the graphemes employed in conventional English spelling in certain words. It remains to consider how dialect difference is a factor in the determination of linguistic forms and therefore affects the relationship between speech and writing.

Let us consider three examples, presented first in their written form—(1) <cant>, meaning "to tilt or slant," or, alternatively, "a jargon," (2) <can't>, the contraction of *can* and *not*, and (3) <Kant>, the German philosopher. The first is pronounced /kænt/ in most dialects of England and America; the second is pronounced /kænt/ in the majority of American dialects, but /ka:nt/ in Standard Southern British and a few American dialects; in the third form, these vowels are reversed for many speakers, so that the pronunciation /ka:nt/ prevails in America, but /kænt/ is the only pronunciation given by Daniel Jones for Standard Southern British. Clearly there is a linguistic difference among these three forms, and English writing represents this fact by employing three different spellings for the forms. In the commonest varieties of British and American speech, however, only two different pronunciations are employed, Britain equating forms (1) and (3), America equating forms (1) and (2). English writing spells all three forms differently, in order to show that they contain three different *diaphonemes*. Diaphonemic spelling enables an American reader to associate the "broad *a*" pronunciation with <Kant>, and the British reader to associate it with <can't>.

The opposite of this situation may be illustrated by the forms pronounced /wayz/, /sayz/, and /ayz/ (that is, the verb-forming suffix). The first and second are spelled <wise> and <size> on both sides of the Atlantic. The verbal suffix is spelled <ize> in America, but <ise> in England. The *pronunciation* of the suffix in both countries reflects the linguistic identity of the form, and the different spellings are a matter of variation in written dialects. All three forms contain the same *diagrapheme,* as indicated by their pronunciations.

We can now say that the linguistic forms that are represented in English speech and writing consist in part of diaphonemes that are different from the phonemes employed by some speakers in some words and different from the phonemes employed by other speakers in other words, and in part of diagraphemes that are different from the graphemes employed in conventional English spelling in certain words. Combining this conclusion with the one previously reached, we might say that English spelling is "dia-morpho-grapho-phonemic," but we cannot say that the linguistic forms represented in speech and writing are "diamorphographophonemes," or the like. Actually the linguistic forms represented in speech and writing include some diaphonemes, some diagraphemes, some morphophonemes, some morphographemes, and, in all those cases that linguists have thus far emphasized, where there is a one-for-one correspondence between phoneme, linguistic form, and grapheme, some mere graphophonemes. We need a name for the class of which these various "emes" are members, and we cannot continue to call it merely "linguistic form," because there are many other linguistic forms, such as "noun," that are not represented directly by phonemes and graphemes. Under these circumstances, I shall venture to coin a new term, *linguon,* to signify the smallest linguistic unit, such as actualized by phonemes in speech and by graphemes in writing. The term is formed on the analogy of *proton, electron, neutron,* etc., in physical science, and is similar to such terms as *phonon, morphon, lexon,* and *semon,* that are used in stratificational grammar.

The abstract nature of such a concept as "the English language" cannot be overemphasized here. Just as one cannot meaningfully say, "I drive the American automobile," so he ought to recognize that when he says, "I speak the English language," he is employing an oversimplified statement to express some such notion as, "I employ a system of speech that is derivable by a list of rules from an abstract structure known as the English language." In terms of the analogy, a given dialect is like a particular make of automobile, say Buick, and my idiolect is perhaps analogous to a particular 1949 Buick sedan I once drove. If we wish to discuss the American automobile in the abstract, we may employ such terms as battery, sparkplugs, brakes, etc., each of which may be thought of as analogous to morpho-phoneme, diagrapheme, etc. Linguons, in these terms, correspond to automobile *parts,* without reference to the make of car or the function of the part.

I should like to test the linguon hypothesis against a particularly recalcitrant body of data: words that contain one of the linguons* //a://, //ɔ://, or //ɔ//. These words are spelled with <a>, <au(gh)>, <aw>, <o>, or <ough>, and pronounced with three, two, or one low back vowel phoneme in different dialects, with considerable variation, in America at least, in the incidence of these phonemes in different words. In order to make the body of data more manageable, only monosyllables containing no more than one postvocalic consonant have been studied. Such an arbitrary restriction may, of course, either simplify or complicate the rules that must be adduced to account for sound-to-spelling correspondences. Any theory of these correspondences must, ultimately, account for all the data.

It may be asked how one can determine what linguons a word contains, since linguons are often not identical to English graphemes or to the phonemes employed in a particular idiolect. This is a particular instance of the general question, how does one formulate a hypothesis, to which the answer is that no one knows. In this particular case, one would, of course, assemble the words under study in their graphic representations along with their principal pronunciations as indicated in dictionaries, linguistic atlases, and other available sources. He would then postulate the linguon constituency of each word in a manner that seemed likely to permit the statement of linguon-phoneme and linguon-grapheme correspondences in terms of the smallest number of rules. One can never be certain that he has found the best formulation—only that one particular formulation is better than another. Thus, it might seem natural to suppose that the words *for, nor, Thor, tor,* and *war* contain the linguon //ɔ://, since all are pronounced with /ɔ:/ in dialects that have this phoneme. If we postulate this linguon in these words, however, we shall require the following rules to convert the linguon into the proper phonemes and graphemes:

(1) //ɔ:// → /ɔ:/†
(2) //ɔ:// → <a> [w__r]
(3) //ɔ:// → <o> [__r]

Of these rules, (1) is required for other words with //ɔ://, and so its statement here does not represent any addition to the required

---

* Linguons will be written between double virgules.

† Rule (1) should be read, "The linguon long open *o* is actualized as the phoneme long open *o*"; rule (2) as, "The linguon long open *o* is actualized as the grapheme *a* in the environment following the linguon *w* and preceding the linguon *r*.

set of rules. Rules (2) and (3), however, are not needed for any other words, and may be described as due to our decision to assign //ɔ:// to the words in question. If we had postulated //ɔ// in *for, nor, Thor, tor,* and *war,* we should have needed the following rules to convert the linguon into the proper phonemes and graphemes:

(4) //ɔ// → /ɔ:/ [___r]
(5) //ɔ// → <o>

Rule (5) is required for other words with //ɔ//, but rule (4) is necessitated by the assignment of //ɔ// to the words in question. Thus, we see that it will be better to assume that *for, nor, Thor, tor,* and *war* contain //ɔ// rather than //ɔ://, because to do so will enable us to convert linguons into the proper phonemes and graphemes with one fewer special rule.

Some 225 monosyllabic words containing no more than one postvocalic consonant phoneme, but containing one of the three vowel linguons in question have been studied. Of these 16 contain //a://, including *ma, pa, calm, palm, par, tar,* and ten other words with postvocalic *r.* Another 131 contain //ɔ//, including *pop, top* (and 11 others with postvocalic *p*), *pot, tot,* (and 12 others with postvocalic *t*), *botch, notch, Scotch, cock, bock* (and 10 others with postvocalic *k*), *cob, bob* (and 10 others with postvocalic *b*), *pod, Tod* (and 8 others with postvocalic *r*). Another 131 contain //ɔ//, including *pop, top* (and 11 others postvocalic *g*), *Tom, bomb, Don, John* (and 5 others with postvocalic *n*), *Poll, doll* (and 3 others with postvocalic *l*), *tong, bong* (and 8 others with postvocalic *ng*), *doff, golf, scoff, off, Goth, moth, wroth, toss, boss* (and 3 others with postvocalic *s*), *posh, bosh, josh, gosh, of, Oz, tor, nor, for,* and *Thor; watt, squat, watch, squad, wan, wash, squash, was,* and *war.* The remaining 78 contain //ɔ://, including *taught, caught, naught, aught, Maugham,* and *Vaughan; ought, bought* (and 4 others with postvocalic *t*), *Sauk, auk, baud, daub, Maude, Paul, maul, Saul, pause,* and *gauze; hawk, pawed, cawed* (and 6 others with postvocalic *d*), *pawn, dawn* (and 4 others with postvocalic *n*), *shawl, yawl, awl, paws, taws* (and 6 others with postvocalic *z*), (*Bryn*) *Mawr, paw, taw* (and 12 others with final //ɔ://); *talk, chalk,* (and 3 others with postvocalic *k*), *tall, call* (and 8 others with postvocalic *l*).

It is found that 21 rules are needed to convert the vowel linguons of these words into their correct English graphemes. Of these 21 rules, 18 relate to the linguon //ɔ://, two relate to //ɔ//, and one relates to //a://. The rules follow:

(1, 2)	//ɔ:// → <au>	[*taught, caught*]
(3)	//ɔ:// → <ou>	[__X +][‡]
(4)	//ɔ:// → <au>	[__X]
(5)	//ɔ:// → <awe>	[*awe*]
(6–10)	//ɔ:// → <aw>	[*shawl, yawl, awl, Mawr, hawk*]
(11, 12)	//ɔ:// → <aw>	[__ +, __n]
(13–16)	//ɔ:// → <au>	[*Paul, maul, Saul, haul*]
(17)	//ɔ:// → <a>	[__l]
(18)	//ɔ:// → <au>	
(19)	//ɔ// → <a>	[w__]
(20)	//ɔ// → <o>	
(21)	//a:// → <a>	

These are ordered rules, which is to say that they must be applied largely in the order in which they have just been presented. Specifically, rules (1–4) must be applied in that order with reference to one another and must precede rule (18). Rule (5) must precede rules (6–12) and rule (18). Rules (6–10) must precede rules (7–18). Rules (11–12) must precede rule (18). Rules (13–16) must precede rules (17–18). Rule (17) must precede rule (18), and, finally, rule (19) must precede rule (20).

Turning to the conversion of these vowel linguons into the phonemes of my idiolect, I find that 20 rules are needed. Since I have only two vowel phonemes, /a:/ and /ɔ:/, in this phonetic area, I need only two rules for //a:// and one rule for //ɔ://. Seventeen rules are required, however, to explain which words with //ɔ// are pronounced with /a:/, which with /ɔ:/.

(1)	//a:// → /ɔ:/	[__ +]
(2–7)	//ɔ// → /a:/	[*doff, Goth, posh, bosh, josh, gosh*]
(8–15)	//ɔ// → /ɔ:/	[*mock, dog, log, fog, hog, gone, on, golf*]
(16–18)	//ɔ// → /ɔ:/	[__r, __ng, __F][§]
(19)	//ɔ// → /a:/	
(20)	//__// → /_/[ǁ]	

The number of rules necessary to make these conversions is due in part to the mixed character of my idiolect. The rules make clear something that I had not previously known: In words that I learned in my native dialect area, rules (16–19) plus one additional rule (18a)—

‡ //X// is a linguon represented by <gh> and /Ø/ (i.e. "zero"). //+// is a linguon representing morpheme boundary.

§ //F// represents any voiceless fricative.

ǁ This rule is to be read, "Replace linguons with phonemes."

//ɔ// → /ɔ:/ [____g]—will account for all of these //ɔ// words except *mock, gone, on,* and *golf.* My pronunciation of *mock* is probably a folk-etymological back formation from *mawkish,* and *golf* could probably be accounted for in a study that includes rules for consonant linguons by a rule that deletes //l// in certain phonetic environments, after which *golf* is accounted for by rule (18). Only *gone* and *on* seem to have been anomalies in my native dialect. Thus, if the effects of dialect mixture are eliminated, only 7 rather than 17 rules are required to account for //ɔ// in my native dialect. Standard Southern British and similar dialects of American English would require only rules (16, 20). Northern Middle West dialects in which //ɔ// becomes /ɔ:/ before //r//, otherwise /a:/, would require only rules (16, 19, 20). Dialects like those of Western Pennsylvania and some parts of the Far West, that have only one low back vowel phoneme, would require only three rules, probably of the form, (1) //a:// → /ɔ/, (2) //ɔ:// → /ɔ/, plus rule (20) from above.

Only nine rules are needed to convert the vowel letters of these words into the correct linguons:

(1)	\<ou\>	→ //ɔ://	
(2)	\<o\>	→ //ɔ//	
(3)	\<au\>	→ //ɔ://	
(4)	\<aw\>	→ //ɔ://	
(5, 6)	\<a\>	→ //ɔ://	[___lk, ___ll]
(7, 8)	\<a\>	→ //ɔ//	[w___, qu___]
(9)	\<a\>	→ //a://	

It should be noted that, in a system that converts consonant graphemes into linguons, rule (8) will be unnecessary, since \<qu\> will already have been converted into //kw//.

Fifteen rules are needed to convert the vowel phonemes of my idiolect into the linguons of English in these words:

(1, 2)	/ɔ:/	→ //a://	[*ma, pa*]
(3–6)	/ɔ:/	→ //ɔ//	[*mock, gone, on, golf*]
(7)	/ɔ:/	→ //ɔ://	[(*Bryn*) *Mawr*]
(8–11)	/ɔ:/	→ //ɔ//	[___g, ___ng, ___r, ___F]
(12)	/ɔ:/	→ //ɔ://	
(13, 14)	/a:/	→ //a://	[___r, ___lm]
(15)	/a:/	→ //ɔ//	

Rule (3) is necessitated by the mixed nature of my idiolect, and rules (6) would not be required in a study that included rules for consonants, since it would come under rule (11) after the deletion of /l/. Standard British English would require only rule (7), rule (10), and a rule of the form /__/ → //__// to indicate the same relationships. The simplest form of Northern Middle West dialect would require rules (7), (10), and (12–15)—a total of six rules. Dialects like that of Western Pennsylvania would require a much longer list of rules, that will not be specified here, in order to sort the one phoneme /ɔ/ into three linguons.

It remains to inquire about the relative difficulty of converting writing to language to speech in these words, on the one hand, as opposed to converting speech to language to writing on the other. The following table indicates the number of rules required to perform these operations in the case of my idiolect, of my native South Midland dialect, of the simplest Northern Middle West dialect, and of Standard Southern British.

	Graph. to Ling.		Ling. to Phon.		Graph. to Phon.	Phon. to Ling.		Ling. to Graph.		Phon. to Graph.
Reed	9	+	20	=	29	15	+	21	=	36
S. Midl.	9	+	10	=	19	13	+	21	=	34
N. Mid. W.	9	+	6	=	15	6	+	21	=	27
British	9	+	2	=	11	3	+	21	=	24

Column 3 is the total of columns 1 and 2, and column 6 is the total of columns 4 and 5. It will be observed that the two total columns indicate that it is always easier to move from writing to speech than it is from speech to writing. The differences are greatest for the relatively "pure" dialects. Since elementary school children ordinarily have much less dialect mixture than adults, the figures for the pure dialects assume increased importance. Of course, we cannot know at this stage of our research whether these relationships will hold when a larger segment of the language is studied.

Superficially these figures suggest the intuitive reaction that it is easier to learn to read than to write. This interpretation will hold, however, only in the normal situation of a subject who knows the spoken language and is trying to learn the written language. If we assume a formerly deaf person who can read and write and is trying to learn the system of English speech, the same figures suggest that it is easier to learn to speak than to comprehend spoken English. One is reminded of Abe Burrows' statement, "I speak French, but I don't understand it."

In conclusion, what has been presented here is what I take to be a set of facts about the relations of speech and writing to a small segment of the English language. What the implications of these facts may be for the organization of reading materials and for classroom procedures in reading instruction will have to be hypothesized by psychologists and reading experts and tested in the laboratory and the classroom. These are not matters upon which linguists may safely pontificate.

T. G. BEVER
T. G. BOWER

How to Read without Listening

INTRODUCTION

Since the article begins with a lucid introduction and summary by the
authors, there is little need for an additional introduction by the editor. As
additional background, I might note that the structural linguistic view of
the relation between the oral and written forms of the language was that
the latter was but a pale reflection of the former. Consequently, the (structural) linguistic textbooks for teaching initial reading are largely based on
the child's building up an association between sound and visual symbol.

Bever and Bower take a quite different view of the relation of the oral
and written forms of the language. They point out that in the transformational model, the hearer imposes an interpretation on the sound that he
hears. That is, he has an "auditory perceptual strategy." This strategy brings
to bear the hearer's knowledge of the structure of his language, in particular
the cycle of rules that regulate the phonological system. According to Bever
and Bower,

> the perceptual segmentation of speech proceeds according to the sur-
> face phrase structure, and the perception of stress and pitch depend
> heavily on an active use of grammar.

Reprinted by permission of the authors from *Project Literacy Reports No. 6*,
(January) 1966, pp. 13–25.

The authors argue that it is possible to go directly from the visual input into the underlying structure of the sentence, skipping entirely the auditory perceptual mechanism. Additional support for this view may be found in Chomsky and Halle's recent book *The Sound Pattern of English* (Harper and Row, 1968), in which the authors argue that the spelling of English words often represents a kind of base form which is closer to semantic units than the actual pronunciation is.

✳

INTRODUCTION AND SUMMARY

It has long been held that reading research should integrate the structural discoveries of linguistic science with practical programs for the analysis and teaching of reading.* Until recently, structural linguistics has been most proficient in the analysis of sound systems. This led to a general preoccupation with mapping the sound system of a language onto the most intuitively and scientifically rational alphabet so that children could use their knowledge of their language to facilitate their reading. Current developments in the formal analysis of syntax, however, offer new insights into what children know when they know a language. These linguistic insights clarify the nature of different kinds of reading habits and thus provide a basis for the discussion of goals in the teaching of reading.

We view the study of reading as an investigation of how a reader's knowledge of his grammar and strategy for auditory sentence perception is recruited in the perceptual processing of written material. Of course, there is more than one way in which the grammar and perceptual habits developed for spoken language are employed in reading. In fact, available data indicate that there are two general strategies for the utilization of grammar in reading. The majority of readers use primarily the perceptual processes used in auditory perception of sentences. Other readers appear to analyze the visual input directly, independently of auditory processes. These "visual" readers comprehend written material better and faster than "auditory readers." Thus we propose that reading can and should be taught as a visual skill, enabling readers to analyze written sentences into their fundamental psychological structure directly, without auditory mediation. If readers can be taught to extract a linguistically correct and psychologically pertinent syntactic and semantic interpretation from the way written

---

* The research on "visual" and auditory readers was carried out at Cornell University. The relevance of the data to linguistic theory was first pointed out by Ragner Rommetveit, who gave a great deal of invaluable advice.

sentences *look* rather than from the way they *might sound*, unconscious dependence on mechanisms learned for auditory perception can be circumvented.

LINGUISTIC STRUCTURE AND
THE DESCRIPTION OF SENTENCES

Linguistic study analyzes those strings of words which are felt intuitively to be acceptable sentences. Intuitions about sentences and the relations between sentences are psychological facts fully as palpable as any other psychological data. Consequently, a theory which accounts for these intuitions is a psychological theory, albeit one which is relatively primitive. This psychological theory of language employs several descriptive levels which occur in the complete analysis of any sentence. For our purposes, we can isolate four structural levels: the analysis of phonology, or sound structure of a sentence; the analysis of the apparent phrase structure of a sentence; the analysis of the underlying of "logical" phrase structure of a sentence; and, the analysis of the semantic structure of a sentence.

Most people concerned with the study of language are familiar with the description of sound systems, since this is the most obvious aspect of language and has been of enduring concern for the past 100 years of linguistic study. At this level the continuous auditory input is analyzed into sequences of discrete segments of sound (phonemes) which are themselves categorized along several descriptive dimensions. For example, the sentence represented in (1a) would be like (1b).

1a. The meat was cold by the pond.
1b. ðə met wəz kold bai ðə pand.

The sequences of phonemes in a sentence are themselves organized into larger segments, words and phrases. For example, sentence (1a) has the hierarchical segmentation into words and phrases shown below. (1c).

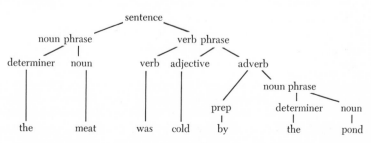

At this level of linguistic analysis it is possible to represent formally the intuitive relations which these phrases bear to each other, like "*subject*," "*predicate*," "*object*" and so on. Consider sentence (1a). The first phrase, "the meat" is clearly the *subject*, the second phrase, "was cold," is the *predicate* and "by the pond" is an *adverbial phrase* modifying the predicate.

The deepest syntactic level represents the basic or "logical" relations which phrases have to each other. Often two sentences have the same apparent grammatical relations, but quite different basic relations: consider sentence (2). Its apparent phrase structure is similar to that shown in (1c) and it is possible to state that "meat" is also the *subject* of "was sold." But at the deeper level "meat" is the *object* of the verb "sell." However, it is in no sense the object of the verb phrase "was sold" in (1a).

The apparent phrase relations often coincide roughly with the underlying relations as in (1a). But this is by no means the general case. In sentences (2), (3) and (4) for instance, the same apparent phrase relations occur but it is immediately clear that the logical relations between the phrases differ from each other and from (1a).

2. The meat was sold by the pond.
3. The meat was sold by the pound.
4. The meat was sold by the poor.

In (2) "the meat" is the underlying object, and in (4) "the meat" is the underlying object while "the poor" is the underlying subject of the action.

Examples of this sort demonstrate conclusively that at least two levels of relations between phrases occur in natural language. In the linguistic enumeration of sentences by a grammar, these levels are elaborated in the reverse order of the one presented above: for example, a grammar generates sentence (4) by starting with the *underlying phrase structure* which produces the underlying structure of sentences. These structures are mapped onto the surface phrase structures by a set of transformations peculiar to a particular language. Finally the phonological component of a language maps the surface phrase structure of a sentence onto a sequence of articulatory movements.

In present grammatical theory, *semantic* analysis provides each sentence with an interpretation presented in terms of a general semantic theory. Each interpretation describes the semantic relation which that sentence bears to other sentences. The semantic analysis of sentences operates on the underlying phrase structure only. Part of the motivation for this is that many superficially different sentences have the same underlying syntactic and semantic structure. For instance, all the sentences and phrases in (5) share the same underlying structure as in Figure 1.

> 5. The poor sold the meat.
> It was the poor who sold the meat.
> It was the meat that the poor sold.
> The selling of the meat by the poor. . . .
> For the poor to sell the meat. . . .
> That the meat was sold by the poor. . . .   etc.

Since the basic semantic relations between the phrases is the same for all these sentences the semantic analysis would have to "de-transform" the superficially different structures back to the common underlying structure. . . .[†] If the semantic analysis applies directly to the underlying structure, an arbitrarily large number of such "de-transformations" will be avoided.

The underlying phrase structure is interpreted in two different directions—on the one hand the semantic rules analyze the meaning of the underlying structure, on the other hand the syntactic transformations and phonological rules map the underlying structure onto a particular surface phrase structure and a particular pronunciation.

THE AUDITORY PERCEPTION OF SENTENCES AND THE PSYCHOLOGICAL REALITY OF THESE LEVELS

Above we have outlined the theory of language behavior which explains certain basic intuitions which speakers have about their language. This theory is *not* a description of how sentences are perceived, produced, or remembered. This theory *is* descriptive of the structure of sentences and thus is a general constraint on the descriptions of sentence perception, production, and memory.

For instance, any description of spoken sentence perception must show how the phonological level, apparent and deep phrase structure levels and semantic interpretations are discovered from the acoustic rendition of the sentence. The perceptual process is represented as bipartite: on the one hand, the linguistic grammar represents what the listener knows about the structure of his language; on the other hand, the auditory perceptual strategy organizes the use of his structural

† Original figures and their references have been omitted.

knowledge to perceive and comprehend the structure of spoken sentences. . . . Recent psycholinguistic research has brought out certain features of this strategy.

It is clear that there is a very close interaction of the phonological and surface phrase structures with the perception of many gross acoustic features of sentences. The research at Haskins Laboratory and elsewhere has shown that the segmentation and discrimination of speech sounds are extremely complex and involves active knowledge of the phonological rules. The perceptual segmentation of speech proceeds according to the surface phrase structure, and the perception of stress and pitch depend heavily on an active use of grammar.

The organization of the linguistic grammar presented above indicates that the perception and comprehension of a sentence involves the discovery of an appropriate underlying phrase structure for which the semantic rules can provide an interpretation. Of course the phonological level is directly represented in speech by many acoustic parameters (although the analysis of these is by no means straightforward). The surface phrase structure can also be expressed in certain acoustic features (e.g., pause, primary stress, pitch, rhythm). But the underlying phrase structure is not represented directly in *any* aspect of pronunciation. Thus auditory sentence perception is formally the analysis of an acoustic signal conveying phonological and surface phrase structure information, into the appropriate underlying structure.

Current linguistic and psychological research indicates that the underlying phrase structure does not interact directly with the perception of the acoustic speech signal. Many experiments, however, indicate that the discovery of the underlying phrase structure is the perceptual goal of the interaction of the lower grammatical levels with the acoustic signal.

Mehler and Carey have demonstrated that subjects use the underlying structure of sentences to form perceptual "sets." Miller, Macmahon, Savin, and others have shown that the larger the number of transformational rules intervene between the apparent and underlying analysis of a sentence, the harder the sentence is to recognize, perceive, or comprehend.

Similar research has shown that subjects remember sentences by decoding them into their underlying structure and memorizing them in that form. Miller and Mehler have found evidence that in sentence learning the underlying structure of sentences is memorized first. Mehler and others have shown that in time errors are made in sentences which tend to simplify their underlying structure.

In brief, then we have the following picture of the auditory perception of sentences. . . . The acoustic signal interacts with the phonological level and surface phrase structure level to produce a gross perceptual analysis of the acoustic signal into sequences of sounds organized into higher order sequences of words and phrases. A grammatically possible underlying phrase structure for this surface phrase structure is then found and is semantically interpreted. This underlying structure is the psychological form on which sentences are remembered.

UNDERLYING STRUCTURE AND
THE PROBLEM OF READING

Corresponding to the auditory analysis of sentences the skill of reading can be viewed as the ability to extract from a *visual* signal the underlying structure of sentences. The information directly available in current orthography is similar to the information available in the auditory signal. The segmentation of the written sequence into letters and words is distinctly represented as are certain major features of intonation and pause (with commas, question marks, etc.).

Of course, by the time he starts to learn to read, every reader has a well-developed perceptual routine for the analysis of spoken language. Consequently, every reader has the choice of how much of the auditory perceptual routine he will use in reading. One extreme, for instance, would be to read every word out loud and then analyze the written sentence with the already developed perceptual routine as though somebody else had spoken it. The other extreme would be to develop an entirely new, entirely visual perceptual strategy for the comprehension of written sentences.

Literally reading the sentence subvocally or out loud is clearly avoided by most readers. Many readers, however, may proceed by mapping the written sequence onto an internal perceptual analysis of what the sounds would have been had they been actually pronounced. Thus there are two extremes in the perceptual strategies which readers might reasonably pursue in the analysis of sentences. The first would utilize as much as possible of the perceptual routine already developed for the perception of spoken sentences, without actually reading sentences aloud. Readers using this strategy could treat reading as a problem in how to map the perceptual analysis of a visual signal onto a corresponding auditory one.

The second strategy would be to use a purely visual perceptual routine independent of the acoustic perceptual routine. Readers using this strategy would develop underlying phrase structure directly from the visual input and then map that onto the underlying phrase structure for auditory sentences. Thus the non-visual reader maps a perceptual analysis of a concrete visual signal onto the analysis of a concrete auditory signal, while the visual reader maps an abstract visual construct onto an abstract auditory construct.

THE EFFICACY OF THESE STRATEGIES
AND THEIR NATURAL OCCURRENCE

A *priori* arguments can be made in favor of either non-visual reading or visual reading. On the one hand, non-visual reading should be relatively easy to learn since it maximizes the use of available psychological processes while visual reading requires the development of entirely new processes. On the other hand, once the two strategies are learned, non-visual readers may be limited in the speed with which they read and the accuracy with which they comprehend and remember. Many features of spoken language perception may limit its use in visual perception by the fact that there is a normal speed at which spoken language proceeds.

Several studies indicate that both visual and non-visual readers occur without special training. Although we are not required to postulate that non-visual readers literally pronounce sentences to themselves, we do claim that they are integrating the visual percept with an auditory one at a low grammatical level. This indicates that non-visual readers should match written and simultaneously spoken sentences better than matching two simultaneously presented written sentences. Visual readers, on the other hand, should show no improvement with audio-visual sentence comparisons. In fact, if required to get all the superficial details of the written sentence correct, visual readers might do generally worse than non-visual readers. This is likely since visual readers proceed *immediately* to the underlying sentence structure, while non-visual readers are more concerned with the phonological and actual surface structure of the sentences.

In a same-difference experiment (Bower, 1966) written sentences were presented tachistoscopically immediately after spoken or written versions and subjects were asked to judge whether the sentences were completely identical or not. (Sentences differed in one misprinted letter.) About 92% of the subjects did much better in auditory-visual comparison than in the visual-visual comparison. The remaining 8%

(N = 18 out of 225 subjects) of the subjects did no better than with the visual-visual comparisons. In fact, although the general comprehension of these subjects was higher than *average*, their general ability to compare the details of pairs of sentences was lower than average for either kind of comparison.

Another prediction about non-visual readers is that they should tend to absorb written material from left to right (in English) since the auditory processing of phonology and apparent phrase structure also proceeds in time. Visual readers, on the other hand, should be free to process the written material in any order to facilitate the direct visual discovery of the underlying phrase structure. In an experiment in which sentences were briefly presented (1–100 msec) the same 92% of subjects who benefited from the auditory presentation, also recognized the briefly presented sentences decreasingly well from left to right. The 8% who were not aided by the auditory presentation did not pick up words in briefly presented sentences particularly from the left or right, but correctly identified words in different positions depending on the particular sentence.

The pattern of words the 8% identified first is quite suggestive. It appeared that the first word recognized was the *underlying* subject regardless of the apparent phrase relation that word had in the apparent phrase structure. Second, this 8% correctly identify the syntactic form of the sentence, even when they get none of the words right. Third, when they do get the words right, they often put the sentence into its simple declarative form (which has a surface structure more similar to the underlying structure than any other type of sentence).

We intend to test these findings using more carefully designed materials. For instance, visual readers should give quite different results on the recognitions of the word "meat" in sentences (1) and (2), while auditory readers should yield similar results for both sentences.

THE SIGNIFICANCE AND NATURAL TEACHING OF VISUAL READERS

Additional data gathered at Cornell indicate that visual readers comprehend faster and better than non-visual readers. They appear to analyze written sentences directly into underlying structures. These underlying structures are not only postulated by linguistic theory as the essential form of sentences, they have also been found psychologically to be the form in which sentences are coded.

We are interested not only in the light these readers may shed on the psychological use of grammar but also in studying methods which may naturally train all readers to see what they read, rather than hear it.

VISUAL READERS AND SPEED READING

The relation of "visual reading" to so-called "speed reading" may seem apparent. It may then seem hopeless to consider a general program in which all children are taught to read "visually" since the methods for teaching "speed reading" are expensive, time consuming, and presuppose a general reading ability. We are not so discouraged for one thing because the visual readers we found appear to have instructed themselves. Secondly, we have shown that visual readers are using their grammar visually in a particular way. This makes it possible for us to use the linguistic grammar in designing printed materials which will bring out automatically the kind of perceptual strategy which visual readers have. For instance, if small print is used, specific features of the linguistic structure can be directly represented. Secondly, we may be able to train readers to be "visual" by presenting sentences tachistoscopically in their underlying structure order. (See Bever & Rosenbaum, 1965, for a discussion of printing methods.)

Although it appears that non-visual reading should be easier to learn, this may not be the case. It is quite likely that some features of writing are arbitrary with respect to auditory analysis. It is also likely that many features of auditory sentence perception are unique to acoustic analysis and arbitrary with respect to visual analysis. Bower (1966) has already found that the attentional process underlying visual reading is docile and easily trained. Thus it may not only be more efficient to be a visual reader, it may also be easier to learn to be one.